Our Hope in Christ

Gerald W. Wrenn

Our Hope in Christ

Table of Contents

Preface

Snap! I just tore the medial lateral ligament in my knee during football practice. I was clipped as I was covering a punt. The trainer came onto the field and he and another player helped me to the sidelines. "It might not be torn. It could just be strained," he said.

He wanted to verify that it was a tear. He said, "After practice, let's go over to the pool and we will rehab." I thought, "Rehab?" I could hardly walk, and when I tried to, my leg would collapse. The pain was killing me.

The trainer said, "Get into the pool and swim over to the other side." As soon as I started swimming, the lower half of my leg floated out to the side at a 90-degree angle. "I guess it is torn." he said.

He took me to the training room and put a cast on my leg from my ankle to the top of my thigh. His final instructions were, "Take a couple of aspirin when you get to the dorm and come see me tomorrow." He gave me some crutches and the assistant trainer took me over to the athletic dorm.

When I arrived, a friend from the team saw the cast and asked what happened. I told him, expecting a reply like "that's too bad." Instead, he asked me a question that stopped me dead in my tracks. "Have you ever asked yourself why you believe what you believe?" The question completely took me by surprise. I was in pain. I do not think that I had ever really thought about it; but I remember thinking, "How could I go through life without knowing the answer to this question?"

Then he asked, "Do you believe that God can do what He promises in His Word?"

"Sure I do," I answered, although I'm not sure that I ever thought about that either. I was more concerned with my pain than some religious discussion.

He then handed me a Bible and said, "Read this." It was open to III John 2.

III John 2 AV

Beloved, I wish above all things that thou mayest prosper and be in health, even as thy soul prospereth.

"Do you believe that it is God's will for you to be healed?" he asked. After several of my, "Yes, but...," he finally got me to the place that I actually thought about what God said in His Word. He got me to be honest with what God's Word said without rationalizing it. I had been to church every Sunday of my life before college, but I never had a question like that put to me.

"If you believe what it says, cut off your cast." Reluctantly I headed for the showers with a screwdriver.

I got in the shower with my brand spanking new cast (knowing that I was going to catch hell from the trainer and the coach the next day, and the guys might think I was crazy), and I took the screwdriver and started to chip away at the cast.

When I finally got it off, I gingerly took some steps, and then I pivoted on it. There wasn't any pain and I could walk!

God healed my knee! For the first time in my life, *I knew* there was a Living God. I had been to church my entire life, but I had never experienced anything like this before.

This event drastically changed the course of my life. For the first time in my life, I knew that God was indeed a delivering God and that He truly cared for me.

A while later my friend said, "Next weekend some of us are going up to Duke University to speak the Word." Well I really was not that kind of guy, but I was overflowing with excitement about what God just did for me, so I agreed to go.

When we arrived we went to a pub to meet a friend from Duke. We talked to folks for an hour or so, but nothing was really going on, so we went back to the dorm where one of our friends lived.

I noticed that the guy at the desk had his knee all wrapped up. I went over and asked him what happened. He told me that he was on the track team, had torn the ligaments in his knee, and he was due for surgery on Monday.

I looked around for my friends but they had gone up to a friend's room to have fellowship before we returned to ECU. Later, I found out that they were praying for me and the young man I was talking to at the desk.

"Are you a Christian?" I asked. "Yes I am," he replied. I read him the same verse my friend read me. I was new to all of this and really did not know much more than that.

I said, "Well, God promises He will heal you according to His Word; do you believe that?" He said, "Really?" I answered, "That's what He wants for His people. The Lord Jesus paid for our healing as well as for our sins. We were healed by his stripes." We turned to I Peter 2:24 and I read it to him, and I said "That's God's Word. He said it, not me."

I shared with him what had just happened to me. I said, "It's available to be healed since you are a Christian." I asked, "Do you want me to minister healing to you?" He said, "Yes I do."

I put my hands on his knee and started to pray. The moment I started, in my mind it was as if an X-ray screen light was turned on. I asked God to heal the torn ligaments I saw, in the name of Jesus Christ. As I spoke the words I felt something move under my hands. I said "Take off your bandage, you are healed."

He quickly got up and took it off. He said, "The pain is gone!" He was doing deep knee bends and jumping around saying, "I am healed!" "I am healed!"

Because my back was to the lobby, I did not know that it was filling up with folks coming back from an evening out. They were just standing there in amazement, watching. After that, we stayed till late in the night speaking God's Word.

I'm no one special, just one of the many God gave his Son for because of His great love. What He has done for me, He has done for all of His children. The only difference may be that someone taught me what was available from God's Word, the Bible. They put it together for me so I could understand it and they taught me how to receive what God promises.

There are many scholars in Christianity who I am sure are much more academically accomplished than I am, but I know that I have experienced the delivering power of God in my life and I know what God wrote to His people in His Word. I cannot deny what I have seen and experienced walking with God as my Heavenly Father.

Miracles like this were commonplace for the remaining two years I was a student at East Carolina University. My senior year I experienced even more confirmations of God's power in my life.

The football season following that torn ligament in my knee, we played against East Tennessee State University. I dove for a pass in front of the split end. He stepped on my spine as I hit the ground. I could not get up. I was having spasms and the pain was awful. At half time, another friend ministered healing to me, and I played the second half.

The next day the trainer sent me to the team Doctor. He examined me and took X-rays of my back. He said, "It looks like at some point you fractured three vertebrae, but they have healed."

Two weeks later, we were playing in the Harvest Bowl against the University of Richmond. On one of the kickoffs I ran down the field and made the tackle. "Off sides!" the referee shouted. "Replay the down."

I was determined I was not going to lose the only tackle I had single handedly made on the kickoff team that season, so I ran down the field recklessly out of control. Wham!! I was blindsided and was hit right on my collar bone. I went off the field thinking the laces on my shoulder pads had torn loose. The trainer pulled my jersey down and said, "It's not your laces. Sit down." It was a compound fracture of the clavicle.

The pain got increasingly worse on the ride home. When I got off the bus someone gave me my coat and tie and I took them in the hand on the side of my injury and I thought I was going to pass out from the pain.

The assistant trainer was taking me to the hospital for surgery, and I asked him to stop to see my friend on the way. Reluctantly, he agreed, and went in to get my friend. He came out and ministered healing to me and said, "Take off your figure eight (the harness that was holding the collar bone together)."

As I was removing the harness, I realized the pain was gone! I began trying every position I could to see if it was really healed. It was. I told the trainer to leave me there, I was not going to the hospital. That night I was doing one-arm pushups to show people what had happened.

The next morning, I was called into the trainer's office to meet with him, the coach, and the team surgeon. They could not believe it, even after I did 25 one-arm pushups. The doctor would not release me to play, but I was determined that God would be glorified in this.

The only pain I had was in the morning when I first got up; it felt stiff. I decided I would not sit on the sidelines as an injured player should. Again, I was called into the coach's office. He told me if I didn't want to lose my scholarship and no longer be on the team, I had to come to practice and watch. I said, "God healed it coach, I can play." He said, "Gerald, you can't play because of insurance liability. If anything happened, the school would be liable. I'm sorry."

I said, "I understand that you have to do what you have to do, but I have to do what I have to do, too. Coach, I'm healed; I can't deny it." So that ended my football career.

Two weeks later, I was home for Thanksgiving. On Thanksgiving afternoon, some of my former high school buddies, who were playing football at other colleges, got together and we played a game of tackle.

My team had the ball. The quarterback said to go down 10 yards and hook and slide away from the coverage. I ran down the field, stopped and went up for the pass and someone took my legs right out from under me. I landed from the peak of my jump, right onto my right shoulder, on the same side I had a compound broken collar bone two weeks earlier.

A friend was driving me to the hospital where my regular orthopedic surgeon was meeting us. I said, "I need to make another call." I called my friends back at ECU. They were eating Thanksgiving dinner.

I heard my friend say, "It's Gerald, he hurt his collar bone again." He ministered to me and I thanked him. Off to the emergency room I went.

When Dr. Atkins saw the X-rays he said, "It looks like you had a hairline fracture maybe six months ago, but nothing to worry about, it's healing just fine." My friend was white as a sheet as I related to the Dr. what had just happened not an hour ago and the two weeks previously. "There is no way in hell that could be," the Dr. said.

I was so excited I had to tell my friend about what God had done for me on the way back to the game. We played for another half hour after we returned.

Afterwards we went to the Ratskeller to share stories and talk about old times. I just could not contain myself, I had to tell everyone what God had been doing for me.

It was like living in the time of the book of Acts.

With all my heart I wanted to learn more so that I could teach others how to walk with the power of God, so they could have the delivering power of God in their lives, too. For the first time in college I knew what I wanted to do with my life.

From that point some forty years ago, my greatest desire has been to know the God that healed me and to walk with Him.

I have had the privilege of seeing God perform His Word both in my life and in the lives of His people.

Repeatedly I have seen God deliver men and women, boys and girls, young and old when they believed the Word of God. It does not matter how huge your need may be, it's a matter of how great your God is. There are no incurable diseases with God, no mental prisons too severe to overcome, no financial holes too deep. There is not a single situation from which He cannot deliver you.

Miracles and deliverance follow those who believe God's Word. Circumstances do not limit God. There is nothing too hard for Him. He is a delivering, living God.

Christianity is not a self-help religion. It is a living, vital spiritual relationship with God as your Father. It is walking with the living God by taking Him at His Word.

Without the certainty of His Word, understanding any particular spiritual matter is sheer folly. With the understanding of His Word, we can once again say with certainty, "Thus says the Lord!"

This book is for people who are hungry, who want real answers in their lives. It's about learning about a Living God and His purposes. It isn't for those who just want to argue about doctrine or only have a scholarly knowledge of religion.

At the time I was first learning how to walk with God, I was taking a comparative religion class. My teacher was a Ph.D. in religion and formerly a Baptist minister who had converted to the Hindu religion. I wanted answers, real answers, not more B.S. I wanted truth that worked, not just more academic knowledge from an intellectual who had no spiritual understanding whatsoever.

You see, this book is really not about me, but about the God I love and serve with all my heart. This is about God's plan concerning the ages that he planned in Christ. It is the story of Christianity as God reveals it to us in His Word. This is only the beginning of my story.

Our Hope in Christ

Introduction

What we believe concerning our hope of salvation will have a dynamic influence on how we live as Christians. The attitude we have regarding our end will affect our entire lives. It will fuel our motivation for how we live, and it will give us the stamina we need to be steadfast, unmovable, always abounding in the work of the Lord.

Our Heavenly Father gave us so rich a hope in Christ that He says it will take Him the whole of eternity, the ages to come, to clearly demonstrate the immeasurable riches of His grace in kindness to us in Christ Jesus. It is my desire that this work will help you appreciate the riches of the glory that the Father has in store for us, His beloved. When we realize our end, it will strengthen our resolve to stand and endure the trials we encounter in this life so we can live in joy and rejoicing until our Lord returns for us. Our hope is the anchor of our souls.

When we are persuaded by the revelation that our Father gives us in the Word of truth, we will live as strangers and pilgrims on the earth because we are unreservedly confident that our Father will perform everything He has promised.

The Scriptures speak of the joys of eternal life in new glorious bodies at His Son's return, deliverance from the wrath to come, rewards for service done in love, pleasures forevermore, and fullness of joy at His right hand in new heavens and a new earth. God and His beloved children will dwell together forever without the tyranny of sin and death, or sorrow or pain.

Our Father says He will make all things new, and that His children, the righteous in Christ, shall live and reign forever in glory. All this great grace and glory is ours because of the accomplished work of Jesus Christ our Lord and the authority that God delivered to him over all principalities, powers, mights, and dominions. We will be firsthand witnesses of the exceeding greatness of His power when God brings every jot and tittle of His will to fulfillment, from the gathering together of His saints in the air, throughout the unending glory of the new heavens and the new earth.

As believers in the Lord Jesus Christ, we have an incorruptible inheritance that will not fade away that is reserved in heaven for us. It is in this certainty of unending glory that we can rejoice even though our present circumstances may at times seem like disappointing misery. Regardless of the times of pain, grief, or sorrow we may encounter today, we can be sure that they are but for a fleeting moment compared to the eternal glory that is guaranteed us when Christ returns for us.

God's Word is full of encouragement for us. What precious truth is ours to dwell on as we deal with the trials of life, in our seasons of depression, in times of sickness, and even in the face of death. We are Christ's and Christ is God's. Therefore, we are more than conquerors through Him Who loves us, regardless of the obstacles we may encounter.

What confident peace is ours when we believe God's Word. Our Father is a delivering God, now and for all times, even from the grave itself. Our final homes will not be decay and corruption in a cold grave, but in the warmth of the Father's glory when Christ returns for us. Such unspeakable joy is ours by the grace of God.

What more can we say but thanks be to God, Who gives us this victory! May God's Word inspire you to stand and rejoice in Christ's coming until you see him face to face and when you are as he is!

As you read and study along with me, please take note:

There are several conventions that I used in this manuscript in an effort to be as clear and helpful as possible:

- Bible verses are in bold print.

- In some cases, multiple verses are presented as one paragraph or passage to avoid the distraction of being broken apart by every verse number.

- I used brackets [ ] within the citation of a Scripture passage to distinguish my remarks from the Scripture. The actual Bible passage is in bold print.

- Greek, Hebrew, and Aramaic words are italicized.

- When I specify a particular word or phrase from a verse, it appears in quotation marks or in bold type in the manuscript.

- At the end of this manuscript, I have provided a list of Suggested Texts for your personal reading and study, some of which I have also referenced with the text.

- I used various translations and versions of the Bible to convey the most accurate understanding of the verse(s) under consideration.

It is helpful to know that there are three major categories of translations:

1. A *literal translation* translates from the original tongues to our language word by word.

2. An *expanded translation* is a translation that reproduces the original with additional alternate meanings or explanatory renderings.

3. A *literal translation according to usage* reproduces the thoughts and meanings of the original. It is based on the words in the original text and their usage in light of the grammatical laws governing Figures of Speech and Eastern oriental expressions (Orientalism) which were common at the time of the writing of God's Word. The literal translation according to usage provides valuable understanding of what is written.

Below are descriptions of the translations and versions used in this manuscript and the abbreviation in the citation if an abbreviation is used.

Authorized Version (AV) is also known as *The King James Version,* (KJV) – 1611. The primary translation sources were the Hebrew *Masoretic Text* and Stephens Greek text of 1550. *The Bishop's Bible* of 1568 (many of the revisers who contributed to this work were bishops, thus the name) was the basis for their translation.

The American Standard Edition (ASV) – 1901. Sources: The *Masoretic Text*, the translation of Westcott and Hort (1881) and that of Tregelles (1857). It is basically the same as the 1885 *English Revised Version*. The ASV incorporates the alterations of the American contributors that were appended in the 1881 version by the English.

Aramaic-English Interlinear New Testament – 1988. *Aramaic Peshitta* version, The Way International, American Christian Press. This work is accompanied by *The Concordance to the Peshitta Version of the Aramaic New Testament,* which includes a dictionary.

English Revised Version (ERV) – 1885. Published in England, this was the revision of the *King James* or *Authorized Version.* Invitations to all the leading Biblical scholars in the United Kingdom were sent out as well as to all the churches of America. Their translation of Greek words was consistent, unlike the Authorized Version. The AV uses similar English words interchangeably for the same Greek word. *The English Revised Version* is one of the most accurate translations.

Interlinear Greek – English Translation by Green – 2005. Source: *Masoretic Text, Textus Receptus* (LITV) - a formal equivalence translation. Considers the pictorial, descriptive nature of the Hebrew; keyed to *Strong's Exhaustive Concordance*; features the Greek texts with a direct English rendering below each word, the literal translation of the Bible in the outside column, and Strong's numbers printed above the Greek words.

Lamsa – 1933. Lamsa translated from the *Peshito*, which is the authorized Bible of the Church of the East. The *Peshito* is the classical Syriac dialect of Eastern Aramaic or Estrangelo Aramaic. Our Lord Jesus Christ spoke Aramaic, as did the Judeans of the first century. The Greek speaking Jews were Hellenists. The Aramaic speaking Jews looked upon the Hellenist as corrupt. The two groups were alienated.

The Life and Epistles of St. Paul by Coneybeare and Howson – 1978: fifteenth printing. The introduction states that the purpose of this work is, "to give a living picture of St. Paul himself, and of the circumstances by which he was surrounded." It gives a historical picture of the times surrounding the writing of the Church Epistles. It is well worth the student's time to read this work.

Moffatt New Translation – 1913. Moffatt used Von Sodon's work as his standard. Moffat was a highly competent Greek Scholar. His translation utilizes the idiomatic words of his day (British).

Murdock New Testament – 1859. This is a literal translation from the *Syriac Peshito* Version by Dr. James Murdock, D.D.

Nestle-Aland Greek-English New Testament (NAGENT) – 1981. The work compares the editions of Tischendorf, Westcott, and Hort, and Weymouth, adopting the agreement of two for his Greek text and placing the third in his apparatus. The critical apparatus contains the variant readings of the *Authorized Version*, the *English Revised Version* of 1881, the *American Standard Version* of 1901, and the Catholic Edition of the *Revised Standard Version*. The work allows the reader to monitor the translators, which is a significant advantage. It lists variants, which makes precise comparisons possible. The work provides informed readers with a basis by which they can judge for themselves which readings more accurately reflect the originals.

New English Bible (NEB) – 1961. Sources: *Masoretic Text*, Greek New Testament although the translators do not identify the specific texts used.

The NEB involved about 24 denominations. The idea behind the work was to incorporate newly gained knowledge of the Greek text of the New Testament as well as of the Greek language itself, which was acquired since the completion of the Revised Version in 1881.

Rotherham's Emphasized Bible – 1872. Published in England, Rotherham's work is even more strictly literal than *Young's Literal Translation*. He places excessive stress on words and phrases.

Revised Standard Version (RSV) – 1952. Source: *Masoretic Text, Nestle-Aland Greek New Testament*; formal equivalent; a revision of the *American Standard Version* (1901), intended to preserve the best of that version while incorporating modern English.

Weymouth New Testament – 1903. This translation is also known as *The New Testament in Modern Speech,* and is translated into "modern" English as used in the nineteenth century from *The Resultant Greek Testament,* which Richard Francis Weymouth did himself. It is most careful with tenses, article, and synonyms. It does not represent a clear picture of the Eastern background of the New Testament. The Preface to the original translation by Weymouth (dated 1902) states that the version was chiefly designed to furnish a succinct and compressed running commentary (not doctrinal) and is to be used side by side with its elder compeers.

The Working Translation (WT) - 2006. By Walter J. Cummins. In his Forward he writes, "The plan of the Working Translation with its notations is to communicate in current, commonly understood English the thought, meaning, and integrity of the God-inspired Scriptures as well as certain distinctive characteristics and flavor of language as used by the writers. To do so requires the careful consideration of those words as they have been preserved in the various printed Greek texts and the older manuscript in Greek and other languages. It is called a "Working Translation" because it is designed to be an ongoing project that may be changed from time to time as more is learned.

The Working Translation is not designed to replace other translations but rather to be a study tool with selected notes regarding vocabulary, grammar, and the tests from which the translation was made. The Working Translation and notes will serve to help students of the Scriptures who are interested in understanding the God-inspired text from which translations and versions have been made." (Page ix.)

Wuest Expanded Translation (WET) – 1981 (NT). Source: *Nestle-Aland Text.* An expanded translation, which contains additional material not distinguished from the text. The writer sought to use as many English words as were necessary to bring out the force and clarity of the Greek text.

Young's Literal Translation of the Holy Bible (YLT) – 1862. First published in England, it uses "the received text" the same as the KJV of 1611. It is known for its strictly literal translation and present tense of Hebrew verbs.

Death and Resurrection

Genesis 3:19

**In the sweat of thy face shalt thou eat bread,
till thou return unto the ground; for out of it wast thou
taken: for dust thou art, and unto dust shalt thou
return.**

John 5:28

**Verily, verily, I say unto you, The hour is coming, and
now is, when the dead shall hear the voice of the Son of
God: and they that hear shall live.**

John 11:25

**Jesus said unto her, I am the resurrection, and the life:
he that believeth in me, though he were dead, yet shall
he live:**

Death

We are mortal beings, meaning that we are subject to death.

How do we speak of realities beyond our finite, known reality? We are faced with two alternatives. We can listen to men, whether religious, scientific or even agnostic, or we can believe what God reveals to us in His Word.

There are many opinions, doctrines, traditions and theories about the realm of death and beyond, but there can only be one truth; one reality.

If we study the Word of God, it eliminates all the guesswork and uncertainty concerning this subject. It alone reveals the Will of God to us. Every other position on the subject has to be weighed against the truth of God's Word if we truly want answers from which we will never have to back-up.

In this section we will deal with death, resurrection, the importance of Jesus Christ's resurrection, the soul, tradition, and difficult scriptures concerning these topics.

Is Death the Door to Eternal Life?

The Word of God teaches all there is to know regarding death and our deliverance from it.

The popular traditional belief is that death is the entrance to eternal life and that it is a welcomed friend.

Movie upon movie personifies life after death. Television series tout their afterlife views. Poets etch their unsubstantiated sentiments into our thinking with their libretto. Philosophers pontificate on the subject as though they are qualified spokespersons.

Are these "the experts" we should trust or should we consult what God reveals to us in His Word?

We should always compare what anyone may say about spiritual matters to the revelation of the Word of God. It alone can separate between the truth and what is error concerning spiritual matters.

Is death the gateway to eternal life? Is it the entrance into glory?

I Corinthians 15:26 AV
The last enemy *that* shall be destroyed *is* death.

God reveals to us that death is an *enemy*. He also tells us that death is the *last* enemy that shall be destroyed.

If you read the obituaries in your local newspaper, you will see that death is still a harsh reality. God gives us His Word that there is a future time when death will be destroyed. The book of Revelation records the time when this will occur.

Revelation 20:14 AV
And death and hell were cast into the lake of fire. This is the second death.

This event will not occur until the end of this heaven and earth.

Revelation 21:1-4 AV
And I saw a new heaven and a new earth: for the first [*protos*, former] heaven and the first [former] earth were passed away; and there was no more sea. And I John saw the holy city, new Jerusalem, coming down from God out of heaven, prepared as a bride adorned for her husband. And I heard a great voice out of heaven saying, Behold, the tabernacle of God *is* with men, and he will dwell with them, and they shall be his people, and God himself shall be with them, *and be* their God. And God shall wipe away all tears from their eyes; and there shall be no more death, neither sorrow, nor crying, neither shall there be any more pain: for the former things are passed away. And he that sat upon the throne said, Behold, I make all things new. And he said unto me, Write: for these words are true and faithful.

When God makes the new heaven and new earth there will be no more death.

I Corinthians 15:50 AV
Now this I say, brethren, that flesh and blood cannot inherit the kingdom of God; neither doth corruption inherit incorruption.

The Word of God teaches us that corruption does not inherit incorruption. Corruption takes place when one dies. Using the figure of speech, *metonymy*, "corruption" is used for "death" in this verse, painting a much more vivid picture of death than the literal truth itself.

The figure of speech, *metonymy*, is founded on relation. The metonymy makes a change for the noun "death" and instead, uses a word that concerns the effect of death, which is "corruption."

"Incorruption" is stated using the same figure of speech. Instead of saying "resurrection life," the figure features the effect of that life – "incorruption."

Corruption or death does not inherit incorruption or resurrection life at the moment one's earthly life terminates. Death is not the entrance into glory, but to corruption and decay. The state of death brings man into a worse state.

The Word of God teaches the exact opposite of tradition. God said, "**Ye shall surely die**" in Genesis 2:17 and the serpent said, "**Ye shall not surely die**" in Genesis 3:4. Whose word proved to be true?

Jesus Christ taught that one must be born again if he is to enter the Kingdom of God.[1] No one who is only flesh and blood can inherit God's Kingdom, nor does death automatically inherit resurrection life upon death. This is not a matter of opinion or theory – this is God's revelation on the subject.

Scripture, whether Old or New Testament, never teaches that death is the saints' hope or that it is the entrance into eternal life.

According to Scriptures, death is not the gateway to eternal life. Mankind does not go to heaven upon death, far from it; he corrupts in the grave.

No one can teach us more about death than God reveals to us in His Word. Life and death are issues under God's hand and His revelation is the only source we can trust for answers concerning them.

As we study the Scriptures, they will reveal the agent, the event and time when God will provide release from death for His people.

---

[1] *See* John 3:3-16.

What is Death?

The Hebrew word for "death" is *maveth* in the Old Testament; *thanatos* is the Greek word used in the New Testament. Since God reveals all that is possible to know about death in His Word, let's consider its testimony.

Genesis 2:7 AV
And the Lord God formed man of the dust *of* the ground, and breathed into his nostrils the breath of life; and man became a living soul.

Man becomes a living soul with "the breath of life."

Psalms 146:4 AV
His breath goeth forth, he returneth to his earth; in that very day, his thoughts perish.

When a person breathes his last breath, he dies. This is the natural end of every human being. Man decomposes and returns to the earth upon death.

The living have "the breath of life," but when they take their last breath they lose life. Death is the loss of life. A person ceases to live at death. Death is the opposite of living.

Genesis 3:19 AV
In the sweat of thy face shalt thou eat bread, till thou return unto the ground; for out of it wast thou taken: for dust thou *art*, and unto dust shalt thou return.

Adam, the whole person, was to return to the ground, not to heaven.

When we read a verse that speaks of "the dead" as though they are "alive," and which contradicts the literal truth, it is using the figure of speech, *prosopopceia* or personification, which attributes intelligence, by words or actions, to inanimate objects or abstract ideas. Some examples of this are found in Isaiah 14:9-11, Ezekiel 32:11-12 and Revelation 6:9-10.

Do the dead have memory in the grave?

Psalms 6:4 and 5 AV
Return, O LORD, deliver my soul: oh save me for thy mercies' sake. For in death *there is* no remembrance of thee: in the grave who shall give thee thanks?

There is no memory in the grave, nor can we give God thanks from it. There is no communion with God in the grave.

The psalmist did not want to die. He asked God to deliver and save him from death. If salvation occurs at death, why would he pray for deliverance from it? We will discuss how God will deliver His people from the grave in detail in a later chapter.

What else does God reveal about the state of death?

Ecclesiastes 9:5, 6, 10 AV
For the living know that they shall die: but the dead know not any thing, neither have they any more a reward; for the memory of them is forgotten. Also their love, and their hatred, and their envy, is now perished; neither have they any more a portion for ever in any *thing* that is done under the sun. Whatsoever thy hand findeth to do, do *it* with thy might; for *there is* no work, nor device, nor knowledge, nor wisdom, in the grave, whither thou goest.

What do the dead know? They know nothing at all. In death, there is no reward. Love, hatred and envy belong to the living – not the dead. There is nothing that the dead have in common with the living.

There is "**. . . no work, nor device, nor knowledge, nor wisdom in the grave. . ..**" There is no mental or physical activity of any kind in death.

Ecclesiastes 9:5 AV
For the living know that they shall die: but the dead know not any thing, neither have they any more a reward; for the memory of them is forgotten.

This record contrasts the living with the dead: **"The living know,"** while **"the dead know not anything."**

Genesis 3:19 AV
In the sweat of thy face shalt thou eat bread, till thou return unto the ground; for out of it wast thou taken: for dust thou *art*, and unto dust shalt thou return.

There is only corruption and decay in death. God originally formed Adam's body from the elements found in the dust of the earth. At death, these elements return to their original state. The soul life expires. If a man is born of the Spirit of God, the Spirit returns to God who gave it. Everything returns to its original state.

Job 7:21 AV
And why dost thou not pardon my transgression, and take away mine iniquity? for now shall I sleep in the dust; and thou shalt seek me in the morning, but I *shall* not *be*.

We know that death is not the same thing as sleep. If I go to sleep at night, it is with the expectation of awakening in the morning; but if I should die, I will corrupt in the grave.

To **"sleep in the dust"** fails to be true to fact, so it has to be a figure of speech in this instance.

The word "sleep" is used in this verse instead of the word "death" using the figure of speech, *euphemism*, which is the exchange of a word that is unpleasant for a word that is more pleasant.

Even though this figure of speech softens the language concerning death's awful sting by referring to it as sleep, it does not diminish the truth about death.

Why does God use the comparison of death to sleep when it concerns His people? He uses it because of the likeness of the comparison. He says that they "sleep" – not "awaken."

When God says that they are dead, He means that they are dead. Had He meant that the dead do not really die, but become alive at death in some other form He would have chosen the word "awaken" – not "sleep."

There are many modern definitions of "sleep," however, Webster defined it very simply. "Sleep is that state of an animal in which the voluntary exertion of his mental and corporeal powers is suspended, and he rests unconscious of what passes around him."[2]

Sleep is the opposite of conscious awareness. The Word of God uses the comparison of death to sleep to teach us that in this sense they are alike.

---

[2] *American Dictionary of the English Language*, by Noah Webster, 1828 reproduction ed.

Psalms 13:3 AV
Consider *and* hear me, O LORD my God: lighten mine eyes, lest I sleep the *sleep of* death;

The **"sleep of death"** and the expression to **"sleep in the dust of the earth"** are figures of speech used for death. Death is not the entry into eternal life or glory.

Death is the natural end of our earthly human existence. It is a loss of life. It is not merely an *event*, but it is a *continuing state* until the time of awakening. When a person breathes his last breath, he enters the death-state.

In *A Critical Lexicon and Concordance to the English and Greek New Testament*, Dr. Bullinger remarks that, "Death is an unbroken slumber till the Resurrection morn when the sleepers shall wake."

Psalms 49:6-9 AV
They that trust in their wealth, and boast themselves in the multitude of their riches; None *of them* can by any means redeem his brother, nor give to God a ransom for him: (For the redemption of their soul *is* precious, and it ceaseth for ever:) That he should still live for ever, *and* not see corruption.

God's Word explicitly teaches that no one can live forever in his natural state as a mortal. His natural end is death and corruption.

There is no such thing as the immortality of the soul, such as when one dies and then passes on to life in another realm. Poets, philosophers, artists, teachers, movie producers or the serpent may speak of it but God does not.

No amount of wealth will keep men from death. What ransom can be provided to God to deliver any man from death? The parenthesis further explains that the redemption of their soul - their life - from death is precious or costly and that it is forever unachievable by any means man may possess.

If a man dies, but he does not really die, but gains eternal life at death, indeed he would "live forever," but this is not the case. When a man dies he does not see life in any form, he sees corruption.

Psalm 49:10 and 11 AV
For he seeth *that* wise men die, likewise the fool and the brutish person perish, and leave their wealth to others. Their inward thought *is*, *that* their houses *shall continue* for ever, and their dwelling places to all generations; They call *their* lands after their own names.

It is sad that man can be so arrogant. It blinds him to the truth.

Psalms 49:12-14 AV

Nevertheless man *being* in honour abideth not: he is like the beasts *that* perish. This their way *is* their folly: yet their posterity approve their sayings. Selah. Like sheep they are laid in the grave; death shall feed on them; and the upright shall have dominion over them in the morning; and their beauty shall consume in the grave from their dwelling.

The natural man cannot forestall death. He is its subject and he comes under its jurisdiction. He is no different than the beasts that perish. Both perish when they breathe their last breath.

If God had not provided a release from death and the grave no one could escape its grasp. "Death" is the natural end of physical life. It is not merely an occurrence, but a continuing state.[3]

Psalms 49:15 AV

But God will redeem my soul from the power of the grave: for he shall receive me. Selah.

The word S*elah*, means "Consider what I say." God promises that He will redeem His people from death and the authority of the grave. While man has nothing in his power that can redeem him from death, God does.

The psalmist said that God will take His people out of *Sheol* at some time.

Isaiah 38:18 and 19 AV

For the grave cannot praise thee, death cannot celebrate thee: they that go down into the pit cannot hope for thy truth. The living, the living, he shall praise thee, as I do this day: the father to the children shall make known thy truth.

Hezekiah was a king that stood for God. He did not look forward to death. He knew that death was a loss of life and there was no victory in it.

Death is not a welcomed friend that leads us into the presence of God, it is an enemy and it is costly to our Lord.

---

[3] Bullinger, E. W. (1999 ed.). *A Critical Lexicon and Concordance to the English and Greek New Testament.* pp 367-370.

The grave is not a place of torment, nor is it the entrance into eternal life. There is no memory or mental activity of any kind in the grave. The grave is where one corrupts and decays.

What is *Sheol*?

In the Old Testament, the Hebrew word *sheol* is translated as "grave," "pit" and "hell" in the King James or Authorized Version. The word appears 65 times in the Scriptures.

If we study the 65 times it appears in the Word of God, we will know all that is available for us to know of the grave.

In the Old Testament, *sheol* and its counterpart, *hades,* in the New Testament are translated as "hell" at times.

Our understanding of the grave must be gleaned from these verses. To help you as you read, I have underlined the word translated from *sheol*. The Word of God interprets itself in the verse where it is written, and in the context, and where it has been used before.

God put the meaning to the words He used, and He expects us to do the same so that we can understand what He is communicating to us.

Genesis 37:35 AV
And all his sons and all his daughters rose up to comfort him; but he refused to be comforted; and he said, For I will go down into <u>the grave</u> unto my son mourning. Thus his father wept for him.

Genesis 42:38 AV
And he said, My son shall not go down with you; for his brother is dead, and he is left alone: if mischief befall him by the way in the which ye go, then shall ye bring down my gray hairs with sorrow to <u>the grave</u>.

Genesis 44:29 AV
And if ye take this also from me, and mischief befalls him, ye shall bring down my gray hairs with sorrow to <u>the grave</u>.

Genesis 44:31 AV
It shall come to pass, when he seeth that the lad *is* not *with us*, that he will die: and thy servants shall bring down the gray hairs of thy servant our father with sorrow to <u>the grave</u>.

Numbers 16:30 AV
But if the LORD make a new thing, and the earth open her mouth, and swallow them up, with all that *appertain* unto them, and they go down quick into <u>the pit</u>; then ye shall understand that these men have provoked the LORD.

Numbers 16:33 AV
They, and all that *appertained* to them, went down alive into <u>the pit</u>, and the earth closed upon them: and they perished from among the congregation.

Deuteronomy 32:22 AV
For a fire is kindled in mine anger, and shall burn unto the lowest <u>hell</u>, and shall consume the earth with her increase, and set on fire the foundations of the mountains.

I Samuel 2:6 AV
The LORD killeth, and maketh alive: he bringeth down to <u>the grave</u>, and bringeth up.

II Samuel 22:6 AV
The sorrows of <u>hell</u> compassed me about; the snares of death prevented me;

I Kings 2:6 AV
Do therefore according to thy wisdom, and let not his hoar head go down to <u>the grave</u> in peace.

I Kings 2:9 AV
Now therefore hold him not guiltless: for thou *art* a wise man, and knowest what thou oughtest to do unto him; but his hoar head bring thou down to <u>the grave</u> with blood.

Job 7:9 AV
As the cloud is consumed and vanisheth away: so he that goeth down to <u>the grave</u> shall come up no *more*.

Job 11:8 AV

It *is* as high as heaven; what canst thou do? deeper than <u>hell</u>; what canst thou know?

Job 14:13 AV

O that thou wouldest hide me in <u>the grave</u>, that thou wouldest keep me secret, until thy wrath be past, that thou wouldest appoint me a set time, and remember me!

Job 17:13 AV

If I wait, <u>the grave</u> *is* mine house: I have made my bed in the darkness.

Job 17:16 AV

They shall go down to the bars of <u>the pit</u>, when *our* rest together *is* in the dust.

Job 21:13 AV

They spend their days in wealth, and in a moment go down to <u>the grave</u>.

Job 24:19 AV

Drought and heat consume the snow waters: *so doth* <u>the grave</u> *those which* have sinned.

Job 26:6 AV

<u>Hell</u> *is* naked before him, and destruction hath no covering.

Psalm 6:5 AV

For in death *there is* no remembrance of thee: in <u>the grave</u> who shall give thee thanks?

Psalm 9:17 AV

The wicked shall be turned [R.V.: returned] into <u>hell</u>, *and* all the nations that forget God.

Psalm 16:10 AV

For thou wilt not leave my soul in <u>hell</u>; neither wilt thou suffer thine Holy One to see corruption.

Psalm 18:5 AV

The sorrows of <u>hell</u> compassed me about: the snares of death prevented me.

Psalm 30:3 AV

O LORD, thou hast brought up my soul from <u>the grave</u>: thou hast kept me alive, that I should not go down to the pit [*bor:*a sepulcher].

Psalm 31:17 AV

Let me not be ashamed, O LORD; for I have called upon thee: let the wicked be ashamed, *and* let them be silent in <u>the grave</u>.

Psalm 49:14 AV

Like sheep they are laid in <u>the grave</u>; death shall feed on them; and the upright shall have dominion over them in the morning; and their beauty shall consume in <u>the grave</u> from their dwelling.

Psalm 49:15 AV

But God will redeem my soul from the power of <u>the grave</u>: for he shall receive me. Selah.

Psalm 55:15 AV

Let death seize upon them, *and* let them go down quick into <u>hell</u>: for wickedness *is* in their dwellings, *and* among them.

Psalm 86:13 AV

For great *is* thy mercy toward me: and thou hast delivered my soul from the lowest <u>hell</u>.

Psalm 88:3 AV

For my soul is full of troubles: and my life draweth nigh unto <u>the grave</u>.

Psalm 89:48 AV

What man *is he that* liveth, and shall not see death? shall he deliver his soul from the hand of <u>the grave</u>? Selah.

Psalm 116:3 AV

The sorrows of death compassed me, and the pains of <u>hell</u> gat hold upon me: I found trouble and sorrow.

Psalm 139:8 AV

If I ascend up into heaven, thou *art* there: if I make my bed in <u>hell</u>, behold, thou *art there*.

Psalm 141:7 AV
Our bones are scattered at <u>the grave's</u> mouth, as when one cutteth and cleaveth *wood* upon the earth.

Proverbs 1:12 AV
Let us swallow them up alive as <u>the grave</u>; and whole, as those that go down into the pit [*bor*]:

Proverbs 5:5 AV
Her feet go down to death; her steps take hold on <u>hell</u>.

Proverbs 7:27 AV
Her house *is* the way to <u>hell</u>, going down to the chambers of death.

Proverbs 9:18 AV
But he knoweth not that the dead *are* there; *and that* her guests *are* in the depths of <u>hell</u>.

Proverbs 15:11 AV
<u>Hell</u> and destruction *are* before the LORD: how much more then the hearts of the children of men?

Proverbs 15:24 AV
The way of life *is* above to the wise, that he may depart from <u>hell</u> beneath.

Proverbs 27:20 AV
<u>Hell</u> and destruction are never full; so the eyes of man are never satisfied.

Proverbs 30:16 AV
<u>The grave</u>; and the barren womb; the earth *that* is not filled with water; and the fire *that* saith not, *It is* enough.

Ecclesiastes 9:10 AV
Whatsoever thy hand findeth to do, do *it* with thy might; for *there is* no work, nor device, nor knowledge, nor wisdom, in <u>the grave</u>, whither thou goest.

Song of Solomon 8:6 AV

Set me as a seal upon thine heart, as a seal upon thine arm: for love *is* strong as death; jealousy *is* cruel as <u>the grave</u>: the coals thereof *are* coals of fire, *which hath a* most vehement flame.

Isaiah 5:14 AV

Therefore <u>hell</u> hath enlarged herself, and opened her mouth without measure: and their glory, and their multitude, and their pomp, and he that rejoiceth, shall descend into it.

Isaiah 14:9 AV

<u>Hell</u> from beneath is moved for thee to meet *thee* at thy coming: it stirreth up the dead for thee, *even* all the chief ones of the earth; it hath raised up from their thrones all the kings of the nations.

Isaiah 14:11 AV

Thy pomp is brought down to <u>the grave</u>, *and* the noise of thy viols: the worm is spread under thee, and the worms cover thee.

Isaiah 14:15 AV

Yet thou shalt be brought down to <u>hell</u>, to the sides of the pit.

Isaiah 28:15 AV

Because ye have said, We have made a covenant with death, and with <u>hell</u> are we at agreement; when the overflowing scourge shall pass through, it shall not come unto us: for we have made lies our refuge, and under falsehood have we hid ourselves:

Isaiah 28:18 AV

And your covenant with death shall be disannulled, and your agreement with <u>hell</u> shall not stand; when the overflowing scourge shall pass through, then ye shall be trodden down by it.

Isaiah 38:10 AV

I said in the cutting off of my days, I shall go to the gates of <u>the grave</u>: I am deprived of the residue of my years.

Isaiah 38:18 AV

For <u>the grave</u> cannot praise thee, death can *not* celebrate thee: they that go down into the pit cannot hope for thy truth.

Isaiah 57:9 AV

And thou wentest to the king with ointment, and didst increase thy perfumes, and didst send thy messengers far off, and didst debase *thyself even* unto <u>hell</u>.

Ezekiel 31:15 AV

Thus saith the Lord GOD; In the day when he went down to <u>the grave</u> I caused a mourning: I covered the deep for him, and I restrained the floods thereof, and the great waters were stayed: and I caused Lebanon to mourn for him, and all the trees of the field fainted for him.

Ezekiel 31:16 AV

I made the nations to shake at the sound of his fall, when I cast him down to <u>hell</u> with them that descend into the pit: and all the trees of Eden, the choice and best of Lebanon, all that drink water, shall be comforted in the nether parts of the earth.

Ezekiel 31:17 AV

They also went down into <u>hell</u> with him unto *them that be* slain with the sword; and *they that were* his arm, *that* dwelt under his shadow in the midst of the heathen.

Ezekiel 32:21 AV

The strong among the mighty shall speak to him out of the midst of <u>hell</u> with them that help him: they are gone down, they lie uncircumcised, slain by the sword. [The figure of speech, *Personification*, is used here where dead people are said to speak. It says they "lie uncircumcised" and were "slain by the sword."]

Ezekiel 32:27 AV

And they shall not lie with the mighty *that are* fallen of the uncircumcised, which are gone down to <u>hell</u> with their weapons of war: and they have laid their swords under their heads, but their iniquities shall be upon their bones, though *they were* the terror of the mighty in the land of the living.

Hosea 13:14 AV

I will ransom them from the power of <u>the grave</u>; I will redeem them from death: O death, I will be thy plagues; <u>O grave</u>, I will be thy destruction: repentance shall be hid from mine eyes.

Amos 9:2 AV

Though they dig into <u>hell</u>, thence shall mine hand take them; though they climb up to heaven, thence will I bring them down:

Jonah 2:2 AV

And said, I cried by reason of mine affliction unto the LORD, and he heard me; out of the belly of <u>hell</u> [the great fish's belly, which was his grave] **cried I,** *and* **thou heardest my voice.**

This last verse is an example of the figure of speech, e*xergasia*, which is "a repetition, so as to work out or illustrate what has already been said."

> a. **"I cried by reason of mine affliction unto the Lord,**
> b. **and he heard me**:
>
> a. *out* **of the belly of hell** [*sheol*] **cried I,**
> b. **and thou heardest my voice."**[4]

In a and *a,* we have Jonah's cry of affliction and in b and *b,* we are told that the Lord heard him. Jonah was dead in the fish's belly for three days and three nights. Before he died, he prayed to the Lord and the Lord heard him. Then, verses 6 and 7 make it clear that Jonah died.

Habakkuk 2:5 AV

Yea also, because he transgresseth by wine, *he is* **a proud man, neither keepeth at home, who enlargeth his desire as <u>hell</u>, and** *is* **as death, and cannot be satisfied, but gathereth unto him all nations, and heapeth unto him all people:**

Young's Analytical Concordance to the Holy Bible tells us that the Hebrew word, *sheol,* is translated as "the grave" 31 times, "hell" 31 times and "pit" 3 times.

In English, the word "hell" equates to the "grave." *Sheol*, translated as the grave, hell or pit, is not a place of torment or punishment; it is the present state of the dead; it is the state of "gravedom." All who have died are in this category.

The Hebrew word *qeber* is the place or spot where the body is buried, whether on land or at sea. *Qeber* is not s*heol* or *hades.* The *American Revised Version* (ARV) did not translate the word s*heol* into English, but instead

---

[4] Bullinger (1992 ed.). Figures of Speech Used in the Bible, p. 400.

used "sheol" in the English translation. For example, in the ARV, Habakkuk 2:5 reads:

Moreover, wine is treacherous; the arrogant man shall not abide. His greed is as wide as Sheol; like death he has never enough. He gathers for himself all nations, and collects as his own all peoples.

What is *Hades*?

In the New Testament, the Greek word equivalent to *sheol* is *hades.* It is used eleven times in the New Testament. It is translated "grave" once and "hell" ten times.

Hades is associated with the pagan imagery of the Greek philosophy. We can thank Plato for making the belief of dying and either going to heaven or hell popular. I will give you an overview of its history in the chapter, "Is the Soul Immortal?"

"As *Hades* (a word of human origin) is used in the New Testament, as the equivalent for the Hebrew word *sheol* (a word of Divine origin), its meaning can be gathered, not from human imagination, but from its Divine usage in the Old Testament. If we know this, we know all that can be known."[5]

The Word of God always connects *hades* with the dead – never with the living. The dead will not live again, *until* Christ raises them from the dead at his coming. This is the only release from the grave or hell.

Listed below are the uses of *hades* in the New Testament.

Matthew 11:23 AV
And thou, Capernaum, which art exalted unto heaven, shalt be brought down to hell [the grave]**: for if the mighty works, which have been done in thee, had been done in Sodom, it would have remained until this day.**

Matthew 16:18 AV
And I say also unto thee, That thou art Peter, and upon this rock I will build my church; and the gates of hell [the grave] **shall not prevail against it.**

---

[5] *Ibid.*

Not even death can prevail against the Church because Christ has the power to raise his saints from it.

Luke 10:15 AV
And thou, Capernaum, which art exalted to heaven, shalt be thrust down to hell [the grave]**.**

Luke 16:23 AV
And in hell [the grave] **he lift up his eyes, being in torments, and seeth Abraham afar off, and Lazarus in his bosom.**[6]

Acts 2:27 AV
Because thou wilt not leave my soul in hell [the grave]**, neither wilt thou suffer thine Holy One to see corruption.**

This verse speaks of the Lord Jesus and that God would not leave him in the grave. He did not see corruption.

Acts 2:31 AV
He seeing this before spake of the resurrection of Christ, that his soul was not left in hell [the grave]**, neither his flesh did see corruption.**

I Corinthians 15:55 AV
O death, where *is* thy sting? O grave, where *is* thy victory?

Death and the grave are used together here. This verse and the previous verse, **"Death is swallowed up in victory,"** are quoted from two Old Testament records, Isaiah 25:8 and Hosea 13:14.

Resurrection will give the believers who die the victory over death and the grave. The Lord Jesus Christ will execute his God-given authority to deliver the saints from death and the grave at his coming.

Revelation 1:18 AV
I *am* he that liveth, and was dead; and, behold, I am alive for evermore, Amen; and have the keys of hell [the grave] **and of death.**

The Lord Jesus Christ has "the keys" that will provide release from death and the grave at his coming.

---

[6] *See* the discussion, *The Rich Man and Lazarus*, in this manuscript.

Not even the Lord Jesus by-passed death. He was dead, and for three days and three nights he was in the grave before God raised him to life again.

Today, he is alive and lives in the heavenlies in his resurrected and glorified body. He was the first to receive the promise of eternal life. He is alive forevermore. God gave him the authority to deliver the dead from the corruption of the grave when he returns.

Revelation 6:8 AV

And I looked, and behold a pale horse: and his name that sat on him was Death, and Hell [the grave] **followed with him. And power was given unto them over the fourth part of the earth, to kill with sword, and with hunger, and with death, and with the beasts of the earth.**

Death is personified here, and he sits on a pale horse. The grave followed him and he killed the fourth part of the earth. Does this sound like the entrance into eternal life?

Revelation 20:13 AV

And the sea gave up the dead which were in it; and death and hell [the grave] **delivered up the dead which were in them: and they were judged every man according to their works.**

This verse is speaking of the second resurrection, that of the unjust. Death and the grave delivered up the dead. The dead were not in heaven, paradise or the *gehenna*. They were dead and in the grave.

Revelation 20:14 AV

And death and hell [the grave] **were cast into the lake of fire. This is the second death.**

"Hell" is the grave and it is associated with death. There is coming a time when both death and the grave will end. Death and the grave are used together in these verses indicating their likeness. The second death will be everlasting destruction.

Jacob, Job, David, and Christ all died, and the Word of God says that they all descended into *sheol* or *hades,* translated as "hell" in the New Testament. It is inconceivable to think that they went to a place of burning torment and eternal punishment, that some imagine hell to be.

Jacob was the father of the nation of Israel.

According to God, Job was a "perfect and upright man."

God made David the king of Israel and He says that David was a man after God's own heart. God told him that Christ would come out of his linage and sit on his throne forever.

Jesus Christ was the Only Begotten Son of God – His Beloved Son, who always did his Father's will.

Are we to believe that these saints went to the hell that Greek philosophy invented and that tradition embraces, a place of torment and eternal punishment? If these saints could not escape "hell" upon death, who could possibly think that anyone else could?

I Corinthians 15:22 AV
The last enemy *that* shall be destroyed *is* death.

Revelation 20:14 AV
And death and hell were cast into the lake of fire. This is the second death.

In the first place, one day, God will destroy "death and hell." Whatever hell is, it has an end – it is not eternal.

In the second place, these men expected to be delivered from the death-state by resurrection. This was the hope of every saint in the Bible that died. Upon death, the wicked as well as the righteous go to hell, which is the grave.

The popular traditional belief concerning hell is a myth. Hell is not used this way in the Word of God.

Sheol or *hades* is "the grave," which is translated into English as "hell" at times, where there are only the dead, which decay and corrupt.

Sheol is not a place of "afterlife" of which some men speak, nor is it the gateway to eternal life. It is not the place of an intermediate state such as purgatory or limbo (these words and what they teach are foreign to the Word of God). The grave is not a place of torment.

These ideas all come from pagan origins. They originated in Babylon, and were perpetuated in Egyptian and Greek philosophy. Early Church theologians incorporated the beliefs into church doctrine in the first four centuries.

The Greek philosophers introduced the immortal soul and its immediate entrance into an everlasting state based on their works, either to heaven and its rewards, or what they called hell and everlasting burning and torment.

These doctrines are not in the Word of God – Old or New Testament. They are the product of Greek philosophy, which became especially popularized by the teachings of Plato.

The Pharisees embraced these traditions at the time of Christ and Christ rebuked them for having such beliefs. I cover this further in this manuscript in the chapter *What Does God's Word Say?* regarding the parable of *"The Rich Man and Lazarus."*

In the early centuries of Christianity, many pagan beliefs were brought into Christianity as it moved away from the doctrine of God's Word. To keep their converts, teachers mingled pagan traditions with "church doctrine."[7]

In summary, what is s*heol*?

- "As to *place*, it is in the earth. It is the place of corruption and decay.

- "As to *nature,* it is put for the state of death, or the state of the dead, of which the grave is the tangible evidence.

- "As to *relation,* it stands in *contrast* with the state of the living. It is the state of "gravedom," a coined word, meaning the dominion or power of the grave. It only has to do with the dead.

- "As to *duration*, the dominion of s*heol* or the grave, will continue until, and end only with, *resurrection*, which is the only exit from it."[8]

Words Confused with *Sheol* and *Hades*

There are some other words used in God's Word that we must consider if we are to understand *sheol* and *hades*. The Greek words g*ehenna, tartarus,* a*bussos* and the Hebrew word, *abaddon*, must be understood from their usage in God's Word. We cannot mix these words with *sheol* or *hades* as though they mean the same thing.

---

[7] Many books trace these doctrines historically. *The Two Babylons*, by Alexander Hislop; *Babylon Mystery Religion* by Ralph Woodrow, and *Highlights of Church History,* by Howard Vos are a few examples. *See* Appendix B: *Works Cited and Suggested Reading.*

[8] Bullinger, E.W. (1999 ed.). *A Critical Lexicon and Concordance to the English and Greek New Testament.*

Gehenna

Matthew 10:28 AV

And fear not them which kill the body, but are not able to kill the soul: but rather fear him which is able to destroy both soul and body in hell [*gehenna*].

Gehenna is a place of burning. The word was first used describing the Valley of Hinnom, where Moloch worshippers burned their children as sacrifices. After Israel's exile, they continually burned the refuse and carrion from Jerusalem there. It is a place of destruction.

Gehenna corresponds to the lake of fire mentioned in the following verses.

Daniel 7:11 AV

I beheld then because of the voice of the great words which the horn spake: I beheld *even* till the beast was slain, and his body destroyed, and given to the burning flame.

Revelation 19:20 AV

And the beast was taken, and with him the false prophet that wrought miracles before him, with which he deceived them that had received the mark of the beast, and them that worshipped his image. These both were cast alive into a lake of fire burning with brimstone.

Revelation 20:10 AV

And the devil that deceived them was cast into the lake of fire and brimstone, where the beast and the false prophet *are*, and shall be tormented day and night for ever and ever.

Revelation 20:14 and 15 AV

And death and hell [the grave] were cast into the lake of fire. This is the second death. And whosoever was not found written in the book of life was cast into the lake of fire.

Gehenna is for the devil, the false Christ, the beast, death, hell and the ungodly that have rejected the Lord Jesus Christ. It is not death or the grave. *Gehenna* is the place where the sentence of the second death will be carried out.

This judgment will occur at the time of the White Throne judgment, at the end of the second heaven and earth. Hell is not a proper translation of *gehenna*.

Tartarus

The word *tartarus* is only used in II Peter 2:4.

II Peter 2:4 AV
For if God spared not the angels that sinned, but cast *them* down to hell [*tartarosas*], and delivered *them* into chains of darkness, to be reserved unto judgment;

Tartarus has nothing to do with death or the grave. It does not concern *men* in any state. It concerns only **"the angels that sinned."**

Tartarus is the place where God imprisoned these spirits until He imposes their sentence in the day of judgment, according to verse 9. Jude 6 affirms that God is holding these spirits for the day of His judgment.

I Peter 3:18-20 reveals that Christ went to these spirits and proclaimed his triumph after his resurrection.

"Hell" is not a proper translation of the word *tartarus*.

Abaddon

Abaddon is a Hebrew word. It is first used in Job 26:6.

Job 26:6 AV
Hell *is* naked before him, and destruction [*abaddon*] hath no covering.

It is always translated "destruction." It appears six times in the Scripture.

Abussos

Abussos is a Greek word. It is translated as the "bottomless pit" five times, "the deep" two times and "bottomless" two times. This word is transliterated into the English language as "abyss."

Luke 8:28-31 AV
When he saw Jesus, he cried out, and fell down before him, and with a loud voice said, What have I to do with thee, Jesus, *thou* Son of

God most high? I beseech thee, torment me not. (For he had commanded the unclean spirit to come out of the man. For oftentimes it had caught him: and he was kept bound with chains and in fetters; and he brake the bands, and was driven of the devil into the wilderness.) And Jesus asked him, saying, What is thy name? And he said, Legion: because many devils were entered into him. And they besought him that he would not command them to go out into the deep.

The word "deep" is the Greek word *abussos.* These devil spirits begged the Lord not to send them into the deep.

Revelation 20:1-3 AV
And I saw an angel come down from heaven, having the key of the bottomless pit and a great chain in his hand. And he laid hold on the dragon, that old serpent, which is the Devil, and Satan, and bound him a thousand years, And cast him into the bottomless pit, and shut him up, and set a seal upon him, that he should deceive the nations no more, till the thousand years should be fulfilled: and after that he must be loosed a little season.

Here *abussos* is translated as "the bottomless pit." Again, it has nothing to do with men. It is a prison capable of holding spirit-beings.

The verses concerning the deep, or abyss, give us insight into a place of imprisonment. This is a place for unclean spirits, which are devil spirits. Neither the grave nor man has anything to do with it.

Jesus Christ's Death and Resurrection

Let's now turn our attention to Jesus Christ's death and resurrection. Why is his resurrection from the dead so important?

Romans 10:9 AV
That if thou shalt confess with thy mouth the Lord Jesus and shalt believe in thine heart that God hath raised him from the dead, thou shalt be saved.

The only prescription for salvation is to confess the Lord Jesus and to believe that God raised him from the dead. Salvation, forgiveness of sin and deliverance from death are contingent on Jesus Christ's resurrection from the dead.

I Corinthians 15:3-8 AV
For I delivered unto you first of all that which I also received, how that Christ died for our sins according to the scriptures; And that he was buried, and that he rose again the third day according to the scriptures: And that he was seen of Cephas [Peter], then of the twelve: After that, he was seen of above five hundred brethren at once; of whom the greater part remain unto this present, but some are fallen asleep. After that, he was seen of James; then of all the apostles. And last of all he was seen of me also, as of one born out of due time.

These verses set forth the divinely inspired history of Christ's resurrection. He was the first to rise from the dead never to die again. These witnesses attest that Jesus Christ indeed arose from the dead.

I Corinthians 15:12-19 AV
Now if Christ be preached that he rose from the dead, how say some among you that there is no resurrection of the dead? But if there be

no resurrection of the dead, then is Christ not risen: And if Christ be not risen, then *is* our preaching vain, and your faith *is* also vain. Yea, and we are found false witnesses of God; because we have testified of God that he raised up Christ: whom he raised not up, if so be that the dead rise not. For if the dead rise not, then is not Christ raised: And if Christ be not raised, your faith *is* vain; ye are yet in your sins. Then they also which are fallen asleep in Christ are perished. If in this life only we have hope in Christ, we are of all men most miserable [most to be pitied].

Salvation and redemption rests on Jesus Christ's resurrection from the dead. If he did not rise from the dead, we are yet in our sins and those who have died have perished forever.

If we trust in a fictitious hope, we ought to be pitied more than all other men because we have believed in a worthless lie. However, that is not the case.

I Corinthians 15: 20-22 AV
But now is Christ risen from the dead, *and* become the firstfruits of them that slept. For since by man [Adam] *came* death, by man [Jesus Christ] *came* also the resurrection of the dead. For as in Adam all die, even so in Christ shall all be made alive.

This takes us back to Adam's condemnation and on to the remedy for it. The Word of God reveals that our resurrection to life is based on Jesus Christ's resurrection from the dead. If he did not rise from the dead, neither will we. If he did rise from the dead, then we have the certain hope that we will rise, also.

I Thessalonians 4:14 Coneybeare and Howson
For if we believe that Jesus died and rose again, so also will God, through Jesus, bring back those who sleep, together with Him.

As God raised Jesus Christ from the dead so He will raise us from the dead, also. By the power of His Word, God created the heavens and the earth. Likewise, Jesus Christ was raised from the dead by the power of God's Word.

Romans 1:3 and 4 Nestle-Aland
The gospel concerning his Son, who was descended from David according to the flesh and designated Son of God in power

according to the Spirit of holiness [God, Who is Holiness] **by his resurrection from the dead, Jesus Christ our Lord,**

Jesus Christ's resurrection from the dead was God's validation that he was indeed the Son of God. He is the only man to die and be raised to eternal life.

Forty days after God raised Jesus from the dead he ascended into the heavens and sat down at the right hand of God.

Acts 2:36 Nestle-Aland
Let all the house of Israel therefore know assuredly that God has made him both Lord and Christ, this Jesus whom you crucified.

God made Jesus both Lord and Christ. If we are to be saved, we must do two things.

Romans 10:9 AV
That if thou shalt confess with thy mouth the Lord Jesus, and shalt believe in thine heart that God hath raised him from the dead, thou shall be saved.

God set the criterion for salvation – not man. He says we must confess Jesus as lord and believe that God raised him from the dead.

God sent the Savior into the world and the Savior did the work required to save us. God stipulates that our part is to confess him as our Lord and believe that God raised him from the dead. The Lord Jesus did the work of salvation; we simply believe it. This is the Divine grace shown us in Christ by Almighty God. We are saved by the grace of God.

The time is soon coming that God will have His Son speak His Word and all who have confessed Jesus is their lord and that God raised him from the dead will receive the salvation that He promised. They will be raised to life the same as Jesus Christ was raised to life.

Jesus Christ's resurrection is crucial if we are to be saved.

The lord Jesus overcame the grave in the glory and power of his resurrected body, never to die again. His second coming will be vastly different from the suffering and shame he endured during his first coming.

Who will deliver us from death? Let's begin by considering the details of Jesus's death.

Isaiah spoke of the Lord's suffering and torture the he would undergo to redeem man:

Isaiah 53:2b New English Bible
. . . his form, disfigured, lost all the likeness of a man, his beauty changed beyond human semblance.

Why did the Lord endure some forty hours of horrific torture that disfigured him to the degree that it was hard to recognize him? He endured it because of his love for God and his dogged commitment to fulfill His Word.

Jesus Christ gave his life for us. He suffered and died in our stead to pay for our sins, for our salvation and redemption.

As we consider Jesus Christ's death, burial, and his resurrection out from among the dead, we need to understand that the four gospel accounts complement one another.

Each gospel record reveals different pieces of information, that when combined, give us a more comprehensive picture of the complete event.[9] For example, one record may contribute details about time, while another gives details of place, while another may mention who was involved, or any combination of these details. The combined records will give us the whole story. This is the principle of scripture build-up.

We must be careful to note events that precede the event under consideration with those that follow the particular record if we are to rightly-divide the Word of God. First, I would like you to consider what Jesus Christ said about his death and resurrection.[10]

John 2:19-22 AV
Jesus answered and said unto them, Destroy this temple and in three days I will raise it up. Then said the Jews, Forty and six years was this temple in building and wilt thou rear it up in three days? But he spake of the temple of his body. When therefore he was risen from the dead, his disciples remembered that he had said this unto them; and they believed the scripture, and the word which Jesus had said.

---

[9] For a more thorough discussion of the Passover Lamb and the events that surrounded the last week of Jesus Christ's life and his resurrection appearances see, *Jesus Christ Our Passover*, by Dr. Victor Paul Wierwille. The resurrection appearances given here are in their chronological order.

[10] *See* also: John 11:25; Matthew 17:9-23; 16:21; 26:32; 27:63; and Mark 9:31.

John 10:17 and 18 AV

Therefore doth my Father love me, because I lay down my life, that I might take it again. No man taketh it from me, but I lay it down of myself. I have power to lay it down, and I have power to take it again. This commandment have I received of my Father.

Matthew 26:53 reveals that Jesus had twelve legions of angels that he could have summoned to his aid had he wanted to escape the cross, but he did not. No man took his life from him; he laid it down as the Passover Lamb to pay the penalty for our sin.

Jesus hung on the cross from about nine A.M. until about three P.M. – the time when the Passover Lamb was to be slain. According to Matthew 27:45, darkness covered the entire land from noon until three P.M.

Before he died, he cried out in triumph!

Matthew 27:46 Lamsa

And about the ninth hour, Jesus cried out with a loud voice and said, *Eli, Eli lemana shabakthani!* My God, my God, for this I was spared!

He cried out in the Aramaic tongue, "***Eli, Eli lemana shabakthani***!" What do the words mean? **"My God, My God, for this I was spared."** This was his destiny! He was giving his life as God's Passover lamb. While the Israelites were killing their Passover lambs, Jesus Christ was dying as the Lamb of God.

His cry was a cry of victory, triumph and conquest! He did not hang on the cross in failure. He accomplished the mission that God sent him to accomplish. Jesus Christ successfully finished the work of salvation and redemption for those who would believe in him. He fulfilled his purpose. He died as the Passover Lamb. By his sacrifice, he accomplished redemption and salvation for whoever would believe regarding him.

Hebrews 10:11-14 AV

And every priest standeth daily ministering and offering oftentimes the same sacrifices, which can never take away sins: But this man [Jesus Christ]**, after he had offered one sacrifice for sins for ever, sat down on the right hand of God; From henceforth expecting till his enemies be made his footstool. For by one offering he hath perfected for ever them that are sanctified.**

This was the purpose in giving his life as the Lamb of God. When a man makes Jesus his Lord and believes that God raised him from the dead, how long is he perfected? The verse says, **"For by one offering he hath perfected for ever them that are sanctified."**

Hebrews 10: 18 AV
Now where remission of these *is, there is* no more offering for sin.

Jesus Christ made the ultimate sacrifice to pay for sin. He gave his life to redeem us from sin and death. His offering was the last sacrifice to be made for sin. According to God's Word, there is nothing more to pay. Our Lord paid the full price for the remission of sin. God requires nothing further.

John 19:30 AV
When Jesus therefore had received the vinegar, he said, It is finished: and he bowed his head, and gave up his spirit.

After three hours of darkness covering the entire land, Jesus cried out his last words, **"It is finished,"** and he died. The temple veil was rent from top to bottom, and rocks were torn apart by a great earthquake that shook the earth. He completely accomplished all that was required for our salvation and redemption. God's seal to this accomplishment was that He raised him from the dead!

When Jesus died, the veil of the temple was rent from the top to the bottom. The veil hung in the temple between the Holiest of All and the Holy place. Only the chief priest could enter the Holiest of All once a year, on the Day of Atonement. He would intercede for the people of Israel as their representative and offer the blood of atonement on the mercy seat, which covered the top of the Ark of the Covenant.

When the veil was rent from the top to the bottom, it was God's witness to Israel that Christ had abolished their separation from Him. In Christ, they now had access to God. The book of Ephesians gives us further insight, revealing that the separation between the Gentiles and God was also done away, when Jesus Christ died.

After the savage torture Jesus endured from Monday evening until Wednesday afternoon at the time of his death, it would have been difficult to recognize him as a man. His face was a bloody pulp. His back was savagely beaten until it looked like a newly plowed field. [11]

---

[11] Psalm 129:3.

Jesus Christ endured about forty hours of the most horrific physical torture and excruciating mental anguish that a man could suffer before he died. He endured it all as our Passover Lamb so that he could redeem and save us. His love motivated him to submit to this shameful treatment and to lay down his life in our stead. He is indeed the Savior.

When did Jesus Christ die? If we will examine the records in the Word of God, they will give us the answer. Let's begin in the gospel of John.

John 19:31-33 AV
The Jews therefore, because it was the preparation, that the bodies should not remain upon the cross on the sabbath day, (for that sabbath day was an high day,) besought Pilate that their legs might be broken, and *that* they might be taken away. Then came the soldiers, and brake the legs of the first, and of the other which was crucified with him. But when they came to Jesus, and saw that he was dead already, they brake not his legs.

The Hebrew day ran from sunset to sunset, not from midnight to midnight as ours does.

The Passover lamb was killed on **"the preparation,"** between three in the afternoon and sunset. The preparation was the day before the Passover.

The Passover was called a high day, a special Sabbath or a holy convocation. These high days or special Sabbaths could fall on any day of the week.

It would be like our celebration of Christmas. If Christmas falls on Wednesday, that day would be a special or high day. If it falls on Sunday, Christmas would take precedence over our regular Sunday.

There were *two* Sabbaths in this particular week, the Passover Sabbath and the regular weekly Sabbath on Saturday. The Passover Sabbath began at sunset. The regular weekly Sabbath began at sunset on Saturday.

This Passover did not occur on the weekly Sabbath. God's Word clearly distinguishes this Sabbath by the parenthesis in John 19:31, **"(for that Sabbath day was an high day)."**

Jesus Christ died as *the* Passover Lamb. He fulfilled all that the Word of God required concerning the Passover sacrifice.[12]

---

[12] The first Passover is recorded in Exodus 12:1-27. Passover instructions after entering the Promised Land are recorded in Deuteronomy 16:4-7, 16.

Numbers 28:16-18 AV

And in the fourteenth day of the first month *is* the passover of the LORD. And in the fifteenth day of this month *is* the feast: seven days shall unleavened bread be eaten. In the first day *shall be* an holy convocation; ye shall do no manner of servile work *therein*:

Christ died on the fourteenth day of the first month. At sunset, the fifteenth day of the same month, the Feast of Unleavened Bread began, which lasted for seven days. The first and seventh days of the feast were called "high days," holy convocations or special Sabbaths.

Jesus Christ died as the Passover Lamb on the fourteenth of Nisan (according to the Hebrew calendar) about the ninth hour of the day, which is about 3 P.M. our time, and he was buried before sunset.

After Jesus died, Joseph of Arimathaea went to Pilate to obtain his body for burial.

Mark 15:42-46 AV

And now when the even was come, because it was the preparation, that is, the day [the words "the day" are not in the Greek texts] before the sabbath, Joseph of Arimathaea, an honourable counsellor, which also waited for the kingdom of God, came, and went in boldly unto Pilate, and craved the body of Jesus. And Pilate marvelled if he were already dead: and calling *unto him* the centurion, he asked him whether he had been any while dead. And when he knew *it* of the centurion, he gave the body to Joseph. And he bought fine linen, and took him down, and wrapped him in the linen, and laid him in a sepulchre which was hewn out of a rock, and rolled a stone unto the door of the sepulchre.

This tells us that it was still the 14th of Nisan, the preparation. Joseph went to Pilate to get his permission to take Jesus' body so that he could bury him. Joseph bought fine linen cloth, took Jesus down from the cross and wrapped him in it. He buried him in a linen cloth, which is the word *sindon* in the Greek.

Joseph did not use traditional grave clothes, which the word *othonion* describes, nor did he anoint Jesus' body with spices and oils according to their burial customs.

Why did he not do this? He believed that Jesus would rise from the dead.

Luke 23:55 AV

And the women also, which came with Him from Galilee, followed after, and beheld the spulchre, and how his body was laid.

The women, who are identified as Mary Magdalene, and Mary the mother of James the less and of Joses, and Salome in Mark 15:40 and 41, observed that Jesus had not been embalmed or wrapped in the traditional grave clothes. They took it upon themselves to prepare spices and oils to properly bury him. It would take time to acquire the spices, oils, and the traditional grave clothes needed. After they left, someone else arrived.

John 19:39-42 AV

And there came also Nicodemus, which at the first came to Jesus by night, and brought a mixture of myrrh and aloes, about an hundred pound *weight*. Then took they [Nicodemus and his servants] **the body of Jesus, and wound it in linen clothes with the spices, as the manner of the Jews is to bury. Now in the place where he was crucified there was a garden; and in the garden a new sepulchre, wherein was never man yet laid. There laid they Jesus therefore because of the Jews' preparation *day*; for the sepulchre was nigh at hand.**

This is the first we have heard of Nicodemus in the records of the burial. He was a wealthy man and he had servants that accompanied him to the sepulcher.

He must have observed that Joseph had not properly embalmed Jesus' body according to their burial customs. Nicodemus brought a mixture of myrrh and aloes, weighing about a hundred pounds. He wound Jesus' body **"in the linen clothes** (*othionion,* burial clothes or grave clothes) **with the spices, as the manner of the Jews is to bury."**

Nicodemus did not believe that Jesus would rise from the dead at this point, which is why he embalmed him.

This burial was completely different from that which Joseph performed. Joseph had gone to Pilate to get permission to take his body from the cross, and he buried him in a linen sheet. Nicodemus came to the sepulcher later and embalmed him with a mixture of myrrh and aloes, which weighed about a hundred pounds, and put the body in traditional grave clothes.

Jesus Christ had two burials by two different men.

The women that followed Jesus continued to gather the materials to embalm him. The women only observed the first burial by Joseph, which according to their customs was not proper.

Matthew 27:62-66 AV

Now the next day, that followed the day of the preparation, the chief priests and Pharisees came together unto Pilate, Saying, Sir, we remember that that deceiver said, while he was yet alive, After three days I will rise again. Command therefore that the sepulchre be made sure until the third day, lest his disciples come by night, and steal him away, and say unto the people, He is risen from the dead: so the last error shall be worse than the first. Pilate said unto them, Ye have a watch: go your way, make *it* as sure as ye can. So they went, and made the sepulchre sure, sealing the stone, and setting a watch.

The day following the preparation was Nisan 15. It began at sunset. This was a special Sabbath, which marked the beginning of the Feast of Unleavened Bread. The day after Jesus' death, the chief priests besought Pilate to seal the entrance to the sepulcher for three days by Roman authority. Pilate told them to make it sure, so they rolled a large stone on the entrance, placed the Roman seal on it and stationed guards to keep watch.

Matthew 12:40 AV

For as Jonas was three days and three nights in the whale's belly; so shall the Son of man be three days and three nights in the heart of the earth.

Jesus Christ, the Son of man, would have to be dead and in the grave for 72 hours or three complete days and three complete nights, if he was to fulfill this prophecy. So far, we have read that he died on the fourteenth of Nisan and he was buried on the same day before sunset.

When did Jesus Christ rise from the dead?

Matthew 28:1 Interlinear Greek-English New Testament, Berry

Now late on Sabbath, as it was getting dusk toward [the] first [day] of [the] week, came Mary the Magdalene and the other Mary to see the sepulchre.

What was the time according to the Scripture? It was late on the Sabbath (our Saturday) before sunset, the seventeenth of Nisan, as dusk approached. Remember that the Hebrew day ended at sunset. Time is specified twice in the verse: it was "**late on the Sabbath**" and "**it was getting dusk . . ..**" It was not yet the first of the week, which would be our Sunday.

Matthew 28:1 Interlinear Greek-English New Testament, Berry

Now late on the Sabbath, [This was the weekly Hebrew Sabbath, Saturday, the seventeenth of Nisan] **as it was getting dusk toward** [the] **first** [day] **of** [the] **week, came Mary the Magdalene and the other Mary to see the sepulcher.**

The weekly Sabbath, which we would call Saturday, ended at sunset, which would have been around six P.M. our time.

It was approaching dusk toward the first day of the week. The Hebrews numbered their days, first, second, third, etc. The Sabbath is the seventh day of the week, our Saturday. We call the first day of the week Sunday.

It was late on the weekly Sabbath, Saturday afternoon before sunset. The guards were watching the tomb, which was still sealed to preserve the evidence that Jesus was dead. The chief priests had done all they could to make the sepulcher inaccessible.

After seeing that the sepulcher was still inaccessible to them, the women left to prepare spices so they could give Jesus a proper burial after the weekly Sabbath ended and the guards were gone.

Matthew 28:2-4 AV

And, behold, there was a great earthquake: for the angel of the Lord descended from heaven, and came and rolled back the stone from the door, and sat upon it. His countenance was like lightning, and his raiment white as snow: And for fear of him the keepers did shake, and became as dead *men*.

The word "behold" introduces a new subject to us. In verse one, we learned that the women, Mary Magdalene and the other Mary, came to view the sepulcher.

They still could not get in to anoint Jesus' body because of the guards and the stone that sealed the sepulcher, so, they left.

After they left, we are told there was a great earthquake and we are told the reason for it. The angel of the Lord descended from heaven and rolled away the stone from the door, and he sat upon it. The guards were petrified with fear.

Christ was raised out from the dead on the seventeenth of Nisan, late on Saturday, the weekly Sabbath, towards dusk. Counting backwards three days and three nights takes us back to his burial on Wednesday, the fourteenth, before sunset. Every gospel record agrees concerning these events.

Jesus Christ was in the grave for three days and three nights as the prophecy foretold.

One Night and One Day	Two Nights and Two Days	Three Nights and Three Days	
14th – Crucifixion and two burials before sunset	15th – High Day	16th --	17th – The Regular Weekly Sabbath The Resurrection takes place late on the Sabbath towards dusk
Sunset	Sunset	Sunset	Sunset
15th - High Day or Special Sabbath Tomb sealed by Roman Authority and watch was set.	16th -	17th – The Regular Weekly Sabbath	18th – The First Day of the Week

According to Hebrew reckoning the night precedes the day. When day and night are mentioned together, it always signifies a full 24-hour period in the Scriptures. Jesus was dead and in the grave for three full days and three full nights.

Jesus died, he was embalmed and buried. He was a dead man. Did he go to heaven upon death? No.

Matthew 12:40 AV
For as Jonah was three days and three nights in the whale's belly; so shall the Son of man be three days and three nights in the heart of the earth.

If anyone should have died and immediately gone to heaven, surely, it should have been the Lord Jesus Christ, but he did not. He died.

Acts 2:31 and 32 AV
He seeing this before spake of the resurrection of Christ, that his soul was not left in hell [hades: the grave]**, neither his flesh did see corruption. This Jesus hath God raised up, whereof we all are witnesses.**

He was embalmed and in the grave for three days and three nights, but God did not leave him in the grave or hell. God raised him out from the dead!

Jesus Christ's Resurrection Appearances

The Word of God gives us an accurate record of Jesus Christ's appearances after his resurrection from the dead. The next chronological event that the Word of God tells us about took place very early the next morning before the sun came up.

John 20:1 AV
The first *day* of the week cometh Mary Magdalene early, when it was yet dark, unto the sepulchre, and seeth the stone taken away from the sepulchre.

This occurred on the first of the week, before daybreak. We call the first day of the week Sunday. Mary came to the sepulcher alone. It was very early and the sun had not yet risen.

The Hebrew months began with a new moon. This was the eighteenth of the month, so the moon would have been at least three quarters full. This would have provided enough light for Mary to see that the stone was removed from the sepulcher. What happened next?

John 20:2 AV
Then she runneth, and cometh to Simon Peter, and to the other disciple, whom Jesus loved, and saith unto them, "They have taken away the Lord out of the sepulchre, and we ["I" according to the texts] know not where they have laid him."

Mary thought that the Pharisees or the Herodians had removed Jesus body from the sepulcher so she ran to tell Peter.

When Peter and the other disciple whom Jesus loved came to the tomb early the first of the week, the record in John 20: 5-9 tells us:

John 20:5-9 AV
And he stooping down, *and looking in*, saw the linen clothes lying; yet went he not in. Then cometh Simon Peter following him, and went into the sepulchre, and seeth the linen clothes lie, And the

napkin, that was about his head, not lying with the linen clothes, but wrapped together in a place by itself. Then went in also that other disciple, which came first to the sepulchre, and he saw, and believed. For as yet [meaning "until then"] **they knew not** [they did not understand] **the scripture, that he must rise again from** [out from among] **the dead.**

Twice the Word of God draws our attention to what these two witnesses *saw.*

The disciple whom Jesus loved outran Peter and arrived at the sepulcher first.

He stooped down to get a better view of what was inside the open sepulcher. He saw the "**linen clothes lying**", the *othionion,* the about a hundred pounds of herbs and linen strips of cloth that had been wound around his body, but he did not go in. He must have been stunned at what he saw.

Then Peter arrived and went into the sepulcher and he "**seeth the linen clothes** [*othionion*] **lie**".

Twice the Scripture points out what these witnesses saw so that we do not miss it.

It was what the first disciple saw that caused him to believe. What he saw convinced him that God had raised Jesus out from among the rest of the dead.

They had never before understood the scripture that he must rise out from among the dead, *until* they saw the linen clothes (*othonion*) lying there.

Just what did these men see? They did not merely see an empty sepulcher or a shroud in it, they saw the linen grave wrappings that Jesus Christ had been wound in – about a hundred pounds worth we were told – lying intact.

These witnesses saw an empty casing without a body in it! They entered the sepulcher and saw the undisturbed linen grave wrappings, exactly as they had been wrapped around Jesus' dead body, with one exception – the body was gone!

How did the resurrected Christ get out of them? He passed right through them in his resurrected body!

He left irrefutable, indisputable, undeniable, concrete proof for the witnesses that he was risen indeed.

Had the linen grave wrappings that they wound around his corpse been unwound or disturbed and left in a pile it would not have been convincing proof that he had risen from the dead.

If they had taken the body somewhere else, they would have taken the grave clothes with the body.

The record further tells us that the napkin or kerchief that covered his face had been removed, folded, and set aside so that the witnesses could clearly see that the linen grave wrappings no longer contained his body.

The witnesses saw an empty shell in the form of the body it had contained. Christ had risen out from among the dead!

Why did the angel of the Lord descend from heaven and roll the stone away from the entrance of the sepulcher? He did it so that the witnesses who came to the grave could gain access to the evidence: that Jesus Christ had risen indeed.

Then the angel sat on the rock so that it could not be put back over the opening.

Christ did not need the stone removed so that he could get *out* of the sepulcher; he passed right through it in his resurrected body.

The angel removed it so that the witnesses could get *in* to see the tangible proof of Christ's resurrection.

These two men were stunned when they beheld the empty grave wrappings lying there in the same position as when they that had contained Jesus' dead body.

He had been wrapped in about a hundred pounds of linen burial wrappings with spices!

A great stone had been rolled over the opening to the sepulcher.

The chief priests had sealed the grave by Roman authority; guards had been posted at the entrance of the sepulcher to ensure that it stayed sealed and three days and three nights had elapsed, the same time that Jonah had been in the whale's belly. Legally, Jesus was a dead man.

The religious leaders, with the support of Pilate, preserved the irrefutable evidence that he had been dead for three days and three nights or seventy-two hours, however, their plans backfired in their faces!

When the witnesses came he was not there, but the burial casing, the linen grave clothes were. The very ones who sought to discredit Christ's resurrection had preserved the evidence of his resurrection from the dead.

The undisturbed empty burial clothes were left as the physical proof of his resurrection from the dead. All the witnesses saw it. It was undeniable. He was risen out from among the dead!

What happened after the two disciples left?

John 20:11-18 AV
But Mary stood without at the sepulchre weeping: and as she wept, she stooped down, *and looked* into the sepulchre, And seeth two angels in white sitting, the one at the head, and the other at the feet, where the body of Jesus had lain. And they say unto her, Woman, why weepest thou? She saith unto them, Because they have taken away my Lord, and I know not where they have laid him. And when she had thus said, she turned herself back, and saw Jesus standing, and knew not that it was Jesus. Jesus saith unto her, Woman, why weepest thou? whom seekest thou? She, supposing him to be the gardener, saith unto him, Sir, if thou have borne him hence, tell me where thou hast laid him, and I will take him away. Jesus saith unto her, Mary. She turned herself, and saith unto him, Rabboni; which is to say, Master. Jesus saith unto her, Touch me not; for I am not yet ascended to my Father: but go to my brethren, and say unto them, I ascend unto my Father, and your Father; and *to* my God, and your God. Mary Magdalene came and told the disciples that she had seen the Lord, and *that* he had spoken these things unto her.

Mary saw two angels inside the sepulcher sitting where Jesus body had been laid and they asked her why she was crying. She thought that Jesus' body had been taken somewhere else. She turned around and Jesus asked her why she was crying and who she was looking for. She thought he was the gardener until he said, "Mary." She recognized his voice and said, "Rabboni."

Jesus said, "**Touch me not; for I am not yet ascended to my Father:**" Christ was the first fruits from the dead. This verse is speaking of Christ presenting himself to his Father, God, as the first fruits from the dead as the true wave offering.

Under the Law, the first fruits of the spring barley harvest were presented to God as an offering by the high priest.

Acting in his office as God's High Priest, the Lord Jesus presented himself to his Father as the first fruits from the dead.

This is what he meant when he said, "**I ascend unto my Father, and your Father; and to my God and your God.**"

Had Mary held him he would have been ceremonially defiled and unclean according to the Law and he could not have fulfilled the Law's requirements concerning the offering.

The wave offering was presented on the day after the weekly Sabbath during the Feast of Unleavened Bread.

We see from this record that Mary could have held him and that he could talk.

Mark 16:9 AV

Now when *Jesus* was risen early the first *day* of the week, he appeared first to Mary Magdalene, out of whom he had cast seven devils. *And* she went and told them that had been with him, as they mourned and wept. And they, when they had heard that he was alive, and had been seen of her, believed not.

Punctuation is a man-made addition. It was non-existent in the uncial or cursive manuscripts from which our English translations were taken. Aldus Manutius invented punctuation marks in the fifteen century. Punctuation does not carry any God-given authority when it comes to interpretation.

The editors of the King James Version of the Bible added the italicized words as well as the punctuation. In Mark 16:9 they added the comma after the word "week." The addition of the comma after the word "week" makes it sound as if he arose on Sunday.

John 20 told us that Jesus first appeared to Mary on the first of the week, not that he arose on the first of the week. For all the records to fit together accurately, if you want a comma in Mark 16:9 it should follow the word "risen." The verse would then read, "**Now having risen, early the first day of the week he appeared first to Mary Magdalene. . .**" Now all the records agree without any discrepancy.

Mary carried out her Lord's instructions as given in John 20:17 and 18. How did the disciples receive her report?

Mark 16:11 AV

And they, when they had heard that he was alive, and had been seen of her, believed not.

No one can do any more than speak the word of the Lord. They did not believe her. Their unbelief was not a reflection on Mary. She did what she was told to do.

They did not expect Jesus to be raised from the dead. They continued mourning, overcome with grief and fear and they continued to prepare spices to embalm him.

They had only seen Joseph's burial of Jesus, so they did not know that Nicodemus had given him a proper burial.

The next chronological event is recorded in Luke 24:1 and Mark 16:2 and 3.

Luke 24:1 AV
Now upon the first *day* of the week, very early in the morning, they came unto the sepulchre, bringing the spices which they had prepared, and certain *others* with them.

Mark 16:2 and 3 AV
And very early in the morning the first *day* of the week, they came unto the sepulchre at the rising of the sun. And they said among themselves, Who shall roll ["did roll" is the Aramaic] **us away the stone from the door of the sepulchre?**

It was still early the first of the week (our Sunday morning), but it was now "**at the rising of the sun**" or sunrise. It was daylight.

The stone had been removed from the sepulcher before they arrived. The women believed that the stone was removed so that they could give Jesus a proper burial. The great stone, which had been sealed by Roman authority, was gone. There is no mention of guards either. Now the women could get in to embalm Jesus or so they thought.

Luke 24:2 AV
And they found the stone rolled away from the sepulchre.

Mark 16:4 AV
And when they looked, they saw that the stone was rolled away: for it was very great.

Mark 16:5-7 AV
And entering into the sepulchre, they saw a young man sitting on the right side, clothed in a long white garment; and they were affrighted. And he saith unto them, Be not affrighted: Ye seek Jesus of Nazareth, which was crucified: he is risen; he is not here: behold the place where they laid him. But go your way, tell his disciples and

Peter that he goeth before you into Galilee: there shall ye see him, as he said unto you.

Are you keeping up with all the different angel appearances? This angel was inside the sepulcher sitting on the right side.

Jesus had already risen from the dead before they arrived. Luke gives us some additional information that compliments the record in Mark. It follows on the heels of the previous incident.

Luke 24:4-8 AV
And it came to pass, as they were much perplexed thereabout, behold, two men stood by them in shining garments: And as they were afraid, and bowed down *their* faces to the earth, they said unto them, Why seek ye the living among the dead? He is not here, but is risen: remember how he spake unto you when he was yet in Galilee, Saying, The Son of man must be delivered into the hands of sinful men, and be crucified, and the third day rise again. And they remembered his words,

Jesus had already risen when the women came to the sepulcher. As the women were considering the astonishing event that occurred - the great stone had been rolled away, Jesus' body was not in the grave clothes, an angel appeared to them and said that Jesus had been raised from the dead. Suddenly, two more angels appear to them in the form of men with garments flashing like lightning. Again, the angels told them that Jesus was risen from the dead and that it occurred the third day. He had risen from the dead. He was alive!

Put yourself in their sandals. How amazed would you be after a series of events as astonishing as these were?

Matthew 28:8 AV
And they departed quickly from the sepulchre with fear [awe] and great joy; and did run to bring his disciples word.

Meanwhile, the guards ran off to report what occurred to the religious leaders.

Matthew 28:11-15 AV
Now when they were going, behold, some of the watch came into the city, and shewed unto the chief priests all the things that were done. And when they were assembled with the elders, and had taken counsel, they gave large money unto the soldiers, Saying, Say ye, His

disciples came by night, and stole him *away* while we slept. And if this come to the governor's ears, we will persuade him, and secure you. So they took the money, and did as they were taught: and this saying is commonly reported among the Jews until this day.

All the bribes on earth could not change the reality of the Lord Jesus' resurrection. God raised His Son from the dead! Romans 1:4, tells us that God marked out Jesus Christ as His Son by his resurrection from the dead. Christ is the first fruits of those who will rise from the dead.

All that God prepared for His people rests on Jesus Christ's resurrection out from among the dead. The purpose of the ages that He purposed in Christ Jesus pivots on God raising His Son from the dead.

None of the Gospels say that Jesus Christ arose on Sunday morning. What they do teach is that Christ appeared to the witnesses on the first of the week.

Saturday evening before dusk, the angel of the Lord rolled the stone away and sat on it. Three days and three nights after his crucifixion and burial, Christ arose from the dead!

The resurrection of Jesus Christ from the dead is the pivot point of the ages. It dominates the witness of his disciples throughout the book of Acts and of the saints to this day.

Luke 24:9-11 AV
And returned from the sepulchre, and told all these things unto the eleven, and to all the rest. It was Mary Magdalene, and Joanna, and Mary *the mother* of James, and other *women that were* with them, which told these things unto the apostles. And their words seemed to them as idle tales, and they believed them not.

He was risen indeed! Did they believe the women's report? The eleven apostles and the others with them thought their report was nothing more than a tale. They were so overcome with grief and fear they could not process the reality of his resurrection. They could not take in the truth of what had occurred.

Peter had seen the empty sepulcher earlier and now he was hearing a report that confirmed that the Lord was risen.

Luke 24:12 AV
Then arose Peter, and ran unto the sepulchre; and stooping down, he beheld the linen clothes laid by themselves, and departed, wondering [marveling] in himself at that which was come to pass.

This was Peter's second visit to the sepulcher. He heard the report by Mary and then of the women and he himself had now seen the empty grave clothes twice.

Peter had been with Jesus on three occasions that he raised people from the dead. The latest episode was when he saw Jesus raise Lazarus from the dead just weeks before.

Peter had heard his Lord teach them that he would rise out from among the dead. He must have thought, "Could it really be true? Is this really happening?" This time Peter left the sepulcher marveling at what had occurred. The day was still young.

Mark 16:12 and 13 AV
After that he appeared in another form unto two of them, as they walked, and went into the country. And they went and told *it* unto the residue: neither believed they them.

How did Christ appear to these two men? He appeared in another, meaning, a different form. His resurrected body could function in new dimensions that his fleshly body could not. This will become more apparent as we consider more of his resurrection appearances. The gospel of Luke enlarges on this event.

Luke 24:13-16 AV
And, behold, two of them went that same day to a village called Emmaus, which was from Jerusalem *about* threescore furlongs. And they talked together of all these things which had happened. And it came to pass, that, while they communed *together* and reasoned, Jesus himself drew near, and went with them. But their eyes were holden that they should not know him.

They did not recognize who he was. Can you imagine their state of mind after all that had taken place?

Luke 24:17-19a AV
And he said unto them, What manner of communications *are* these that ye have one to another, as ye walk, and are sad? And the one of them, whose name was Cleopas, answering said unto him, Art thou

only a stranger in Jerusalem, and hast not known the things which are come to pass there in these days? And he said unto them, What things?

Had they believed that Christ would rise from the dead they would not have been sad.

Cleopas asked Jesus if he just got off the bus, so to speak. It would have been like saying, "Are you the only stranger in Jerusalem? Don't you know what has happened?"

Jesus acted as if he did not know and asked, "What things?"

Luke 24:19b-24 AV
And they said unto him, Concerning Jesus of Nazareth, which was a prophet mighty in deed and word before God and all the people: And how the chief priests and our rulers delivered him to be condemned to death, and have crucified him. But we trusted that it had been he which should have redeemed Israel: and beside all this, today is the third day since these things were done. Yea and certain women also of our company made us astonished, which were early at the sepulchre; And when they found not his body, they came, saying, that they had also seen a vision of angels, which said that he was alive. And certain of them which were with us went to the sepulchre, and found *it* even so as the women had said: but him they saw not.

The men rehearsed all the recent events to Jesus. This was the third day since he had been crucified, which would make it the fourth day. They had heard the reports that he was risen . . . but as yet they did not believe.

Luke 24:25-29 AV
Then he said unto them, O fools, and slow of heart to believe all that the prophets have spoken: Ought not Christ to have suffered these things, and to enter into his glory? And beginning at Moses and all the prophets, he expounded unto them in all the scriptures the things concerning himself. And they drew nigh unto the village, whither they went: and he made as though he would have gone further. But they constrained him, saying, Abide with us: for it is toward evening, and the day is far spent. And he went in to tarry with them.

Jesus Christ did not share his resurrection experiences with them; instead, he opened the Word of God to them. He went through the entire Old Testament pointing out the prophecies that concerned him.

Here was the only man ever raised from the dead to receive the promise of eternal life. Hebrews 12:2, calls him the author and finisher of the faith. He is the only one who believed the promise of God and actually received it. God raised him from the dead and gave him eternal life. Forty days later, he would ascend into the heavenlies and sit down at the right hand of the throne of God.

On the day of his resurrection, what did he do? He spent time with two saints who hoped that Jesus was the Christ, the redeemer of Israel. These two had been with the disciples when the women brought the report that he was alive. They heard that certain others went to the sepulcher and found it as the women said, but they did not see Jesus. They were confused and perplexed about what had occurred. Now the resurrected Christ himself was teaching them, yet they did not recognize him.

Luke 24:30-32 AV
And it came to pass, as he sat at meat with them, he took bread, and blessed *it*, and brake, and gave to them. And their eyes were opened, and they knew him; and he vanished out of their sight. And they said one to another, Did not our heart burn within us, while he talked with us by the way, and while he opened to us the scriptures?

He was their guest, yet he took the bread from them and blessed it, which only the host would do according to Eastern hospitality. Suddenly they recognized who he was and he vanished right before their eyes. What a record!

What did they talk about after his disappearance? **"Did not our heart burn within us, while he talked with us by the way and while he opened to us the scriptures?"** God's Word will always burn in the hearts of those who believe it.

Luke 24:33 and 34 AV
And they rose up the same hour, and returned to Jerusalem, and found the eleven gathered together, and them that were with them, Saying, The Lord is risen indeed, and hath appeared to Simon.

When the two disciples returned to Jerusalem they found the eleven gathered together (Thomas was absent), as well as others, and they heard them report that, "**The Lord is risen indeed, and hath appeared to Simon**".

Luke 24:35 AV
And they [Cleopas and the other disciple] **told what things *were done* in the way, and how he was known of them in breaking of bread.**

The eleven and the others were now getting multiple reports that confirmed that Christ had indeed risen from the dead.

Mark 16:12 and 13 AV
After that he appeared in another form unto two of them, as they walked, and went into the country. And they went and told *it* unto the residue: neither believed they them.

They still did not believe in spite of all the witnesses' reports. What is it going to take to get them to believe?

John 20:19 AV
Then the same day at evening, being the first *day* of the week, when the doors were shut where the disciples were assembled for fear of the Jews, came Jesus and stood in the midst, and saith unto them, Peace *be* unto you.

It was now the evening of the first day of the week (our Sunday evening). After receiving reports of Christ's resurrection throughout the day, surely you would think that they were overjoyed.

Where were the disciples? They were hiding behind closed doors in fear. Not only did they not believe the reports, they were overcome by the fear of being found out by the Jews. Then suddenly Jesus appeared in their midst and said, "Peace be unto you." Where did he come from? Who let him in?

Luke 24:36-44 AV
And as they thus spake, Jesus himself stood in the midst of them, and saith unto them, Peace *be* unto you. But they were terrified and affrighted, and supposed that they had seen a spirit. And he said unto them, Why are ye troubled? and why do thoughts arise in your hearts? Behold my hands and my feet, that it is I myself: handle me, and see; for a spirit hath not flesh and bones, as ye see me have. And when he had thus spoken, he shewed them *his* hands and *his* feet. And while they yet believed not for joy, and wondered, he said unto them, Have ye here any meat? And they gave him a piece of a broiled

fish, and of an honeycomb. And he took *it*, and did eat before them. And he said unto them, These *are* the words which I spake unto you, while I was yet with you, that all things must be fulfilled, which were written in the law of Moses, and *in* the prophets, and *in* the psalms, concerning me.

Even after Jesus suddenly appeared to them behind locked doors, they were still terrified, afraid and troubled. He had completed his offering to the Father, so He let them touch him and observe his hands and feet. He ate with them. He did all he could to comfort them and put them at ease.

What did the Lord do to convince them of his resurrection? He opened God's Word and showed them that he had fulfilled all that was written of him. He repeatedly took his disciples back to the testimony of God's Word.

Mark 16:14 adds that, **"he upbraided them for their unbelief and hardness of heart."**

Luke 24:45-48 AV
Then opened he their understanding, that they might understand the scriptures, And said unto them, Thus it is written, and thus it behoved Christ to suffer, and to rise from the dead the third day: And that repentance and remission of sins should be preached in his name among all nations, beginning at Jerusalem. And ye are witnesses of these things.

Jesus Christ opened the Word of God and explained to them that what he did was necessary to fulfill the scriptures.

The Old Testament in the Hebrew canon is divided into the Law, the Psalms and the Prophets. He went throughout the Scriptures explaining everything from his suffering and death to his resurrection to them.

He put the Word of God together for them so that they could believe it.

John 20:18-24 AV
Mary Magdalene came and told the disciples that she had seen the Lord, and *that* he had spoken these things unto her. Then the same day at evening, being the first *day* of the week, when the doors were shut where the disciples were assembled for fear of the Jews, came Jesus and stood in the midst, and saith unto them, Peace *be* unto you. And when he had so said, he shewed unto them *his* hands and his side. Then were the disciples glad, when they saw the Lord. Then said Jesus to them again, Peace *be* unto you: as *my* Father hath sent

me, even so send I you. **And when he had said this, he breathed on** *them*, **and saith unto them, Receive ye the Holy Ghost: Whose soever sins ye remit, they are remitted unto them;** *and* **whose soever** *sins* **ye retain, they are retained. But Thomas, one of the twelve, called Didymus, was not with them when Jesus came.**

This record tells us that Thomas was the disciple who was not present. Later Jesus appeared to him.

John 20:26-31 AV
And after eight days again his disciples were within, and Thomas with them: *then* **came Jesus, the doors being shut, and stood in the midst, and said, Peace** *be* **unto you. Then saith he to Thomas, Reach hither thy finger, and behold my hands; and reach hither thy hand, and thrust** *it* **into my side: and be not faithless, but believing. And Thomas answered and said unto him, My Lord and my God. Jesus saith unto him, Thomas, because thou hast seen me, thou hast believed: blessed** *are* **they that have not seen, and** *yet* **have believed. And many other signs truly did Jesus in the presence of his disciples, which are not written in this book: But these are written, that ye might believe that Jesus is the Christ, the Son of God; and that believing ye might have life through his name.**

Jesus Christ gave his disciples proof of his resurrection. Twice when he appeared to them, he told his disciples, "**Peace be unto you.**" He allowed them to touch him and view his hands that had been spiked to the tree. He showed them his side that was pierced with the spear.

The same Jesus that the chief priest and members of the Sanhedrin conspired to crucify rose from the dead.

The disciples could see, hear and touch him. He could veil his identity or reveal himself. He had the ability to appear or to vanish. He could also eat.

God gave us these records so that we might believe that Jesus is the Christ, the Son of God; and that by believing regarding him we could have eternal life.

II Peter 2:4 and Jude 6 are both records that concern the spirits that God imprisoned. I Peter 3: 18-20 reveals that Christ went to declare his triumph to the imprisoned spirits in his resurrected body.

His resurrected body was capable of ascending into the heavenlies where he now lives in the presence of God.

His spiritual body could function in new dimensions that his human body could not. Time and space did not limit his movement.

I Corinthians 15:44 and 45 Rotherham
It is sown a body of the soul, it is raised a body of the spirit; - if there is a body of the soul, there is also of the spirit: Thus, also, it is written - The first man, Adam, became, a living soul, the last Adam, a life-giving spirit.

The book of Acts reveals that he was lifted up from the earth into heaven.

Acts 1:9-12 AV
And when He had spoken these things, while they beheld, He was taken up; and a cloud received Him out of their sight. And while they looked stedfastly toward heaven as He went up, behold, two men stood by them in white apparel; Which also said, "Ye men of Galilee, why stand ye gazing up into heaven? This same Jesus, which is taken up from you into heaven, shall so come in like manner as ye have seen Him go into heaven."

The same Jesus that the leaders of Israel murdered arose from the dead. Forty days later this same Jesus was lifted up from the earth into the heavens.

Where did his ascension into heaven occur? He was on the Mount of Olives.

Zechariah 14:4 AV
And His feet shall stand in that day upon the mount of Olives, which is before Jerusalem on the east, and the mount of Olives shall cleave in the midst thereof toward the east and toward the west, *and there shall be* a very great valley; and half of the mountain shall remove toward the north, and half of it toward the south.

He was on the Mount of Olives when he ascended. The same Jesus will return to the earth and stand on the same mount from which he ascended.

There was no more pain, agony, sorrow or death in the Lord Jesus' resurrected body – only life and that eternal! Even though his mortal body had been mutilated by torture and crucifixion, his resurrected body was glorious.

These things were written so that we could believe that Jesus was the Christ, the Son of God and that by believing we could have eternal life through him.

The records of the vision that God gave His Son on the Mount of Transfiguration, our Lord's resurrection appearances after God raised him from the dead and his ascension into the heavenlies not only reveal glimpses of what Jesus' resurrected body was like; they give us a preview of what our glorified bodies will be like, also.

Is the Soul Immortal?

Today, it is commonly believed that the soul is immortal. Where does this belief originate? Is this the teaching of the Word of God?

Genesis 2:7 AV
And the LORD God formed man *of* the dust of the ground, and breathed into his nostrils the breath of life; and man became a living soul.

As far as the Word of God reveals, a living soul consists of a body and soul. **"The breath of life"** made Adam a **"living soul."** When a man breathes his last breath, he dies. The Word of God does not speak of the soul existing outside of the body after death.

Genesis 2:16 and 17 AV
And the LORD God commanded the man, saying, "You may surely eat of every tree of the garden, but of the tree of the knowledge of good and evil you shall not eat, for in the day that you eat of it you shall surely die.

Adam's condemnation for disobeying God was that in the day that he ate the fruit of the tree of knowledge of good and evil, he would surely die.

Genesis 3:4 AV
But the serpent said to the woman, "You will not surely die."

The serpent, which was the spirit-being, the devil, was the one who said, **"You will not surely die."** The devil said this – not God. The devil is the one who started the lie of the immortality of the soul, not the One True God.

Is the soul immortal?

Psalm 22:29 AV

All they that be fat upon the earth shall eat and worship: all they that go down to the dust [the grave] **shall bow before him: and none can keep alive his own soul.**

Psalm 89:48 Lamsa

Who is the man who lives and shall not see death? Shall he deliver his soul from the hand of Sheol [the grave]**?**

Matthew 10:28 AV

And fear not them which kill the body, but are not able to kill the soul: but rather fear him which is able to destroy both soul and body in hell [ghenna].

These examples from God's Word reveal that there is no such thing as the immortality of the soul. There is an end to soul life, which is death. The soul can die and, furthermore, it can be destroyed.

The Word of God teaches that there is no human life without both the body and soul being united in the same person. Souls don't exist outside of the body after death.

Nimrod initiated the belief in Babylon. Later, Zoroaster in the Assyrian-Babylonian culture, embraced the immortality of the soul. The Persians believed in disembodied souls. Daoism adopted the belief in the Chinese culture. Many of the ancient cultures accepted the idea of the immortality of the soul.

The doctrine is found in many of the ancient cultures and world religions. The doctrine of the immortality of the soul was the major tenet of the Egyptians in their idea of the afterlife. The Pharaohs built the pyramids and stocked them with their treasures for the afterlife. Oftentimes, their servants would even commit suicide so they could serve their master in the afterlife. They believed that upon death, one passed to the afterlife.

Did God give the doctrine of the immortality of the soul to Israel in the Old Testament? Kaufmann Kohler's treatise in *The Jewish Encyclopedia* says:

> The belief that the soul continues its existence after the dissolution of the body is nowhere expressly taught in Holy Scripture. The belief in the immortality of the soul came to the Jews from contact with Greek thought and chiefly through the philosophy of Plato, its principle exponent, who was led to it

through Orphic and Eleusinian mysteries in which Babylonian and Egyptian views were strangely blended.

The Greek philosopher Plato, who lived from 427 to 347 B.C., believed that at death the body and the soul were separated, but he said that it was not the end of the soul. He said that the soul was indestructible. He believed in the immortality of the soul and its eternal reward or punishment after death. He was a student of Socrates (469-347 B.C.) who believed the same, as did Pythagoras before him (570-490 B.C.). [13]

The Greek historian and geographer, Strabo, was familiar with Plato and his ideas when he discussed Indian religion in his history and descriptions of peoples around the world. He compared Indian beliefs with Plato's. "They invent fables also, after the manner of Plato, on the immortality of the soul, and on the punishments in Hades, and other things of this kind." [14]Strabo, *The Geography of Strabo*.

The International Standard Bible Encyclopedia, 1960, Vol. 2, p. 812, on the subject entitled "Death," says "We are influenced always more or less by the Greek, Platonic idea that the body dies, yet the soul is immortal. Such an idea is utterly contrary to the Israelite consciousness and is nowhere found in the Old Testament."

Is the immortality of the soul a New Testament doctrine in God's Word? The German Church historian Philip Schaff, in the *New Schaff-Herzog Encyclopedia of Religious Knowledge*, in the article on "Platonism and Christianity" says:

Many of the early Christians found peculiar attractions in the doctrines of Plato, and employed them as weapons for the defense and extension of Christianity, or cast the truths of Christianity in a Platonic mold.

The doctrines of the Logos and the Trinity received their shape from Greek Fathers, who, if not trained in the schools, were much influenced, directly or indirectly, by the Platonic philosophy, particularly in its Jewish-Alexandrian form. That

---

[13] Source: Kaufmann, Kohler. *Immortality of the Soul* (late Hebrew, "hasharat ha-nefesh;" hayye 'olam"), at http://www.jewishencyclopedia.com/articles/8092-immortality-of-the-soul. Retrieved February 2016.

[14] Roller, Duane W. (2014). *The Geography of Strabo: An English Translation, with Introduction and Notes.*

errors and corruptions crept into the Church from this source cannot be denied.

Among the most illustrious of the Fathers who were more or less Platonic, may be named Justin Martyr, Athenagoras, Theophilus, Ireneus, Hippolytus, Clement of Alexandria, Origen, Minutius Felix, Eusebius, Methodius, Basil the Great, Gregory of Nyssa, and St. Augustine.

Plato gives prominence also to the doctrine of a future state of rewards and punishments. At death, by an inevitable law of its own being, as well as by the appointment of God, every soul goes to its own place, the evil gravitating to the evil, and the good rising to the supreme good.

The Baker's Evangelical Dictionary of Theology[15] says: "Speculation about the soul in the sub apostolic church was heavily influenced by Greek philosophy. This is seen in Origen's acceptance of Plato's doctrine. . .."

The influence of Philo, the Jewish Platonist, was keenly felt in the great theological school at Alexandria. "Its object, like that of Philo, was to unite philosophy with revelation, and thus to use the borrowed jewels of Egypt to adorn the sanctuary of God. He endeavored to reconcile the Mosaic Law with Greek philosophy to make the Mosaic Law acceptable to the Greek mind."[16]

Philo was one of the first to utilize the allegorical method of interpretation of the scriptures. This method of interpreting a text regards the literal sense as the vehicle for a secondary, more spiritual and more profound sense. The words in the text are ignored, and the emphasis is placed entirely on a secondary sense, so that the original words or events have little or no significance [this is called spiritualizing the scriptures]. The literal sense of the scripture is altogether ignored in this method for a "more spiritual and more profound sense," which is left up to the mind of the individual interpreter.[17]

It would seem that the purpose of the allegorical method is not to interpret Scripture, but to pervert the true meaning of Scripture,

---

[15] Elwell, W. A. (Editor). (1996). *The Evangelical Dictionary of Theology 2nd Ed*. Submission by Carl Schultz, p. 1037.

[16] Farrar, F. (2003 ed.). *History of Interpretation.*

[17] Ramm, B. (1970*). Protestant Biblical Interpretation: A Textbook of Hermeneutics.* p. 21.

albeit under the guise of seeking a deeper or more spiritual meaning.[18]

As we continue with the history of the early church, it will become clearer how Greek Philosophy and the allegorical method of interpretation influenced church doctrine.

Origen (185-254 A.D.) was the first to attempt a systematic theology of church doctrine based on the allegorical method of interpretation. He formalized the allegorical interpretation of Scripture. According to Howard Vos, "He held that the literal meaning of the Scripture conceals a deeper meaning available only to the mature believer. The hidden meaning which he found sometimes bore little or no relationship to the literal."[19]

To move away from the ordinary grammatical meaning of the original language and not allow the Word of God to interpret itself is dangerous license indeed. This removes the Word of God as our reference for truth and substitutes men's thoughts and ideas in its place. (Elwell 1996)

Origen embraced Plato's teachings and believed in the immortality of the soul. He believed that at death, the soul departed to an everlasting state of reward or everlasting punishment. "Origen was the exegetical oracle of the early church, till his orthodoxy fell into disrepute."[20]

In, *Origen De Principiis*, he wrote:

> . . . The soul, having a substance and life of its own, shall after its departure from the world, be rewarded according to its deserts, being destined to obtain either an inheritance of eternal life and blessedness, if its actions shall have procured this for it, or to be delivered up to eternal fire and punishments, if the guilt of its crimes shall have brought it down to this . . .. [21]

He also believed that men's souls existed as fallen spirits before the birth of the individual, which accounted for man's sinful nature.[22]

Origen joined the speculations of Plato with certain parts of the Bible and called his philosophy Neo-Platonism. Origen wrote around 200 A.D.,

---

[18] Pentecost, J. Dwight (1964 ed.). *Things to Come: A Study in Biblical Eschatology.* p. 5.

[19] Vos, Howard F. (1960). *Highlights of Church History.* p. 18.

[20] Schaff, P. (2006). *History of the Christian Church, Vol. II, 3rd Ed.* p. 521.

[21] Donaldson, J. and Roberts, A. (Eds.) (1956). *The Ante-Nicene Fathers, Vol. IV: Fathers of the Third Century.* p. 240.

[22] Vos, Howard F. (1960). *Highlights of Chruch History.* p. 19.

"Souls are immortal, as God Himself is eternal and immortal!" He openly professed to be a true "Platonist, who believed in the immortality of the soul."[23]

The Catholic Encyclopedia, remarking on "the Platonic School," says "The great majority of the Christian philosophers down to St. Augustine were Platonists."

In Werner Jaeger's, *"The Greek Ideas of Immortality," Harvard Theological Review*, Volume LII, July 1959, Number 3, he says, "The immortality of man was one of the foundational creeds of the philosophical religion of Platonism that was in part adopted by the Christian church."

Another influential teacher at the close of the second century was Tertullian of Phoenicia, North Africa. He wrote: "For some things are known, even by nature: the immortality of the soul, for instance, is held by many. . . .. I may use, therefore, the opinion of Plato, when he declares: 'EVERY SOUL IS IMMORTAL.'" (*Ante-Nicene Fathers*, Vol. III, p. 547).

There were always a few who held to the Word of God recorded in the Church Epistles, during the first century. They rejected the immortality of the soul. The Word of God teaches the resurrection of the dead by the authority God vested in the Lord Jesus Christ at his coming.

By 68 A.D., Paul wrote in his second letter to Timothy saying that all Asia had turned away from him and the revelation of the Mystery of Christ. Toward the end of Paul's life, he wrote:

II Timothy 4:3 and 4 AV
For the time will come when they will not endure sound doctrine; but after their own lusts shall they heap to themselves teachers, having itching ears; And they shall turn away *their* ears from the truth, and shall be turned unto fables.

The truth of the Word of God was all but lost by the end of the First Century. The truths revealed by God in His Word were mingled with pagan doctrines, traditions and customs to keep their pagan converts.

Many other writers were influenced by Plato, Aristotle, and Virgil and they dominated the philosophy of Western "Christian" theology during the early Middle Ages.

Augustine, 354-430 A.D., also from North Africa, believed like Plato, that death meant the destruction of the body but not the soul. He endorsed

---

[23] Donaldson and Roberts (1956). *The Ante-Nicene Fathers, Vol. IV.* pp. 314, 402.

Plato's philosophy of the immortality of the soul in his book, *The City of God*. The book was a philosophical history through Biblical and secular history. He wrote that the soul ". . . is therefore called immortal, because in a sense, it does not cease to live and to feel, while the body is called mortal because it can be forsaken of all life, and cannot by itself live at all." (*Ante-Nicene Fathers*, Vol. 2, 1995, p. 245.)

Augustine's theology became the standard for the Roman Catholic Church. He was one of the first to make Scripture conform to the interpretation of the church, according to the church historian Farrar.

> . . . It was Augustine's formulation of Christian Platonism that was to permeate virtually all of medieval Christian thought in the West. So enthusiastic was the Christian integration of the Greek thought that Socrates and Plato were frequently regarded as divinely inspired pre-Christian saints . . ..[24]

Thomas Aquinas (1225-1274 A.D.) crystallized the doctrine of the immortal soul in, *The Summa Theologica*. He wrote that the soul cannot be destroyed. Although unfinished, the *Summa* is "one of the classics of the history of philosophy and one of the most influential works of Western literature."[25]

Throughout the *Summa*, he cites Christian, Muslim, Hebrew, and Pagan sources including but not limited to Christian Sacred Scripture, Aristotle, Augustine of Hippo, Avicenna, Averroes, Al-Ghazali, Boethius, John of Damascus, Paul the Apostle, Dionysius the Areopagite, Maimonides, Anselm, Plato, Cicero, and Eriugena.[26]

The Roman Catholic theologian stamped the doctrine of the immortality of the soul permanently on the Christian-professing world.

Fifty years later, Dante Alighieri wrote the famous poem, *The Divine Comedy*. From his imagination, he depicted hell, purgatory, and paradise for the common man. More of this poem is believed today in the Christian religion than the revelation of God's Word.

---

[24] Farrar (2003 ed.). *History of Interpretation.*

[25] Garcia, J.E., Reichberg, G.M. and Schumacher, B.N. (Eds.) (2003). *Thomas Aquinas, Summa Theologiae (ca. 1273), Christian Wisdom Explained Philosophically* by James F. Ross in *The Classics of Western Philosophy: A Reader's Guide.* p. 165.

[26] Source: Thomas Aquinas at *http://www.wikipedia.com.*; Retrieved May 2014.

Just before the Protestant Reformation, the Roman Catholic Church leaders gathered for the Lateran Council of 1513. At the Council they decreed:

> Whereas some have dared to assert concerning the nature of the reasonable soul that it is mortal, we, with the approbation of the sacred council, do condemn and reprobate all those who assert that the intellectual soul is mortal, seeing, according to the canon of Pope Clement V, that the soul is immortal and we decree that all who adhere to like erroneous assertions shall be shunned and punished as heretics.

Anyone who dissented from the Council's decree was "shunned and punished as heretics." They were turned over to the civil authorities, and history records the atrocities these dissenters endured for believing the Word of God. Not only did this doctrine become religious dogma in the medieval church, but those who rejected the Council's ideas became branded as heretics; they were persecuted and punished.

The personal ideas of the influential pagan Greek philosophers helped to mold the thinking of the entire Christian-professing world. Today in Western thought, the doctrine of the immortality of the soul has become a central tenet.

During the Reformation, some early Protestants cast off the doctrine of the immortality of the soul. Martin Luther declared that the Bible did not teach the immortality of the soul (*Defense, Proposition No. 27*)[27]. "Luther held that the soul died with the body, and that God would hereafter raise both the one and the other" (*Historical View*, p. 344).[28] Luther spoke out against the Roman Catholic Church's doctrine because it deviated from the

---

[27] "However, I permit the Pope to establish articles of faith for himself and for his own faithful such are: That the bread and wine are transubstantiated in the sacrament; that the essence of God neither generates nor is generated; that the soul is the substantial form of the human body that he [the pope] is emperor of the world and king of heaven, and earthly god; that the soul is immortal; and all these endless monstrosities in the Roman dunghill of decretals in order that such as his faith is, such may be his gospel, such also his faithful, and such his church, and that the lips may have suitable lettuce and the lid may be worthy of the dish." From *Assertio Omnium Articulorum M. Lutheri per Bullam Leonis X. Novissimam Damnatorum* (Assertion of all the articles of M. Luther condemned by the latest Bull of Leo X), article 27, as found in the *Weimar edition of Luther's Works, vol. 7*, pp. 131, 132.

[28] Source: *www.theberean.org/ Daily Verse and Comment: Ezekial18:4*. Retrieved January 2013.

Word of God. He vigorously taught against allegorical interpretation of God's Word and the perversions it brought into Christianity.

William Tyndale, who was responsible for translating and printing the first New Testament in English said:

> In putting departed souls in heaven, hell, or purgatory you destroy the arguments wherewith Christ and Paul prove the resurrection. The true faith putteth the resurrection; the heathen philosophers, denying that, did put that souls did ever live. If the soul be in heaven, tell me what cause is there for the resurrection?[29]

Luther, Tyndale and a host of other reformers returned to the Scriptures as it interpreted itself, denouncing the allegorical method of interpretation. This is one of the major reasons for the Reformation. These leaders went to the Word of God for their doctrine concerning the hope of salvation, death and resurrection – not to the authority of church doctrine, councils' decisions, philosophy, tradition or allegorically spiritualizing the interpretation of the scriptures.

Today, Plato's philosophy on the immortality of the soul dominates so-called Christian theology. Compare his philosophy with a sermon by one of the most famous Christian teachers of our day:

> . . . You are an immortal soul. Your soul is eternal and will live forever. In other words, the real you - the part of you that thinks, feels, dreams, aspires, the ego, the personality - will never die. . .. your soul will live forever in one of two places - heaven or hell . . . whether we are saved or lost, there is conscious and everlasting existence of the soul and personality. [30]

As discussed previously, John 4:24 says that **"God is spirit,"** not flesh and blood having soul life. Spirit is eternal life; soul life is mortal. Breath life is the life of the human body and it is mortal, not eternal. Spirit and soul are not the same. God sent His Son, the Lord Jesus Christ so that we could have spirit life, which is eternal life. The Word of God teaches that every

---

[29] Daniell, David S. (Ed.) (2000). *William Tyndale: God's Great Love for Humankind: for God so loved the world.*

[30] Graham, Billy. (1983). *Peace with God, Revised and Expanded.* Chapter 6, paragraphs 25 and 28.

man will most certainly die if the Lord tarries. The Word of God says that the soul not only can die but furthermore, it can be destroyed.

The ungodly will be raised in the resurrection of the unjust, be judged out of the books, sentenced to the second death and cast into the lake of fire to be destroyed, according to the Word of God.

Biblically, the word "hell," Sheol or *hades*, is the grave. There is no consciousness, thought, pain, work, no life of any kind in death. It is not the place of burning fire and eternal torture brought to us from Greek mythology.

Gehenna is the place where the sentence of the second death will be carried out for the ungodly. The ungodly will be destroyed, not burn forever.

Let's continue to read what the Word of God reveals:

I Corinthians 15:52 and 53 AV
In a moment, in the twinkling of an eye, at the last trump: for the trumpet shall sound, and the dead shall be raised incorruptible, and *we* shall be changed. For this corruptible must put on incorruption, and this mortal *must* put on immortality.

The Word of God reveals that the members of the Church, who are living when Christ returns, will put on immortality at the same time that the dead (sleeping) members of His Church, who have deteriorated in the grave, will be raised, incorruptible. The revelation says nothing about "the soul" being immortal.

The saved of the Church of the Grace of God will inherit eternal life on the Day of Redemption, the day that Christ Jesus our Lord returns for the members of his body, to gather together both the living saints and those who have died . . . at the same time.

There is no life after death except by resurrection and that by the Lord Jesus Christ at his coming according to the Word of God. Resurrection involves raising the whole person to life. Its teachings do not include the disembodied spirits of the dead.

We cannot elevate anyone's words above God's Word. The Word of God is the only trustworthy, reliable reference for truth concerning spiritual matters. If we allow it to interpret itself, from its own words, we will have the word of truth. Why not learn from God by taking Him at His Word?

Colossians 2:8 AV

Beware lest any man spoil you through philosophy and vain deceit, after the tradition of men, after the rudiments of the world, and not after Christ.

We should know why we believe what we believe. The Word of God does not teach what Plato taught. Greek philosophy, mythology and the religious traditions derived from these men have nothing to do with God's Word. The revelation of the Word of God has been mixed with Greek philosophy and pagan mythology and "baptized" as Christian doctrine today.

With the Reformation, believers returned to the Word of God as their only reference for truth concerning spiritual matters, and they discovered God's revelation once again. Regrettably, many theologians since that time have returned to the teachings of ancient Babylon, Egypt and Greece.

The allegorical method of interpretation embraced by many theologians has perverted the Word of God and blinded the minds of those who desire to know its truth.

How many Christians do you know believe that when you die, you will immediately go to heaven if you are good or, you will burn in hell? These ideas did not come from the Word of God. The soul is not immortal.

Ask yourself, who started the lie, **"Ye shall not surely die"**?

Christ's Words versus Tradition

Today, some teach that when the body dies, the soul automatically goes to heaven to live and then comes back at some future time for the body.

Wherever the Word of God speaks of resurrection life, it speaks of the whole person living again. This will only occur when Christ raises the dead at his coming. There are no partial or intermediate steps to eternal life.

John 6:38-40 AV
For I came down from heaven, not to do mine own will, but the will of him that sent me. And this is the Father's will which hath sent me, that of all which he hath given me I should lose nothing, but should raise it up again at the last day. And this is the will of him that sent me, that every one which seeth the Son, and believeth on him, may have everlasting life: and I will raise him up at the last day.

John 6:44 AV
No man can come to me, except the Father which hath sent me draw him: and I will raise him up at the last day.

John 6:53 and 54 AV
Then Jesus said unto them, Verily, verily, I say unto you, Except ye eat the flesh of the Son of man, and drink his blood, ye have no life in you. Whoso eateth my flesh, and drinketh my blood, hath eternal life; and I will raise him up at the last day.

Four times in John 6, Jesus Christ said "**I will raise him up**." He will raise the same person that lived previously. It is *you yourself,* the individual, that which makes you who you are, that he will raise to life again.

When did he say he would raise him? He said "**. . . at the last day**," not at the time of one's death.

John 14:1-3 AV

Let not your heart be troubled: ye believe in God, believe also in me. In my Father's house are many mansions: if *it were* not *so*, I would have told you. I go to prepare a place for you. And if I go and prepare a place for you, I will come again, and receive you unto myself; that where I am, *there* ye may be also.

What did Jesus Christ say? **"I will come again, and receive you unto myself; that where I am, *there* ye may be also."** Oh no, he must have meant to say "You will die and come to me, and I will receive you." Is that what he said? No, he said **"I will come again, and receive you unto myself; that where I am, *there* ye may be also."**

Deliverance from death will occur at the return of Christ. When he returns, he will execute the authority God gave him to raise His people from the dead. This is true of Israel and it is true of the Church of the Grace of God.

All hinges on the power that God gave Christ over death and the grave. He will execute this power at his coming. There is no resurrection from the dead or change for the living except by his authority, and it will only occur at his coming.

Where did we get the popular belief that we die and go to heaven or hell? It comes to us from Babylon, Egypt and Greek philosophy. It is the belief inspired by the old serpent concerning the immortality of the soul.[31] These religious leaders embraced the teaching. This doctrine throws the door wide open to the teachings of spiritualism.

This is not what the Word of God teaches. Adam's condemnation was **"thou shalt surely die,"** not evolve into a spiritual being after death. Who was it that said **"Ye shall not surely die"**? The old serpent, the devil made the statement – not God.

There is no substantiation in the Word of God for the teaching propounded by the spiritualists. The only life after death will come by resurrection, by Christ's authority and it will only occur at his coming.

The only way to reach the conclusion that you become alive upon death is to add, delete or change the Word of God. The old serpent has worked hard to pervert what God's Word says ever since the garden.

---

[31] *See* the discussion, *Is the Soul Immortal?* in this manuscript.

Revelation 1:18
I *am* he that liveth, and was dead; and, behold, I am alive for evermore, Amen; and have the keys of hell [the grave] **and of death.**

Jesus Christ is the only one who holds the keys to the grave and death. There is no release from death except by his authority. He will exercise this power at his coming.

The spiritualist teaching that we die and go to heaven, negates the order of resurrection, the time of resurrection and the power of the Lord's authority over death.

I Thessalonians 4:16 and 17 AV
For the Lord himself shall descend from heaven with a shout, with the voice of the archangel, and with the trump of God: and the dead in Christ shall rise first: Then we which are alive *and* remain shall be caught up together with them in the clouds, to meet the Lord in the air: and so shall we ever be with the Lord.

This revelation to the Church defines the order, the time and the power that brings us our release from death and this world. The dead and living of the Church will be caught up together, at the same time, by the Lord's power and authority. This occurs at his coming, not at death.

I John 3:2 and 3 AV
Beloved, now are we the sons of God, and it doth not yet appear what we shall be: but we know that, when he shall appear, we shall be like him; for we shall see him as he is. And every man that hath this hope in him purifieth himself, even as he is pure.

Our hope is in Christ. When he shall appear, then we shall be like him.

Romans 1:3 and 4 Young's Literal Translation
Concerning His Son, (who is come of the seed of David according to the flesh, who is marked out Son of God in power, according to the Spirit of sanctification, by the rising again from the dead,) Jesus Christ our Lord;

God declared Jesus Christ as His Son by raising him out from the dead. Consider what Jesus Christ said to the Sadducees when they questioned him about the resurrection.

Luke 20:36 AV

Neither can they die any more: for they are equal unto the angels; and are the children of God, being the children of the resurrection.

After these saints are resurrected from the dead, they cannot die again. God will declare them as His children by resurrection, the same as He did with His Son, Jesus Christ our Lord.

Romans 8:22 and 23 Moffett

To this day, we know the entire creation sighs and throbs with pain; and not only so, but even we ourselves, who have the Spirit as a foretaste of the future, even we sigh deeply to ourselves as we wait for the redemption of the body that means our full sonship.

When Christ Jesus the Lord comes to gather his saints of the Church together, we will receive our full sonship. Today, we have the gift of holy spirit, which is the down payment or earnest deposit of our inheritance until the time of its acquisition. The holy spirit is the spirit of sonship. When Christ returns for the church, we will receive the full sonship, the redemption of the body.

If we are alive at Christ's coming, that which is mortal will take on immortality. If we have died, we will be raised incorruptible. The whole creation awaits the manifestation of the sons of God.

Our bodies will be better than the earthly tents we live in today. In Christ, we will have deathless, glorious, spiritual bodies like Christ's glorious body.

We will no longer have the *promise* of eternal life, we will have the *reality* itself.

We will no longer have to struggle against the so-called "god" of this world and be vexed with evil every day. Our life will no longer be subject to disappointing misery that only ends in death.

We will inherit eternal life, and it will take our Father the whole of eternity to demonstrate the riches of His grace in kindness to us in Christ.

With the kindness of a loving Father, God will bestow His beloved children with the riches of His glorious grace beyond anything that we could ask or think.

Christ will come to save, redeem, and transform us to be like him. He will entirely preserve us – body and soul and spirit – and we will be without blame at his coming.

Ephesians 2:7 ASV

That in the ages to come he might show the exceeding riches of his grace in kindness toward us in Christ Jesus:

We know very little comparatively about every spiritual blessing that our Father has prepared for us in the heavenlies throughout the ages to come. It is going to take Him the whole period - eternity - to demonstrate all of His kindness that He has purposed for us in Christ.

The scope of our glorious hope has not been fully disclosed to us, but we have the certainty of God's Word revealed to us that we are joint-heirs with Christ, and he assures us that we will be glorified together with him.

Our loving Heavenly Father was the mastermind of this glorious redemption. When God placed Adam in the garden, it was paradise. God says that everything He made was "very good."

Likewise, the glory that our Father has prepared for us in the last Adam,[32] Christ Jesus, will be glory beyond anything we can ask or think. . . and that, forever. To say that we will not be disappointed in our expectation of hope in Christ is truly an understatement.

II Thessalonians 2:13 and 14 AV

But we are bound to give thanks alway to God for you, brethren beloved of the Lord, because God hath from the beginning chosen you to salvation through sanctification of the Spirit and belief of the truth: Whereunto he called you by our gospel, to the obtaining of the glory of our Lord Jesus Christ.

In Christ, we are the **"beloved of the Lord."** What was God's purpose in calling us? He called us "**to the obtaining of the glory of our Lord Jesus Christ**." The riches of grace that God purposed in Christ for His people are staggering.

Much of what God has prepared for us in eternity remains an enigma today, but we know that we are joint-heirs with Christ and that we will obtain the glory of our Lord Jesus Christ.

David said of his hope, in Psalm 16:10 and 11, that God would show him the path of eternal life and in His presence there would be fullness of joy and pleasures forevermore.

---

[32] "And so it is written, The first man Adam was made a living soul; the last Adam *was made* a quickening [life-giving] spirit." I Corinthians 15:45 AV.

Could there be any less "**fullness of joy and pleasures forevermore**" for us, when we are glorified together with Christ as joint-heirs?

We have seen the need for the hope of redemption and salvation from the Word of God. God's solution to Adam's condemnation, the loss of the spirit, the loss of his dominion, physical death and his access to the tree of life in paradise, was to provide a Redeemer.

Jesus Christ is the woman's seed, the Redeemer of man. His work made it possible for anyone who confesses Jesus as their Lord and believes that God raised him from the dead to be saved. From that point on, God sees the saved one "in Christ," and He says that we fully share with Christ in all that he accomplished.

We are no longer united with Adam as men of the flesh. We are united with Christ as men of the spirit. We now identify with Christ Jesus and we share in his accomplishments. Our hope is in Christ! When he returns for us, he will deliver us from the disappointing misery that the old serpent brought upon both man and the creation. It is Christ in you, the hope of glory!

What Does God's Word Say?

As we have seen, tradition and the Word of God do not usually agree. The truth of God's Word always makes sense, while tradition usually prevents us from understanding the Word of God and leaves us with confusion.

If we are to rightly-divide the Word of God, every verse concerning the identical subject must agree. If there seems to be a problem in understanding a particular verse or passage, we must understand the difficult passage in light of the many passages that are clear. The Word of God will interpret itself; it will unfold the meaning to us if we will consider its testimony.

We cannot pull a statement or verse out of its context and use it in a way that contradicts the many scriptures that are clear and understandable.

We are now going to consider some misquoted or misunderstood scriptures and apply the principals of Biblical study to allow the Word of God to interpret itself.

To Die is Gain

One section that is wrestled from its context is Philippians 1:20- 24. Some use this section to teach that death is a gain, because, *they say*, that death is the entrance to eternal life. Is this what this section is teaching?

The context begins in verse 12.

Philippians 1:12 AV
But I would ye should understand, brethren, that the things *which happened* unto me have fallen out rather unto the furtherance of the gospel;

The context that follows, concerns **"the furtherance of the gospel."** He rejoiced that Christ was proclaimed, whether he was in prison or not; whether some spoke of Christ out of contention or out of love and good will.

He set himself for the furtherance of the gospel, whether it was by his life or by his death.

Philippians 1:20-24 AV
According to my earnest expectation and *my* hope, that in nothing I shall be ashamed, but *that* with all boldness, as always, *so* now also Christ shall be magnified in my body, whether *it be* by life, or by death. For to me to live *is* Christ, and to die [for the furtherance of the gospel] ***is* gain. But if I live in the flesh, this *is* the fruit of my labour: yet what I shall choose I wot** [know] **not. For I am in a strait betwixt two** [living or dying]**, having a desire to depart, and to be with Christ; which is far better** [this third option was far better than either living or dying]**: Nevertheless to abide in the flesh *is* more needful for you.**

Paul was being pressed between two things, life and death according to verse 20, and to either live or die according to verse 21. The apostle Paul was concerned for the furtherance of the gospel whether by his life or by his death.

He was in a tight spot or strait, which could result in his living and proclaiming the gospel or dying in prison if that would further the gospel. His concern was the furtherance of the gospel.

However, verse 23, introduces a third possibility which is amplified by the figure of speech *Pleonasm* or Redundancy. The figure uses more words than the grammar requires for the purpose of amplifying them. The latter part of the verse reads, **"which is far better",** but the Greek reads, *"pollo* (much) *mallon* (more) *kreisson* (better). The third possibility is amplified above either living or dying.

What was his inner passion, his yearning that was "much, more better" or far, far better than either living or dying?

The words **"to depart,"** in the Greek are not the infinitive mood of the verb "depart;" they are, *eis to analusai* **"unto the return."** *Analuo* means, "to return."

The verse reads, "For I am in a strait betwixt two [living or dying], (having a desire for the return and to be with Christ; which is far, far better [than either living or dying])."

The words in verse 23 digress from the two options that pressed on Paul in the flesh – life or death. Verse 23 introduces a third possibility. The third option should be set in a parenthesis.

He ached for the return[33] of Christ. Only then would Paul be with Christ and delivered from the two situations that were pressing on him. Christ's return was far, far better than living or dying.

As I Thessalonians 4:16 and 17 teach, both we which are alive and remain unto the coming of the Lord and the dead in Christ will both be caught up together in the clouds to meet the Lord in the air – at the same time. This is the only possible way to be with the Lord.

II Thessalonians 2:1 teaches us that when our Lord Jesus Christ comes, we will be gathered together unto him. This is the hope of glory.

I Corinthians 15:23 again teaches us that the time of our resurrection is **"at his coming."** Verses 51-54, teach us that the dead will be raised and the living will be changed at the same time – at the last trump. This victory only comes through the Lord Jesus Christ at his coming.

Colossians 3:4 teaches us that, **"When Christ, who is our life, shall appear, then shall ye also appear with Him in glory."**

Ephesians 4:31 and 1:13 and 14 teach us that we are sealed with the holy spirit until the day of redemption. **"The day of redemption"** is the day that the Lord will descend out of heaven to redeem those he purchased with his life. This is called **"the day of the Lord Jesus Christ"** and **"the day of Christ"** in Philippians 1: 6 and 10.

All these scriptures reveal that the time of our redemption from the grave and this present evil world will be on a particular day – the day when Christ returns to gather his Church.

I Thessalonians 5:23 ERV says, **"May the God of peace himself sanctify you wholly; and may your spirit and soul and body be preserved entire, without blame at the coming of our Lord Jesus Christ."** This is the day of our salvation.

I Corinthians 15:26 says that the last enemy to be destroyed is death. If death is an enemy, how can we say that "to die is gain," meaning that it is the time of entrance into eternal life? The only release for the dead believer is at the return of Christ, when he will raise the members of his body unto eternal life.

---

[33] The word used in Philippians 1:23 is *analuo*, which means to loosen back again; therefore, to return. The Greek reads, *eis*, unto, *ton*, the, *analusai* to return again. It means, "to return back." The word is used here and by the lord in Luke 12:36, where it is translated "return." Christ uses the word speaking of his return from heaven. See pp. 206 and 207; 415 and 416; 492 in Bullinger, E.W. (1975 ed.). *Figures of Speech Used in the Bible: Explained and Illustrated.*

The revelation in Philippians 1:23 cannot contradict the truth that God has revealed to us at every other place. The time that we receive eternal life cannot vary from one record to another or from one church to another. We cannot take the seemingly difficult passage and erect a different doctrine based on it.

The difficult passage must be understood in light of the many passages that are clear. Truth cannot contradict itself. Doctrine is not obscure, nor does it require us to embellish what is written and let loose upon it with our own ideas. The Word of God will interpret itself in the verse, the context or how it has been used before.

The difficulty comes from embracing the teaching of tradition[34] instead of the Word of God.

"…Today shalt thou be with me in paradise."

What about the statement that Jesus Christ made to one of the malefactors that was crucified with him, recorded in Luke 23:43 in the King James Version? **"Verily I say unto thee, Today shalt thou be with Me in paradise."**

How could the Lord say that the malefactor would be with him in paradise that very day? He died that day and he was dead for three days and three nights before his resurrection. On the day of his death he was in the grave, not paradise.

After his resurrection from the dead, he was on earth for another forty days before he ascended into heaven. He was not in paradise those forty days.

When he ascended, did he ascend into paradise or the heavenlies? The Word of God says he ascended into the heavenlies. The understanding of this verse has to fit with every other scripture on the subject.

Does one go to paradise upon death? What is paradise?

The word "paradise" is the Greek word *paradeisos*. In the Septuagint, the Greek translation of the Old Testament, it is used in Genesis 2:8 and it is translated into English as "garden."

---

[34] *See* the discussion, *"Is the Soul Immortal?"* in this manuscript.

Genesis 2:8-15 AV

And the LORD God planted a garden eastward in Eden; and there he put the man whom he had formed. And out of the ground made the LORD God to grow every tree that is pleasant to the sight, and good for food; the tree of life also in the midst of the garden, and the tree of knowledge of good and evil. And a river went out of Eden to water the garden; and from thence it was parted, and became into four heads. The name of the first *is* Pison: that *is* it which compasseth the whole land of Havilah, where *there is* gold; And the gold of that land *is* good: there *is* bdellium and the onyx stone. And the name of the second river *is* Gihon: the same *is* it that compasseth the whole land of Ethiopia. And the name of the third river *is* Hiddekel: that *is* it which goeth toward the east of Assyria. And the fourth river *is* Euphrates. And the LORD God took the man, and put him into the garden of Eden to dress it and to keep it.

Adam lived in the Garden of Eden or paradise. The garden contained everything he needed. God provided everything to the end He says that it was "**very good**." It was Adam's responsibility to dress and keep it.

After Adam disobeyed God and ate of the tree of the knowledge of good and evil, God passed sentence and ordered Adam's condemnation and expelled him from the garden. Now he had to live under the condemnation of his sin and death.

Genesis 3:23 and 24 AV

Therefore the LORD God sent him forth from the garden of Eden, to till the ground from whence he was taken. So he drove out the man; and he placed at the east of the garden of Eden Cherubims, and a flaming sword which turned every way, to keep the way of the tree of life.

No man had access to the tree of life after that time. God had the entrance to the garden or paradise guarded by armed Cherubim, which are powerful spirit beings. Had man eaten of the tree of life he would have remained in an unredeemable state forever.

The tree of life will not be available again until the time that God again grants access to it in the new earth, of which Revelation 22 speaks.

Revelation 22:1-4 AV

And he shewed me a pure river of water of life, clear as crystal, proceeding out of the throne of God and of the Lamb. In the midst

of the street of it, and on either side of the river, *was there* the tree of life, which bare twelve *manner of* fruits, *and* yielded her fruit every month: and the leaves of the tree *were* for the healing of the nations. And there shall be no more curse: but the throne of God and of the Lamb shall be in it; and his servants shall serve him: And they shall see his face; and his name *shall be* in their foreheads.

The *tree of life* is not found again until the time of *the new earth* spoken of in Revelation 21.

Revelation 21:1-5 AV
And I saw a new heaven and a new earth: for the first [former] heaven and the first [former] earth were passed away; and there was no more sea. And I John saw the holy city, new Jerusalem, coming down from God out of heaven, prepared as a bride adorned for her husband. And I heard a great voice out of heaven saying, Behold, the tabernacle of God *is* with men, and he will dwell with them, and they shall be his people, and God himself shall be with them, *and be* their God. And God shall wipe away all tears from their eyes; and there shall be no more death, neither sorrow, nor crying, neither shall there be any more pain: for the former things are passed away. And he that sat upon the throne said, Behold, I make all things new. And he said unto me, Write: for these words are true and faithful.

You can read the rest of chapter 21 to 22:5 for the whole record concerning the new heaven and earth. Revelation 2:7 foretells of this time.

Revelation 2:7 AV
He that hath an ear, let him hear what the Spirit saith unto the churches; To him that overcometh will I give to eat of the tree of life, which is in the midst of the paradise of God.

The Word of God tells us that the tree of life will be **"in the midst of the paradise of God."** This speaks of the future time when God will make all things new again in the new heaven and earth.

The word "paradise" only occurs two other times in the New Testament; in Luke 23:43 and II Corinthians 12:4. Let us first read the record in II Corinthians.

II Corinthians 12:1-4 AV
It is not expedient for me doubtless to glory. I will come to visions and revelations of the Lord. I knew a man in Christ above fourteen

years ago, (whether in the body, I cannot tell; or whether out of the body, I cannot tell: God knoweth;) such an one caught up to the third heaven. And I knew such a man, (whether in the body, or out of the body, I cannot tell: God knoweth;) How that he was caught up into paradise, and heard unspeakable words, which it is not lawful for a man to utter.

The word for **"caught up"** is *harpazo* in the Greek and it means "to catch away *or* snatch away *or* carry off." It is used 13 times in the Word of God.

Paul was *caught away* by revelation to the future time of the third heaven and paradise. The revelation was so vivid that he did not know whether he was physically there or not. God did not permit Paul to write about it.

As we have seen from the record in the book of Revelation, and here in II Corinthians, paradise will not occur again on earth until the times of the *third* heaven and earth. These two records make it clear that paradise concerns a yet future time on earth.

With the understanding of paradise from the Word of God, let us read the record in Luke 23:43.

Luke 23:43 AV
And Jesus said unto him, Verily I say unto thee, Today shalt thou be with me in paradise.

How could Jesus tell the malefactor, **"Today shalt thou be with me in paradise"**? Does this fit with the other records that mention paradise in the New Testament? The answer is obvious. No, it does not. How then are we to make sense of this?

Remember, there was no punctuation in the original texts. Aldus Manutius introduced punctuation in the 15th century. When the editors of the Bible added punctuation marks they did it by their own judgment. Punctuation does not carry any Divine authority concerning interpretation, so if we omit it, it does not change the Word of God. Let's read the verse without the punctuation.

"And Jesus said unto him verily I say unto thee today thou shalt be with me in paradise."

The expression, "I say unto thee today" or "I say unto you this day" is a common Hebrew idiom that emphatically stresses the words that follow. **"Verily I say unto you this day . . . thou shalt be with me in paradise."**

In the Greek, **"I say unto thee today. . ."** is in the present tense. **"Thou shalt be with me in paradise"** is in the future tense. Jesus told the malefactor the day that they were being crucified, that in the future, when paradise was once again available on earth, he would surely be with him.

The malefactor died that day and he will remain in the grave until the time of the resurrection of the just. At some time in the future he will be with Christ in paradise on the earth.

Do you see what one little comma can do? Punctuation may be useful for reference, but it *cannot* be used for the purpose of interpretation. It does not carry any God-given authority. It is an editorial edition to the text. It is man-made. It is not of Divine origin.

Every Scripture concerning the identical subject must agree without contradiction if we are to rightly-divide God's Word and have the Word of truth.

We cannot take a scripture that may be difficult for us to understand and use it in a contradictory way with other scriptures that are clear and understandable. The difficult verse or word must fit with all the other clear scriptures concerning the same subject.

Every reference to paradise concerns a place on earth. Heaven is always a place above the earth.

Paradise *is* paradise and heaven *is* heaven. They are two distinct, separate places. The two cannot be used interchangeably.

It is not a matter of what you or I may think, but a matter of the revelation knowledge of God's Word that is important. His Word must be our only reference for truth concerning spiritual matters.

The Rich Man and Lazarus

When Jesus Christ used the parable of the rich man and Lazarus in the Gospel of Luke, he was in a confrontation with the Pharisees who did not believe the Word of God.

A parable is a figure of speech, which is a repeated or continued simile – an illustration by which one set of circumstances is likened to another. The likeness is generally only in some special point.

> The resemblance is to be sought for in the scope of the context, and in the one great truth which is presented, and the one important lesson which is taught; and not in all the minute details with which these happen to be associated.

> The thing, or history, or story may be true or imaginary; but the events must be possible, or likely to have happened; at any rate those who hear must believe that they are possible events, though it is not necessary that the speaker should believe them.[35]

Those who say that when you die you go to heaven, which they erroneously call paradise, often refer to this parable for their argument. Is that what Jesus Christ was saying in this parable?

Let us begin in verse 14 with the immediate context to find the answer.

Luke 16:13 and 14 AV
No servant can serve two masters: for either he will hate the one, and love the other or else he will hold to the one, and despise the other. Ye cannot serve God and mammon. And the Pharisees also, who were covetous, heard all these things: and they derided him.

To whom was Christ speaking? He was speaking to the Pharisees. These religious leaders were covetous and when they heard what Christ said, they derided him. This gives us the reason for what he is about to say.

Luke 16:15 AV
And he said unto them, Ye [the Pharasees] are they which justify yourselves before men; but God knoweth your hearts: for that

---

[35] Bullinger (1975 ed). *Figures of Speech Used in the Bible: Explained and Illustrated.*

which is highly esteemed among men is abomination in the sight of God.

This vividly exposes the character of the Pharisees to whom he was speaking. Many of the things that they believed and taught were opposed to the Word of God.

In chapter 11, these men said that Jesus Christ cast out devils through Beelzebub, the chief of the devils. (In John 8:44 the Lord told the scribes and Pharisees, **"*Ye* are of *your* father the devil, and the lusts of your father ye will do"**).

Later, in Luke 11, the Lord Jesus called them **"fools and hypocrites."** He said that they hindered those who wanted to learn God's Word. They prevented God's people from knowing the truth that God revealed in His Word.

These men made the Word of God of none effect by replacing it with their traditions. They held their traditions in high regard, but their traditions were an abomination in the sight of God.

Their deceitful handling of the Word of God brought about the Lord's scathing reproof in 11:37-54. He condemned them for their traditions, saying some six times, **"Woe unto you."**

Luke 16:16 and 17 AV
The law and the prophets *were* until John: since that time the kingdom of God is preached, and every man presseth into it. And it is easier for heaven and earth to pass, than one tittle of the law to fail.

These men changed the Word of God to suit their own purposes, usually for money, but Christ told them that it would be easier for heaven and earth to pass away, than for one tittle of the law to fail. A tittle is a small ornament in the Hebrew language.

In the next verse, Luke 16:18, Christ quoted the law concerning divorce to them. The Pharisees added many of their own petty grounds for divorce, which were contrary to the Law.

In the context, he then turns to their traditions concerning death and the afterlife. This is yet another instance in which they made the Word of God of none effect by their tradition.

Before we read the parable, I would like you to read what Christ said immediately following it.

Luke 17:1 and 2 AV

Then said he unto the disciples, It is impossible but that offences [stumbling blocks] will come: but woe *unto him*, through whom they come! It were better for him that a millstone were hanged about his neck, and he cast into the sea, than that he should offend one of these little ones.

There should not be a chapter division separating 16:31 and 17:1. Immediately following the parable, Christ spoke to his disciples. What he said sounds very similar to what he told the Pharisees in chapter 11 concerning their teachings. He calls their teachings offenses or stumbling blocks and pronounces their condemnation for the damage they did to God's People. What the Lord says in these verses agrees with what he told the Pharisees, **". . . woe unto you!"**

In the parable of the rich man and Lazarus the Lord is speaking to the Pharisees. He used their own teachings, which he put in the mouths of the characters in the parable, to rebuke them. The parable is addressed to the Pharisees and it is based on their teachings. Their traditions openly contradicted the truth of the Scriptures. In this record, Christ used the Pharisees' own erroneous teachings to condemn them.

Remember, for a parable to be effective what is said must be believed to be true by those who hear it. The parable does not necessarily have to be true in fact, but the hearers have to believe that what is said is possible.

Luke 16:19-28 AV

There was a certain rich man, which was clothed in purple and fine linen, and fared sumptuously every day: And there was a certain beggar named Lazarus, which was laid at his gate, full of sores, And desiring to be fed with the crumbs which fell from the rich man's table: moreover the dogs came and licked his sores. And it came to pass, that the beggar died, and was carried by the angels into Abraham's bosom: the rich man also died, and was buried; And in hell he lift up his eyes, being in torments, and seeth Abraham afar off, and Lazarus in his bosom. And he cried and said, Father Abraham, have mercy on me, and send Lazarus, that he may dip the tip of his finger in water, and cool my tongue; for I am tormented in this flame. But Abraham said, Son, remember that thou in thy lifetime receivedst thy good things, and likewise Lazarus evil things: but now he is comforted, and thou art tormented. And beside all this, between us and you there is a great gulf fixed: so that they which would pass from hence to you cannot; neither can they pass

to us, that *would come* from thence. Then he said, I pray thee therefore, father, that thou wouldest send him to my father's house: For I have five brethren; that he may testify unto them, lest they also come into this place of torment.

The expressions of **"died, and was carried by the angels into Abraham's bosom," "and in hell he lift up his eyes, being in torments"** and **"a great gulf,"** etc., are examples of what the Pharisees believed. They embraced the teachings of Plato concerning death and the immortal soul.

They believed that the dead were not *really* dead, but that they were alive and that they could communicate with the living. In the parable, the rich man wanted to send a dead one to the living to testify to those of his father's house to testify to his five living brethren. This is what spiritualists believe and purport to do in a séance. These men believed in an afterlife.

The Pharisees also believed that the dead were separated by a great gulf between them. On one side of the gulf there were flames of torment and on the other side there was paradise. As we have seen from the Word of God, none of these ideas is true, but the Pharisees believed that they were. These beliefs all came from pagan origins.

The Pharisees boasted that Abraham was their "Father," so in the parable, the Lord Jesus put his words in Abraham's mouth. His purpose was to condemn the Pharisees for their devilish traditions.

Every detail of this story can be traced back to the traditions that the Pharisees taught and believed – not to anything that the Word of God declares as doctrine.

The Pharisees' traditions can be found in the *Talmud*. Their traditions were passed down in many of the early Christian writings,[36] and Greek Apocryphal books of the 1st and 2nd centuries B.C. also contain them.

John Lightfoot, in *A Commentary on the New Testament from the Talmud and Hebraica*, documents their beliefs (Volume xi, pp.165-167 and Volume xii, pp. 159-168).[37]

Alfred Edersheim, in *The Life and Times of Jesus the Messiah*, refers to these same traditions concerning death and the afterlife.[38] Dr. Bullinger, in

---

[36] *See* the discussion, *Is the Soul Immortal?* in this manuscript.

[37] Lightfoot, John. (1989). *A Commentary on the New Testament from the Talmud and Hebraica*.

[38] Edersheim, Alfred. (1993 ed.). *The Life and Times of Jesus the Messiah*.

Selected Writings, devotes three pages to the discussion of the Pharisees' traditions concerning the afterlife on pages 135-137.[39]

At the end of the parable, Christ delivers the punch line by putting his words in Abraham's mouth:

Luke 16:29-31 AV
Abraham saith unto him, They have Moses and the prophets; let them hear them. And he said, Nay, father Abraham: but if one went unto them from the dead, they will repent. And he said unto him, If they hear not Moses and the prophets, neither will they be persuaded, though one rose from the dead.

The Lord said that they did not need someone from the dead to speak to them. They had the Word of God that Moses and the prophets wrote. He further told them that if they would not hear Moses and the prophets, meaning God's Word, they would not believe even if one rose out from among the dead . . . and he was right!

The Lord placed the witness of the Scriptures and the witness of the resurrection side by side. Time and again he asserted the absolute authority of God's Word concerning spiritual matters. We must always weigh what men may say about spiritual matters against the teaching of the Word of God. The Scriptures are the benchmark of truth.

As the Pharisees rejected Christ during his earthly ministry, they rejected him after his resurrection from the dead, also.

This parable does not reinforce the teaching of the Pharisees – it does just the opposite – it condemns it.

The Lord used the beliefs of the Pharisees in this parable to make his point: their beliefs did not agree with the teaching of the Word of God. Compare what the Pharisees believed with the teaching of God's Word, which was the point to the parable. Christ said, **"Let them hear Moses and the prophets!"**

What do "Moses and the prophets" say about resurrection? These are a few examples of what Moses and the prophets taught about it.

- Exodus 3:6 and ff

- Job 14:1-13; 19:25 and 26

---

[39] Bullinger, E.W. (1960). *Selected Writings*.

- Psalm 16:9-11; 17:15; 21:1-7; 23; 49:15 (this whole Psalm contrasts Israel's hope with the death of the ungodly); 73:24 and 25

- Isaiah 25:8; 26:19 (compare the end of the wicked in 26:14 and 19 b with the end of the righteous in 26:19a)

- Ezekiel 37:11-14 (Israel's restoration clearly includes resurrection)

- Daniel 12:2

- Hosea 6:2 and 3; 13:14

What scripture did Jesus Christ use to teach the doctrine of resurrection?

Matthew 22:31 and 32 AV
But as touching the resurrection of the dead, have ye not read that which was spoken unto you by God, saying, I am the God of Abraham, and the God of Isaac, and the God of Jacob? God is not the God of the dead, but of the living.

Jesus Christ established the doctrine of resurrection on the words that God spoke to Moses, which are recorded in Exodus 3:6. The only way that God will be able to fulfill His covenant promises to Abraham, Isaac and Jacob is in resurrection.

The Word of God declares that these men are dead today, but at a future time, Christ will raise them out from their graves.

Matthew 22:29 AV
Jesus answered and said unto them [the Sadducees], "Ye do err, not knowing the scriptures, nor the power of God.

Instead of sending them a disembodied spirit from a dead one (which they believed to be alive upon death), Christ directed them to the Word of God. No one comes from the dead without resurrection and that only occurs when Christ returns and raises them.

The Word of God teaches that the dead are not alive in any form today. All in *hades,* which is the grave according to the Word, are dead and they will remain so until Christ raises them to life. Christ is the only one to whom God has given this authority.

The Word of God says that the dead know nothing at all. Love and hatred belong to the living, not the dead.

There is no work, nor devise in the grave. The dead have nothing in common with the living.

No one can return from the dead to communicate with the living.

There is no torment in the grave.

There is no intermediate state such as purgatory.

Heaven is not paradise and paradise will not exist again until the third heaven and earth.

To die is not to live in any state. It is to corrupt and decay until the time of resurrection.

We have read all of these things in the Word of God concerning death and the grave. Compare this to what the Lord told them in chapter 11.

Luke 11:52 AV
Woe unto you, lawyers! for ye have taken away the key of knowledge: ye entered not yourselves, and them that were entering in ye hindered.

These men were charged with making God's Word known to His people; instead, they kept God's people from understanding His Word by their wicked teachings.

Matthew 15:3 AV
But he answered and said unto them, Why do ye also transgress the commandment of God by your tradition?

Matthew 15:6b AV
Thus have ye made the commandment of God of none effect by your tradition.

Matthew 15:9 AV
But in vain they do worship me, teaching *for* doctrines the commandments of men.

Instead of their heretical traditions, they should have taught God's people His Word. The Pharisees made the Word of God of no effect by their traditions and they kept God's People from understanding God's Word.

In this parable, Jesus Christ condemns their devilish teachings concerning "the afterlife" – not validates them. He refers to the Pharisees when he says to his disciples, "**. . . Woe unto them through whom offenses** come! It would be better for him that a millstone were hanged about his neck and he cast into the sea, than that he should offend** [be the cause of stumbling] **one of these little ones"** [Matthew 18:6; Mark 9:42: Luke 17:2]. Their teachings were the offenses and the cause of stumbling that the Lord was addressing.

Surely, after all we have read from the Word of God, we could not possibly think that in this parable Christ contradicts every other truth in God's Word concerning death and resurrection. How could anyone consider replacing the truth of God's Word concerning death and resurrection, with the Pharisees' beliefs contained in this parable? Christ denounced them.

Jesus Christ said that if they would not believe the Word of God, they would not be persuaded though one was raised out from the dead. His resurrection meant nothing to the Pharisees; cursed children that they were.

Romans 10:9 reveals that one must confess Jesus as Lord and *believe that God raised him from the dead* if he is to be saved. They believed neither.

The Vision on the Mount of Transfiguration

Jesus Christ endured the shame and the cross because of the joy that was set before him. What was the joy that God set before him that enabled him to endure the torture, which resulted in his being disfigured more than any other man? What was the joy that enabled him to lay his life down as the Passover lamb? To find the answer, let us begin in the gospel of Luke.

Luke 9:28-32 AV
And it came to pass about an eight days after these sayings, he took Peter and John and James, and went up into a mountain to pray. And as he prayed, the fashion [appearance] **of his countenance was altered** [*heteros*: became different. In Matthew 17:2, it tells us that he was *transfigured* before them, meaning he changed forms. His face did shine as the sun, and His raiment was as white as absolute light], **and his raiment *was* white *and* glistering** [to flash as with lightening]. **And, behold, there talked with him two men, which were Moses and Elias: Who appeared** [being seen] **in glory, and spake of his decease** [exodus or departure from mortal life] **which he should accomplish at Jerusalem. But Peter and they that were with him were heavy with sleep: and when they were awake, they saw his glory, and the two men that stood with him.**

Where are Moses and Elijah today?

Deuteronomy 34:5 and 6 AV
So Moses the servant of the LORD died there in the land of Moab, according to the word of the LORD. And he buried him in a valley in the land of Moab, over against ethpeor: but no man knoweth of his sepulchre unto this day.

God told Joshua that, **"Moses My servant is dead. . .."** in Joshua 1:2. Moses will remain in the grave until the resurrection of the just.

What about Elijah; is he dead or is he alive in heaven? To answer this question will take a little more work.

II Kings 2:11 AV
And it came to pass, as they still went on, and talked, that, behold, *there appeared* a chariot of fire, and horses of fire, and parted them both asunder; and Elijah went up by a whirlwind into heaven.

This record is quoted to prove that Elijah did not die like all other men, but that he is alive in heaven. We know that what we are reading is true; however, we should not arrive at a conclusion that contradicts all the many clear scriptures concerning death and resurrection. It is dangerous license to read something into the Word of God that it does not say.

Every record concerning the subject has to agree if it is the truth of the Word of God. We dare not hold up a record that we may not understand and make it the benchmark of truth concerning the subject. Let's allow the Word of God to speak for itself.

II Kings 2:16 and 17 AV
And they said unto him, Behold now, there be with thy servants fifty strong men; let them go, we pray thee, and seek thy master: lest peradventure the Spirit of the LORD hath taken him up, and cast him upon some mountain, or into some valley. And he said, Ye shall not send. And when they urged him till he was ashamed, he said, Send. They sent therefore fifty men; and they sought three days, but found him not.

Why would the sons of the prophets want to send men to search for Elijah on earth if he ascended into the heavens to live forever? These men were not fools. They knew that their master was not to die that day; that is why they wanted to search for him.

How does what we are reading here fit with what the gospel of John says?

John 3:13 AV
And no man hath ascended up to heaven, but he that came down from heaven, *even* **the Son of man which is in heaven.**

This record says that no man has ascended to heaven. Jesus Christ, the Son of man, is the only man in heaven according to the Word of God. Elijah did not ascend into heaven to live forever. A chariot of fire separated Elisha from Elijah that day and by a whirlwind he went up into heaven; but there is more information that we need to consider.

King Jehoram (who is also called Joram), King Ahab's son, began his reign in Israel the same year that Elijah was removed by the whirlwind (see II Kings 1:17).

II Kings 8:16 AV
And in the fifth year of Joram the son of Ahab king of Israel, Jehoshaphat *being* **then king of Judah, Jehoram the son of Jehoshaphat king of Judah began to reign. Thirty and two years old was he when he began to reign; and he reigned eight years in Jerusalem.**

The king of Judah was Jehoshaphat and his son's name was Jehoram, also. Jehoram, the king of Judah, began to reign in the fifth year of the reign of Israel's king Jehoram.

Neither Jehoram, king of Israel, nor Jehoram, the king of Judah, walked with God.

II Chronicles 21:5 also says that Jehoram king of Judah was 32 when he began to rule and that he reigned for eight years. If you add the 5 years that Israel's king reigned, to the 8 years of the king of Judah's reign you get 13 years. Judah's king died 13 years after Elijah was removed by the whirlwind.

II Chronicles 21:12-15 AV
And there came a writing to him from Elijah the prophet, saying, Thus saith the LORD God of David thy father, Because thou hast not walked in the ways of Jehoshaphat thy father, nor in the ways of Asa king of Judah, But hast walked in the way of the kings of Israel, and hast made Judah and the inhabitants of Jerusalem to go a whoring, like to the whoredoms of the house of Ahab, and also hast slain thy brethren of thy father's house, *which were* **better than**

thyself: Behold, with a great plague will the LORD smite thy people, and thy children, and thy wives, and all thy goods: And thou *shalt have* great sickness by disease of thy bowels, until thy bowels fall out by reason of the sickness day by day.

Who wrote the letter? Elijah the prophet wrote it.

The first part of the letter deals with the king's past actions, while the latter part speaks of what is going to occur in the future.

From the wording, it appears that Elijah wrote the letter after Jehoram killed his brethren and committed the whoredoms. The letter concludes by foretelling that the king would have a great sickness by the disease of his bowels and it would lead to his death.

II Chronicles 21:19 AV
And it came to pass, that in process of time, after the end of two years, his bowels fell out by reason of his sickness; so he died of sore diseases. . .

The letter was delivered 11 years after Elijah was removed from Elisha by the whirlwind. How could he write this letter if he was in heaven? Elijah was still alive and on earth somewhere.

Elijah died like all other men because it is appointed unto man once to die according to Hebrews 9:27 and he was a man.

Romans 5:12 ff teaches us that Adam's condemnation passed upon all men, so death passed upon all men. James 5:17 says that Elijah was a man subject to like passions as we are. He was mortal and subject to death.

II Kings 2:3 and 5, tell us that the Lord was about to remove Elisha's master from being his head, which means from being his master.

Elijah's ministry was winding down and Elisha's public ministry was commencing. There was to be a change of leadership from Elijah to Elisha that day. Elisha picked up Elijah's mantle, which was the symbol of the prophet's office.

Elijah went up by a whirlwind into heaven. Biblically, heaven may be any place above the earth. We know that he did not ascend to the throne of God to live forever. God removed Elijah to another location by a whirlwind. The whirlwind lifted Elijah up above the earth and set him down somewhere unknown to them. We are not told where he lived after he concluded his public ministry or when he died, but what is written here cannot contradict the scriptures that are clear and understandable.

God's Word reveals that 11 years later, Elijah wrote the letter to Jehoram, so he did not die before then. As suddenly as Elijah came on the scene in I Kings 17:1, his public ministry ended. The Word of God does not give us the details of his death.

If we consider all the scriptures concerning the subject, we will know all that we can know about it. The hardest thing many times is changing our minds to believe the revelation of the Word of God. We do not need to embellish the record with our ideas. We simply do not know any more than the Word of God reveals.

When Jesus "saw" Moses and Elisha in glory, he saw them by revelation, by the manifestation of word of knowledge. They were not actually alive in the glory of the heavenlies. He saw them by revelation – it was a vision.

Matthew 17:9 AV
And as they were coming down from the mountain, Jesus commanded them, saying, Tell the vision to no man, until the Son of man be risen from the dead.

Matthew 17:9 tells us that this was a *vision,* meaning Christ *saw* it by revelation as did those with him.

The Lord saw Moses and Elijah appear in glory with him by revelation. Jesus had not entered his glory yet. He was about to suffer and die.

Moses and Elijah were not in glory when they lived on the earth, nor are they in glory now. They are dead. They are corrupting in the grave awaiting the resurrection of the just.

This vision is Divine revelation concerning the future glory that they will receive in resurrection.

God links the suffering and death of which Christ was about to face, with the glory he would receive in the future because he believed and accomplished that which God asked of him.

God revealed this glory to Christ so that he could see the result of the sacrifice that he was about to accomplish in Jerusalem. God set this joy before him so that he could endure what lay before him.

Matthew 17:4-5 AV
Then answered Peter, and said unto Jesus, Lord, it is good for us to be here: if thou wilt, let us make here three tabernacles; one for thee, and one for Moses, and one for Elias. While he yet spake, behold, a

bright cloud overshadowed them: and behold a voice out of the cloud, which said, This is my beloved Son, in whom I am well pleased; hear ye him.

The **"bright cloud"** overshadowed them. In the Old Testament, the cloud symbolized the immediate presence and power of God.[40] In it was manifested the glory of God. For an example, look at Exodus 40:34-38.

Exodus 40:34-38 AV
Then a cloud covered the tent of the congregation, and the glory of the LORD filled the tabernacle. And Moses was not able to enter into the tent of the congregation, because the cloud abode thereon, and the glory of the LORD filled the tabernacle. And when the cloud was taken up from over the tabernacle, the children of Israel went onward in all their journeys: But if the cloud were not taken up, then they journeyed not till the day that it was taken up. For the cloud of the LORD *was* upon the tabernacle by day, and fire was on it by night, in the sight of all the house of Israel, throughout all their journeys.[41]

Returning to Matthew 17:5, God then said to them out of the bright cloud, **"This is my beloved Son, in whom I am well pleased; hear ye him."** Peter refers to this event in his second epistle.

II Peter 1:17 and 18 AV
For he received from God the Father honour and glory, when there came such a voice to him from the excellent glory, This is my beloved Son, in whom I am well pleased. And this voice which came from heaven we heard, when we were with him in the holy mount.

The record reveals that Jesus received "honour and glory" from God the Father. These same words are used in connection with Aaron's garments when he was consecrated to minister unto God in the priest's office.

Exodus 28:2 AV
And thou shalt make holy garments for Aaron thy brother for glory and for beauty.

---

[40] Thayer, J.H. (1981). *The New Thayer's Greek-English Lexicon of the New Testament Coded with Strong's Concordance Numbers.* p. 242, #1982.

[41] See also Leviticus 16:2; Exodus 13:21 and 22; 16:10; Numbers 9:15; Isaiah 6:4; Matthew 17:5. This is the *Shechina.*

". . . for glory and for beauty," are the same words in the Septuagint as the words used in II Peter 1:17. God directed that the garments that Aaron should wear as the High Priest would be for glory and beauty.

Hebrews 2:9 AV
But we see Jesus, who was made a little lower than the angels for the suffering of death, crowned with glory and honour; that he by the grace of God should taste death for every man.

Here we have the Greek words again, *doxa kai time,* **"glory and honour."** What was the purpose of the high priest's garments?

Exodus 28:3 AV
And thou shalt speak unto all *that are* wise hearted, whom I have filled with the spirit of wisdom, that they may make Aaron's garments to consecrate him, that he may minister unto me in the priest's office.

The garments were to consecrate him so that he could minister unto God in the office of the priest. Verse 4b, says, **". . . and they shall make holy garments for Aaron they brother, and his sons, that he may minister unto Me in the priest's office."** God repeats the purpose of the garments for Aaron so that we cannot miss it.

On the mount, Jesus, **"was transfigured before them: his face did shine as the sun, and his raiment was white as the light."** Luke 9:29 says, **"And as he prayed, the fashion of His countenance was altered, and His raiment *was* white *and* glistering."** Jesus was transfigured before them; he took a different form, that of his glory. His face shone as the sun and his raiment was white and glistering, which means flashing like lightning. The garments he wore were garments of heavenly glory and honor.

The vision concerned Jesus Christ's decease that he would accomplish in Jerusalem and his future glory as the High Priest, who lives forever to make intercession for the saints.

God installed His Beloved Son, Jesus Christ, into the office of High Priest on the Mount. In the revelation, which was a vision, they beheld the glory and beauty of the priestly garments that he wore and the glorious body he would have after his resurrection, ascension into the heavenlies and his seating at the right hand of God.

The transfiguration on the mount followed the first announcement of his death to his disciples.

Looking unto Jesus the author and finisher of *our* faith; who for the joy that was set before him endured the cross, despising the shame, and is set down at the right hand of the throne of God.

Our Lord, Jesus Christ, was the Princely Leader, the only one to both start and finish the course of believing God's Word to the end of actually receiving eternal life. He is the only one to ascend into the heavens so far. He is the only one to sit down at the right hand of the throne of God in the heavenlies.

On the mount, he saw a glimpse of the glory of which he would partake. The vision of Moses and Elijah in glory, who spoke with him about his exodus, was the joy set before him that helped him endure the shame and suffering of his impending exodus.

Enoch's Translation

Hebrews 11:5 AV
By faith Enoch was translated that he should not see death; and was not found, because God had translated him: for before his translation he had this testimony, that he pleased God.

Spiritualists use this verse to say that Enoch did not die, but that God took Enoch to heaven because he pleased Him. Then they go to 12:1, **"Wherefore seeing that we also are compassed about with so great a cloud of witnesses. . .."** They say this means that men who have died are alive in heaven; they are a great cloud of witnesses to us. They say, since they are alive in heaven they can communicate with us.

Is this the teaching of God's Word? We have covered every verse on death and resurrection in the Word of God and the spiritualists teaching is not found in them. The Word of God will interpret itself in the verse, in the context or it will have been explained previously. We must also consider the biblical usage of words used in the verse.

Let's begin in verse 13.

Hebrews 11:13 AV
These all died in faith, not having received the promises, but having seen them afar off, and were persuaded of *them*, and embraced

them, **and confessed that they were strangers and pilgrims on the earth.**

All those mentioned in the preceding verses – Abel, Enoch, Noah, Abraham and Sara – all died believing the promises that God made to them but they did not receive them. They believed what the Word of God promised; they were persuaded of the promises, they saw them afar off, they embraced them and confessed them, but they did not receive the reality of the promise.

God will fulfill His promises to them in resurrection. Verse 35 calls it the **"better resurrection."** Verse 39 concludes the record saying, **"And these all, having obtained a good report through faith, received not the promise."**

There is only one who has received them thus far.

Hebrews 12:1 AV
Wherefore seeing we also are compassed about with so great a cloud of witnesses, let us lay aside every weight, and the sin which doth so easily beset *us*, and let us run with patience the race that is set before us,

We are **"compassed about"** with the examples of those listed in chapter 11, who believed God's Word regardless of what happened to them because of God's promise of resurrection. They ran the race set before them with patience. The next verse takes us a step further.

Hebrews 12:2 AV
Looking unto Jesus the author and finisher of *our* faith; who for the joy that was set before him endured the cross, despising the shame, and is set down at the right hand of the throne of God.

The word **"Looking"** is *aphorao*. It means, "looking away from". Looking away from the examples of those who came before and looking unto Jesus, the Author and Finisher of [THE] faith.

The reason we are to look away from all of the wonderful examples given in chapter 11 unto Jesus is because he is the only one who began believing God's promise of eternal life and actually received it. God raised him from the dead; he ascended into heaven and sat down at the right hand of God in the heavenlies. He is the only one to receive the promise.

The book of Hebrews sets forth this truth repeatedly. Notice the underlined words.

Hebrews 1:3b AV
. . . when he had by himself purged our sins, <u>sat down on the right hand of the Majesty on high;</u>

Jesus Christ was the Author, the Princely leader who completed, who accomplished that which no one else could. He is the only man to ascend into the heavenlies and sit down on the right hand of the Majesty on high.

Hebrews 5:9 AV
And being made perfect, <u>he became the author of eternal salvation</u> unto all them that obey him;

He was "the author," *archegos*, the leader, founder, or princely-leader.

Hebrews 6:19 and 20 AV
Which *hope* we have as an anchor of the soul, both sure and stedfast, and <u>which entereth into that within the veil; Whither the forerunner is for us entered,</u> *even* <u>Jesus</u>, made an high priest for ever after the order of Melchisedec.

"The veil" is the curtain that separated the Holy Place from the Holy of Holies in the Tabernacle. The High Priest of Israel would enter the Holy of Holies with the blood of the lamb and sprinkle it on the mercy seat to make atonement for Israel's sins. The earthly tabernacle was patterned after the original one in the heavenlies.[42] Christ is the forerunner. He entered the veil into the Holiest of All in the heavenlies.

Hebrews 8:1 and 2 AV
Now of the things which we have spoken *this is* the sum: We have such an high priest, <u>who is set on the right hand of the throne of the Majesty in the heavens</u>; A minister of the sanctuary, and of the true tabernacle, which the Lord pitched, and not man.

The Lord Jesus Christ is Israel's high priest forever. He is seated in the true tabernacle in the heavenlies. He sits at the right hand of the throne of the Majesty in the heavens. This tabernacle is the real one – the original – after which the earthly one was patterned.

Hebrews 9:11 and 12 AV
But Christ being come an high priest of good things to come, by a greater and more perfect tabernacle, not made with hands, that is

---

[42] *See* Hebrews 8:1, 2, 5: 9:23, 24.

to say, not of this building; Neither by the blood of goats and calves, but <u>by his own blood he entered in once into the holy place, having obtained eternal redemption</u> *for us*.

In the Greek, "holy place" is plural. It is speaking of, "the holiest." In the tabernacle, God sat above the Ark of the Covenant on the Mercy Seat in the Holiest of All. Jesus Christ entered the original Holiest of All, the one in the heavenlies and offered his own blood for our eternal redemption. He was the Lamb of God. Christ's offering of his life and God's acceptance of it is the grounds for our eternal redemption.

Hebrews 9:24 AV
For Christ is not entered into the holy places made with hands, *which are* the figures of the true; <u>but into heaven itself, now to appear in the presence of God for us:</u>

Hebrews 10:11 and 12 AV
And every priest standeth daily ministering and offering oftentimes the same sacrifices, which can never take away sins: <u>But this man, after he had offered one sacrifice for sins for ever, sat down on the right hand of God;</u>

Hebrews 12:2 AV
Looking unto Jesus the author and finisher of *our* faith; who for the joy that was set before him endured the cross, despising the shame, <u>and is set down at the right hand of the throne of God.</u>

I underlined the words in these verses to point out *why* Jesus was the Author and Finisher of the faith. These verses make it obvious. No one else began believing the promises and received the end of their believing, which was eternal life. No one else has been resurrected from the dead and received eternal life. No one else has ascended into the heavenlies. The Lord Jesus actually sat down at the right hand of the throne of God.

All the wonderful believers mentioned in chapter 11 believed the promises; they were persuaded of them, embraced them, confessed them, yet they did not receive the reality promised them. They all died without receiving the promises. Christ Jesus the Lord is the only one to receive the promises.

Since the Lord Jesus Christ is the only one to be raised to resurrection life, ascend into the heavenlies and sit down at the right hand of God, Enoch could not have been translated into heaven as some assert.

The records in Genesis 5:21-24, Jude 14 and Hebrews 11:5 are the only records that mention Enoch.

In Hebrews 11:5, what does the word "translate" mean? The word "translate" in Hebrews 11:5 is *metathesis,* and it means "to put or place in another place, to transport." Enoch was transported from one place to another.

Let's read Genesis 5:22 from the Lamsa Bible translated from the Aramaic. **"And Enoch found favor in the presence of God, and disappeared; for God took him away."**

Tyndale reads, **"And then Henoch lived a godly life, and was no more seen, for God took him away."** God took him from one place to another. It does not say he took him to heaven.

The word "see" is *eidon,* and it means "to see; implying not the mere act of seeing, but the actual perception of the object."

What does the Word of God say concerning the subject? God took Enoch from where he was and transported him to another location so that he did not actually see anyone die, because he lived a godly life and pleased God. He did not take him to heaven.

Enoch died like all other men.

A Textual Difficulty

Matthew 27:52 and 53 AV
And the graves were opened; and many bodies of the saints which slept arose, And came out of the graves after his resurrection, and went into the holy city, and appeared unto many.

These verses stand at odds with the clear body of scriptures that concern death and resurrection in the Word of God. How do we solve the glaring contradiction that these verses introduce?

Once we are certain that the contradiction is not due to our preconceived ideas about the subject and we have checked the verse for figures of speech, Orientalisms, and the biblical definition of the words, we must check the context and other Scriptures that deal with the same subject.

If after this we still have what seems to be a contradiction, we will have to check the texts from which the translation was made.

In the book, *Jesus Christ our Passover,* on page 257, Dr. Victor Paul Wierwille writes:

Matthew 27:52 and 53 are clearly added by scribes. Manuscript 354 in Venice, Italy, omits these verses. Though other textual documentation for this has not yet been found, it must be realized that the earliest manuscript including this section of Matthew 27 dates from the fourth century A.D. These verses must be an addition since they are contradictory to other scriptures which teach us that the dead are dead and will remain so until Christ returns. Until that time, only Christ has been raised bodily from death unto everlasting life. Textual critics as well as marginal notes in other old manuscripts have recognized these verses as later interpolations. The phrase 'after his resurrection' in Matthew 27:53 demonstrates the passage is totally out of context, obviously a scribal addition.

When we read the verses in the immediate context, this becomes obvious.

Matthew 27:50-53 AV
Jesus, when he had cried again with a loud voice, yielded up the ghost. And, behold, the veil of the temple was rent in twain from the top to the bottom; and the earth did quake, and the rocks rent; And the graves were opened; and many bodies of the saints which slept arose, And came out of the graves after his resurrection, and went into the holy city, and appeared unto many.

Christ "yielded up the ghost." He died as the Passover Lamb on Wednesday, the 14th of Nisan. His resurrection did not occur for three more days. He was raised from the dead late on the Sabbath, on Saturday towards sunset, the 17th.

The verses here say that Jesus yielded up the ghost, meaning he died, the temple veil was rent, the earth quaked and the rocks rent. The Lord would not get up from the dead for another three days and three nights, yet the next two verses skip ahead to the time after his resurrection. Read the next verse in the context.

Matthew 27:54 AV

Now when the centurion, and they that were with him, watching Jesus, saw the earthquake, and those things that were done, they feared greatly, saying, "Truly This was the Son of God.

The centurion, ". . .saw the earthquake and those things that were done." The verse speaks of the events surrounding Jesus' death, not his resurrection. Let's continue to read the verses that follow.

Matthew 27:55-60 AV

And many women were there beholding afar off, which followed Jesus from Galilee, ministering unto Him; Among which was Mary Magdalene, and Mary the mother of James and Joses, and the mother of Zebedee's children. When the even was come, there came a rich man of Arimathaea, named Joseph, who also himself was Jesus disciple: he went to Pilate, and begged the body of Jesus. Then Pilate commanded the body to be delivered. And when Joseph had taken the body, he wrapped it in a clean linen cloth, and laid it in his own new tomb, which he had hewn out in the rock: and he rolled a great stone to the door of the sepulchre, and departed.

The context continues to deal with the events surrounding Jesus' death and burial, not his resurrection. Verses 52 and 53, leap over these events and go to the time following his resurrection. They do not fit with the order of the context.

Many verses clearly state that the dead are dead and they will remain that way until Christ returns and raises them to life. He is the only one to whom God gave this vast authority.

Why is there not a single reference to dead saints coming out of their graves and making appearances in Jerusalem? The Gospels report that the risen Lord had multiple encounters with his disciples. There are at least five different angel appearances recorded after his resurrection. They confirmed that Jesus Christ was indeed raised from the dead, but there is not another record that mentions any encounter with dead saints that were raised. You would think that if such a phenomenal event had occurred, surely, another record would speak of it.

Jesus Christ's resurrection is the only resurrection crucial to redemption. The revelation of his resurrection from the dead validates and substantiates that Jesus Christ is God's Son, Israel's Messiah and our Savior and Lord.

Romans 10:9 AV

That if thou shalt confess with thy mouth the Lord Jesus, and shalt believe in thine heart that God hath raised him from the dead, thou shalt be saved.

One must believe in the resurrection of the Lord Jesus from the dead in order to be saved.

The verses in Matthew 27: 52 and 53 do not fit with the context or with the teaching of the many clear scriptures concerning death and resurrection. There is no mention of what these verses say in any other record in God's Word. We can only conclude that a scribe added them sometime later.

If these saints indeed had come out of their graves, they died a second time, for God's Word says that Jesus Christ is the only man to ascend into the heavens.[43]

Ye Shall Never Die

We need to consider the record in John 11:26 concerning resurrection.

John 11:26 AV

And whosoever liveth and believeth in Me shall never die. Believeth thou this?

As it stands, this verse contradicts about every other scripture we have read. We must not forget that the Word of God interprets itself in the verse, in the context or how it has been used before.

Let's begin in the context.

John 11:20- 25 AV

Then Martha, as soon as she heard that Jesus was coming, went and met him: but Mary sat *still* in the house. Then said Martha unto Jesus, Lord, if thou hadst been here, my brother had not died. But I know, that even now, whatsoever thou wilt ask of God, God will give *it* thee. Jesus saith unto her, Thy brother shall rise again. Martha saith unto him, I know that he shall rise again in the resurrection at the last day. Jesus said unto her, I am the

---

[43] *See* John 3:13.

resurrection, and the life: he that believeth in me, though he were dead, yet shall he live:

The Lord said that her brother Lazarus shall rise again. He was dead at the time of this conversation. Martha agreed that he shall rise again in the resurrection at the last day. Then Jesus said that he was the resurrection and the life. He that believed in him, though he was dead, he shall live. The word "yet" is not in the text.

So, thus far everything agrees with every other scripture concerning resurrection. When will it occur? The Word says, "at the last day." Who will orchestrate it? The Lord Jesus will orchestrate it. Who will rise from the dead? He will raise those who believe in him.

But, the next verse contradicts all doctrine from Genesis to Revelation concerning death and resurrection.

John 11:26 AV
And whosoever liveth and believeth in Me shall never die. Believeth thou this?"

As it reads, it does not fit with the scriptures in the context or what has been said before; or for that matter any later revelation given to Israel.

The words are understandable in the verse. There are no Orientalisms.

There is a figure of speech of repeated negation. The word "never" is translated from two Greek negatives *ou* and *me*. It would be like we would say, "No, no." The usage strengthens the assertion and emphasis, which makes it a most solemn and emphatic assertion.

Some people make the leap to say that this means that you do not really die but live on in another form at death. This idea is not helpful if we are to allow the Word of God to interpret itself. How could we interpret this verse in a way that contradicts every other clear scripture? How do we resolve the problem?

Let's check the Greek and Aramaic texts to see if we can gain some added insight:

John 11:26 Interlinear Greek English New Testament
And everyone who lives and believes on me, in no wise shall die forever.
και πας ο ζων και πιστευων εις εμε ου μη αποθανη εις τον αιωνα πιστευεις τουτο

The Stephens Greek text, from which the King James or Authorized Version was translated, has the word "forever" after die. The Greek is *eis ton aiona*. This now agrees with every other scripture on the subject. How does the Aramaic read?

John 11:26 Murdock (translation of the Aramaic)
And every one that liveth, and believeth in me, will not die for ever. Believest thou this?

The Aramaic-English Interlinear New Testament translation is the same as the Greek. They both agree. The problem lies in the translation of the original languages into the English.

Everyone who lives and believes in the Lord Jesus Christ will absolutely not die forever. The raising of Lazarus from the dead proved it. It was an object lesson to teach that the Lord Jesus had the power to raise the dead. The Lord Jesus Christ will come again and raise those who believe in him out from among the dead.

The Lord Jesus also raised two others from the dead: the daughter of the ruler of the synagogue and the widow's son at Nain. If they were not actually dead, but alive and living in heaven, why would he raise them from the dead and bring them back here?

Verse 39 says that Lazarus had been dead for four days and was corrupting and verse 44 plainly states that Lazarus was dead, not alive in heaven.

John 11:43 and 44 AV
And when He thus had spoken, He [Jesus] cried with a loud voice, "Lazarus, come forth." And he that was dead came forth, bound hand and foot with graveclothes: and his face was bound about with a napkin. Jesus saith unto them, "Loose him, and let him go."

The Word of God says what it means and it means what it says. It makes sense, while tradition usually confuses us about the truth. "Dead" means *dead*. "Resurrection" means *resurrection* and "at his coming" means *at his coming*.

The Word of God always interprets itself. We should study God's Word to show ourselves approved unto Him as workmen that do not need to be ashamed of our workmanship, by rightly dividing the word of truth.

The Lord Jesus is the only one with the power to raise the dead and the Word of God teaches us that it will occur at his coming.

Christ's Second Coming

Overview

Did the Old Testament saints realize that the coming of Christ would involve a first coming and a second coming?

Acts 1:6 AV

When they therefore were come together, they asked of Him, saying, "Lord, wilt Thou at this time restore again the kingdom to Israel

Throughout his ministry, Christ's followers wanted to take him and make him king. They did not understand. They thought that he came to restore Israel's kingdom at that time.

Acts 1:7 AV

And He said unto them, "It is not for you to know the times or the seasons, which the Father hath put in His own Power."

They did not realize the larger purpose of the ages that the Father accomplished in Christ Jesus.

Acts 1:9-11 AV

And when He had spoken these things, while they beheld, He was taken up; and a cloud received Him out of their sight.

And while they looked steadfastly toward heaven as He went up, behold, two men stood by them in white apparel:

Which also said, "Ye men of Galilee, why stand ye gazing up into heaven? This same Jesus, Which is taken up from you into heaven, shall so come in like manner as ye have seen Him go into heaven."

The two messengers said that he would come again.

Christ's first coming began with his birth, and it spanned more than 30 years before it ended when he ascended into heaven. Likewise, his second coming will span a period of time. It will involve different purposes that the Father has put within his power.

If we are to understand the second coming of Christ, we will have to allow God's Word to reveal it.

When we inductively consider the cumulative teaching of the Word of God, it becomes apparent that his second coming consists of two distinct stages. The word *parousia* means "the being or becoming present, (from *pareimi*, "to be present") hence, presence, arrival. . ."[44] *Parousia* denotes both an arrival and a consequent presence with.

To understand Christ's *Parousia*, we will need to understand the purpose of his coming in each stage. We will also need to consider the times in which he comes and the people involved, as well as where it occurs.

First, Christ will come for his Church, which is called, "the body of Christ" in Ephesians 1:23. He will gather together both the saints who are alive and those who have died into the heavenlies. From the moment of our gathering together, he will continually be present with us.

All of the Church, both living and dead, will be gathered together at the same time. The Church will be caught up in the clouds to meet the Lord in the air, and so will we ever be with the Lord.

The purpose of the first stage will be to deliver, to redeem, and to save the members of his body, the Church. The Church will be gathered together unto their Lord in the clouds. They will depart from the earth and ascend with him into the heavenlies. His coming for the Church will be the conclusion of the Administration of the Grace of God.

The second stage of his *Parousia* involves his revelation to the world in the period of the Day of the Lord.

The second stage begins sometime after the gathering together of the Church. The purpose of the second stage of the Lord's coming is to carry out God's judgment on the earth. It will involve Israel and the Gentiles – not the Church in the Administration of the Grace of God. The Word of God refers to this stage of his coming as "the Day of the Lord," and it will involve the Lord's coming to the earth.

This coming will fulfill God's covenants with Israel as well as the Old Testament prophecy concerning it. The Lord spoke of these times during his first coming. The book of Revelation deals with his coming to the earth as the King of kings and Lord of lords.

---

[44] Bullinger (1999). *A Critical Lexicon and Concordance to the English and Greek New Testament.*

The Day of the Lord involves the fulfilling of the covenants that God made with the nation of Israel. It will be the time when the nations are judged, as well as, the Devil, and the fallen angels, the beast, and the false prophet, and those who followed him.

There are two words that are translated "the end:" *sunteleia* and *telos*. The times that cover the extended period of the end times is the *sunteleia*. This period is marked with distinct signs and seasons. It includes every event that leads up to the very end. The climax or the very end of the age is the *telos*.

The Old Testament prophets foretold of the Day of the Lord. Jesus Christ also spoke of his second coming. Both the apostle Paul and the apostle Peter spoke of it. It is the subject of the book of Revelation, written by the apostle John.

This period concludes God's conflict with the Devil and the spirit-beings in the heavenlies that followed him, and with the men on earth who rebelled against Him. The controversy began when the angel Lucifer, also known as the Devil, rebelled against God and was cast out with the angels that followed him. It continued with the ruin of God's order in the second heaven and earth with the entrance of sin and death.

In this period, the Lord will deal with the conclusion of sin, death, the curse, paradise lost, the denial to the tree of life, and the son of man's lost dominion in the earth.

The Lord's Day is the subject of the book of Revelation. Revelation is the compliment to the book of Genesis.

Genesis is a book of beginnings. Revelation deals with the Day of the Lord and the close of the age.

In the Day of the Lord, the Lord will put down all rule, authority, and power. He will rule until all enemies are under His feet.

The last two chapters of Revelation deal with the new heavens and new earth. In the fullness of times, Christ will head up all things in both the heavens and in the earth.

God will make all things new in the third heaven and earth. This period will be a time of unending glory in the presence of God and the Lamb.

There is only "one hope", but it has various stages. There is much we do not understand today about future times such as we read of in the book of Revelation, but it will be apparent to the people who live at that time.

We should be confident of the coming of the Lord Jesus Christ for his church. He has given us a clear understanding of where it will take place, its place in the purpose of the ages, who will participate, and the glory we will share with Christ when we see him face to face and he changes us to have glorious bodies like his.

The First Stage

I Thessalonians 4:15-18

For this we say unto you by the word of the Lord, that we which are alive and remain unto the coming of the Lord shall not prevent them which are asleep.

For the Lord himself shall descend from heaven with a shout, with the voice of the archangel, and with the trump of God: and the dead in Christ shall rise first:

Then we which are alive and remain shall be caught up together with them in the clouds, to meet the Lord in the air: and so shall we ever be with the Lord.

Wherefore comfort one another with these words.

The Gathering of the Church

When will the dead in Christ receive eternal life? When will the living ones receive immortality? Where will the Church of the Grace of God meet Christ? What is the hope of the Church during the Administration of the Grace of God? Will we undergo judgment with the ungodly of the world? Should we fear Christ's coming for us?

I Corinthians 15:51-54 AV
Behold, I shew you a mystery; We shall not all sleep, but we shall all be changed,

In a moment, in the twinkling of an eye, at the last trump: for the trumpet shall sound, and the dead shall be raised incorruptible, and we shall be changed.

For this corruptible must put on incorruption, and this mortal must put on immortality.

So when [indicating the time when this occurs] **this corruptible shall have put on incorruption, and this mortal shall have put on immortality, then** [indicating time] **shall be brought to pass the saying that is written, Death is swallowed up in victory.**

The word "**Behold**" directs our attention to the beginning of a new subject. This word is not a mere interjection, but a verb, which instructs us to look and observe what we see, to observe attentively.

"Behold" is one of several words used as *asterismos*, the figure of speech that calls attention to a thing by acting like an asterisk. The word "behold" is used this way, as is "verily" or "yea."[45]

What are we directed to mark and attentively observe? The asterisk marks the mystery revealed to us in verse 51 and following.

---

[45] Bullinger (1975 ed). *Figures of Speech Used in the Bible: Explained and Illustrated.*

If this revelation had been known previously, it could not have been a mystery. What is this secret? Saints[46] will yet be living when Christ returns to raise the saints of the Church who have died.

The saints who are living at the time of Christ's return will be changed from mortal to immortal at the same time that the dead in Christ are raised to life according to the Word of God.

The mortal, the saints who are alive, will put on immortality at the same time that the dead saints, who have corrupted in the grave, will be raised as incorruptible. This is when **"death is swallowed up in victory"** for the members of the body of Christ, the Church.

It is apparent that this has not yet occurred.

I Corinthians 15:22 and 23 AV
For as in Adam all die, even so in Christ shall all be made alive.

But every man in his own order: Christ the firstfruits; afterward they that are Christ's at his coming.

The dead in Christ will be made alive "**at his coming**."

I Corinthians 15:21 AV
For since by man came death, by man came also the resurrection of the dead.

Death is the last enemy that shall be destroyed. Death is not the portal that leads to eternal life. The Word of God reveals that it is an enemy, but there is a day coming that we will be released from its authority over us.

I Thessalonians also declares God's revelation concerning the Lord's return for his Church.

I Thessalonians 4:13 and 14 AV
But I would not have you to be ignorant, brethren, concerning them which are asleep, that ye sorrow not, even as others which have no hope. For if we believe that Jesus died and rose again, even so them also which sleep in Jesus will God bring with him.

There are several points we need to take into consideration in these verses. First of all, as it stands, the verses read awkwardly, and this makes it

---

[46] "Saint" is the name given to God's people or to spirit messengers. They are holy ones. The saints referred to here are believers in the Lord Jesus

difficult to understand them. When this occurs in translation, it may be due to a figure of speech.

There are two figures used here that when understood make the verses intelligible.

Of what does God not want us ignorant? He does not want us ignorant of "**them which are asleep**."

God uses a figure of speech here called *euphemy*. *Euphemy* uses a softer word for a harsher word. By using the word "sleep" for "death," it softens the emotional sting that accompanies death. God, by Divine Design, emphasizes that death for those in Christ is like sleep, in that we will be awakened from it, the same as we are from sleep.

There are two words for "sleep" in the Greek language. *Katheudo* means, "to intentionally go to sleep," as we do every night. The word used here is *koimaomai*. It means, "to fall asleep *involuntarily*." It is used to describe the earthly death-state of the saints.

Those who are not "in Christ" have no hope of awakening unto eternal life when the Lord returns. The unsaved will be raised in the resurrection of the unjust[47] and be *condemned to the second death*. Their end will be destruction.

Notice that the verse says, "**. . . them which are asleep**," indicating that currently they are dead.

"**For if we believe that Jesus died and rose again, even so. . .**" All the gospel records concur on these points. Jesus Christ died and he was in the grave for three days and three nights. God raised him from the dead, and he ministered on the earth for another forty days before he ascended into the heavenlies.

Romans 1:1-4 Weymouth New Testament
Paul, a bondservant of Jesus Christ, called to be an Apostle, set apart to proclaim God's Good News,

Which God had already promised through His Prophets in Holy Writ, concerning His Son,

Who, as regards His human descent, belonged to the posterity of David,

---

[47] John 5:29b and Revelation 21:8.

But as regards the holiness of His Spirit was decisively proved by His Resurrection to be the Son of God - I mean concerning Jesus Christ our Lord,

God confirmed that Jesus Christ was His Son by raising him from the dead. No other man has ever been raised to life never to die again.

In I Thessalonians 4:14, the words **"even so"** tell us that what follows will be compared with what came before.

As we believe that Jesus died and rose again, **even so**, we believe that God – through Jesus – will bring those that sleep, out from among the dead. The verses that follow will further clarify and define this order.

Dr. E. W. Bullinger, in *Figures of Speech Used in the Bible*, explains that this verse contains the figure of speech, *ellipsis*, which is a figure involving the omission of a word or words. This figure draws our attention to the remaining words. The omitted words are understood from the context. By supplying the omitted words from the previous clauses, it would read **"As we believe that Jesus died and rose again, in like manner** [we believe] **that them which are asleep will God (by Jesus) bring with him** [from the dead]."

I Thessalonians 4:14 Conneybeare and Howson
For if we believe that Jesus died and rose again, so also will God, through Jesus, bring back those who sleep, together with him.

As Jesus died and rose again, so the dead in Christ will rise again from the dead. God, by His agent Jesus (the same Jesus they crucified) will lead those who sleep the sleep of death [Psalm 13:3], out from among the dead.

Christ will bring them from where? The context teaches us that they:

- **"are asleep"** in verse 13
- **"them also which sleep"** in verse 14
- **"are asleep"** in verse 15
- **"the dead in Christ"** in verse 16
- In verse 17, is the pronoun **"them,"** referring to **"the dead in Christ"** mentioned in the previous verse.

The entire context teaches that the Lord Jesus Christ will bring them *from the dead*. This agrees with what we learned in I Corinthians 15.[48]

---

[48] *See* also I Corinthians 15:36-50.

We do not need to be sorrowful as the others who have no hope, because when Christ returns for his Church, he will raise the saints who are dead from their sleep, and they will live again and that forever.

The next three verses reveal the *timing* of this event. They reveal when the dead in Christ will live again.

I Thessalonians 4:15-18 ASV
For this we say unto you by the word of the Lord, that we that are alive, that are left unto the coming of the Lord, shall in no wise precede them that are fallen asleep.

For the Lord himself shall descend from heaven, with a shout, with the voice of the archangel, and with the trump of God: and the dead in Christ shall rise first;

then we that are alive, that are left, shall together with them be caught up in the clouds, to meet the Lord in the air: and so shall we ever be with the Lord.

Wherefore comfort one another with these words.

Here we have "**the word of the Lord**" concerning Christ's coming for the Church.

This is not a theological *theory*, nor is it a religious *tradition* that originated in spiritualism and was later adopted as so-called Christian doctrine.

A council, convention or committee of men did not vote on this, nor was it Paul's view, nor is it my interpretation.

This is "**the word of the Lord**"! It is revelation knowledge from our Lord given for our comfort and believing. Anyone can read it and understand. There is nothing confusing about it. There is only confusion when we read what God reveals in His Word and try to make it fit with tradition.

There is no other hope of eternal life for the believer in Christ Jesus. The Word of the Lord reveals and defines every element of our hope to us.

We will forever be *with* our Lord, whether we are alive when he comes or we have fallen asleep. We have this on the Lord's own authority. Look in the book of Ephesians:

Ephesians 4:30 WT
Likewise, do not grieve the Holy Spirit, that is to say, God, by Whom you were sealed until the day of redemption.

Christ Jesus the Lord will come for the members of his body, the Church, on the Day of Redemption. This is called "**... the coming of our Lord Jesus Christ, and *by* our gathering together unto Him**" in II Thessalonians 2:1. There is no other way of being with the Lord than God reveals to us in His Word.

Both the members of the body of Christ who have fallen asleep and those who are alive and remain unto the coming of the Lord shall be caught up together, at the same time.

The Opening Scene of Eternity for the Church

I Thessalonians 4:16 and 17 AV
For the Lord himself shall descend from heaven with a shout, with the voice of the archangel, and with the trump of God: and the dead in Christ shall rise first:

Then we which are alive and remain shall be caught up together with them in the clouds, to meet the Lord in the air: and so shall we ever be with the Lord.

These verses contain the figure of speech, *protimesis*, which "increases the emphasis of a particular statement by setting forth the order in which the things treated stand, or take place."[49]

- **The Lord himself descends. . .**

- The dead in Christ rise **first**

- **Then** we which are alive are caught up together

- **And so** shall we ever be with the Lord.

First, the Lord himself descends from heaven. He gives the command for his saints to assemble – both the living and those who are dead.

---

[49] Bullinger (1975 ed.). *Figures of Speech Used in the Bible: Explained and Illustrated.*

"For the Lord himself shall descend from heaven with a shout . . ."
The word for "shout" is *keleusma* which is a command that assembles.

In the sport of crew, this word is used for the shout that gives the rowers the timing for their strokes so that they can synchronize their efforts. It is how hunters call their dogs to assemble. Our Lord will assemble his Church, both living and dead at the same time, by the word of his command.

As he exercised his authority to raise Lazarus from the dead and said, "Lazarus, come forth!" so he will exercise the vast authority under his hand in this coming day. When he gives the command, every member of the body of Christ will come forth unto eternal life, whether by rising from the dead or by transformation.

When the heavenly trumpet of assembly sounds, the dead in Christ shall rise first.

In the Old Testament there is a record describing how Moses was to assemble the congregation of Judea when there was a need for them to be gathered together.

Numbers 10:1-7 AV
And the LORD spake unto Moses, saying,

Make thee two trumpets of silver; of a whole piece shalt thou make them: that thou mayest use them for the calling of the assembly, and for the journeying of the camps.

And when they shall blow with them, all the assembly shall assemble themselves to thee at the door of the tabernacle of the congregation.

And if they blow but with one trumpet, then the princes, which are heads of the thousands of Israel, shall gather themselves unto thee.

When ye blow an alarm, then the camps that lie on the east parts shall go forward. When ye blow an alarm the second time, then the camps that lie on the south side shall take their journey: they shall blow an alarm for their journeys.

But when the congregation is to be gathered together, ye shall blow, but ye shall not sound an alarm.

There were two purposes for blowing the trumpets: one for assembly and another for alarm. It is obvious that there were different purposes and times the trumpets were to be blown. This is important to understand concerning the coming of Christ.

When Christ returns to gather the Church together, the heavenly trumpet will sound to assemble the saints.

The dead in Christ will rise first. Then, the saints that are alive and remain on the earth will be changed from mortal to immortal. Together they will be caught up into the clouds to meet the Lord in the air, and then he will lead the victory procession into the heavenlies.

The dead in Christ will be gathered together to meet the Lord in the air at the same time that the living ones are received up into glory. As members of the body of Christ, every one of us will partake of this event at the same time.

The majesty of this victory processional will surpass the magnificence of any scene that Hollywood has ever depicted with its Technicolor, HD, 3-D and digitized surround-sound on IMAX. Just picture the reality that these verses declare!

The Lord descends from the right hand of the throne of God in the heavenlies in all of his power and majesty.

By the way, what does the Lord's glory look like? When Christ was transfigured on the Mount, the vision prefigured his glory.

Matthew 17:2 AV
And was transfigured before them; and His face did shine as the sun, and His raiment was white as the light.

Luke 9:29 adds,
And as he prayed, the fashion [appearance] **of His countenance** [face] **was altered** [became different], **and His raiment was white and glistering.** [The word "glistering" means "to flash as lightening"].

Verse 32 tells us that Peter, James and John saw his glory. Peter refers to this event in the record of II Peter.

II Peter 1:16-18 AV
For we have not followed cunningly devised fables, when we made known unto you the power and coming of our Lord Jesus Christ, but were eyewitnesses of his majesty.

For he received from God the Father honour and glory, when there came such a voice to him from the excellent glory, This is my beloved Son, in whom I am well pleased.

And this voice which came from heaven we heard, when we were with him in the holy mount.

Peter, James and John were eyewitnesses of his majesty. They heard God's confirmation that Jesus Christ was His Beloved Son.

They knew firsthand of the power and coming of our Lord Jesus Christ. The revelation on the mountain was a foreshadowing, a preview of the glory that the Heavenly Father reserved for His Beloved Son.

When Christ Jesus descends to gather his Church together, we will behold his glory! We will see him face to face, and be like him.

By the grace of God, we are God's beloved children, and we will be glorified together with Christ Jesus our Lord.

There is no greater privilege than to be a member of the body of Christ. Solely by the grace of God and the accomplished work of the Lord Jesus Christ, every member in the body of Christ fully shares in this hope.

Every spiritual blessing in the heavenlies is ours in Christ. We are joint-heirs with him, and we will obtain the glory of our Lord Jesus Christ.[50] What a revelation!

I Thessalonians 4:16 and 17 AV
For the Lord himself shall descend from heaven with a shout, with the voice of the archangel, and with the trump of God: and the dead in Christ shall rise first:

Then we which are alive and remain shall be caught up together with them in the clouds, to meet the Lord in the air: and so shall we ever be with the Lord.

At the sound of the heavenly assembling trumpet and with his majestic command, the Lord will initiate the immense power that his Father gave him.

The graves that previously held the dead in Christ as prisoners, will give up their captives, and his living saints will be transformed, from mortal to immortal. Both will have glorious bodies fashioned like their Lord's glorious body.

Both the living and the dead of the Church are caught up and away together in the clouds, to meet the Lord in the air.

---

[50] I Thessalonians 2:14.

The words translated "**caught up**" are the Greek word *harpazo*. It literally means, "to snatch by authority." The Latin word is *raptus* from which we get the word "rapture."

The Lord will snatch us from the earth up into the cloud, *nephele*. This cloud is a particular, distinct cloud. In the Septuagint, *nephele* is the word used of the cloud that led Israel in the wilderness. It is the cloud that overshadowed them on the mountain of transfiguration. It is used of the *Shechina* glory associated with the glory of God.

Acts 1:9 AV
And when he had spoken these things, while they beheld, he was taken up; and a cloud received him out of their sight.

Christ was taken up and a cloud received him out of their sight. Like the Lord, we will be caught up, "**. . . in the clouds, to meet the Lord in the air.**" This is even more significant than we may first notice.

Ephesians 2:1 and 2 AV
And you hath he quickened, who were dead in trespasses and sins;

Wherein in time past ye walked according to the course of this world, according to the prince of the power of the air, the spirit that now worketh in the children of disobedience:

Today, one of the devil's titles is, "**the prince of the power of the air.**" Christ Jesus our Lord will gather us together in the air, and this prince will be powerless to stop it. We will be loosed from this crooked and perverse world and from death itself if it has overtaken us.

The fullness of time will have come for Christ Jesus the Lord to be united with the members of his body, the Church, and together they will ascend into the heavenlies with all the divine pomp and circumstance attached to it.

The Greek for "**meet**" in I Thessalonians 4:17, is *apantesis*. It means "to meet and return with."[51]

The word is used of dignitaries when they visited cities. Their coming would be received with great pomp and circumstance. While they were still

---

[51] "When a dignitary paid an official visit (*parousia*) to a city in Hellenistic times, the action of the leading citizens in going out to meet him and escort him back on the final stage of his journey was called the *apantesis*." Bruce, F.F. (1982). *I and II Thessalonians: Word Biblical Commentary Series, Vol.45*: p.102.

well beyond the city, an envoy of officials would be sent to meet the caravan of dignitaries and escort them the rest of the way.

The citizens would line the streets from the entrance to the palace, strewing them with palm branches. Once they arrived at the palace, greetings, and ceremonial speeches usually followed. After the public ceremony for the dignitary concluded, they would enter the palace together for private festivities, hosted by the local official.

When we win a victory in war or in athletics, we celebrate it. We have victory celebrations, parties, parades, we sing and rejoice, and the victors are introduced to prominent dignitaries. Honors are bestowed. Recognition and awards are given for sacrifice and achievement in the arena. This victory processional and celebration will be more glorious than any other in history.

Christ Jesus our Lord gathers us together and then leads us in a victory processional into the heavenlies. It will be the affair of the ages, the greatest celebration of any ever known. The Heavenly Father has planned for this gala affair for ages!

Christ will lead us home, and we will be welcomed as members of his body, as joint-heirs with him. The super conquerors will be lead into the heavenlies by their head and Lord.

The Father will finally have His children home. It will be a time of indescribable joy.

We will be welcomed home by our Father, our Lord, principalities, powers, mights, dominions, and an innumerable company of angels - His entire heavenly host.

Just think; this is only the opening scene of eternity for us! It will take our Father the ages to come – all of eternity – to show us all the exceeding riches of His grace. His kindness will be beyond anything we could ever ask or think.

Man has never witnessed anything that even remotely parallels this event. Every single believer since the beginning of the Age of Grace and the Mystery will be gathered together with Christ into the heavenlies, into eternal glory.

Our Lord will lead us into our Father's presence in the heavenlies where we will enjoy rest, glory, and fullness of joy as citizens of the heavenlies.

I Thessalonians 4:17 AV
Then we which are alive and remain shall be caught up together with them in the clouds, to meet the Lord in the air: and so shall we ever be with the Lord.

The word "**so**" means "thus" or "in this manner." The word is emphatic: "**. . . and so shall we ever be with the Lord.**"

I Thessalonians 4:18 AV
Wherefore comfort one another with these words.

The Lord gave us these words for our comfort. At his return, all who are members of the body of Christ, the Church, will live again and that forever. Our hope is of life, comfort, rest, fullness of joy, and glory. We should comfort and encourage one another with His Words.

II Thessalonians 2:1 AV
Now we beseech you, brethren, by the coming of our Lord Jesus Christ, and by our gathering together unto him,

Christ's coming for the Church is "in the air." He will come for the members of his body to deliver them from death and from this earth. Our Lord will gather us together unto himself and lead us into the heavenlies to obtain our inheritance.

Let's briefly summarize what we have learned concerning the first stage of his *Parousia*.

To what administration does this coming belong?

It is the conclusion of the Administration of the Grace of God, which began on the Feast of Pentecost following Christ's resurrection from the dead, his ascension into the heavenlies, and his seating at the right-hand of God.

Who does this stage of his *Parousia* concern?

It involves the Church, which is the body of Christ. It involves both the living and the dead in Christ. We will both be caught up together at the same time.

What is this part of the *Parousia* called in the Word of God?

- It is "**the day of Jesus Christ**."[52]

---

[52] Philippians 1:6.

- It is "**the coming of our Lord Jesus Christ and our gathering together unto Him.**"[53]
- It is when both the living of the Church "**shall be caught up together with them** [the saints that he raises from the dead] **in the clouds to meet the Lord in the air.**"[54]
- It is "**the departure.**"[55]
- It is "**the day of redemption.**"[56]
- It is when the Church "**will obtain salvation by our Lord Jesus Christ.**"[57]
- It is when the Church will be "**received up into glory.**"[58]

When will it occur?

It will take place "**at his coming.**"[59] It occurs before the Day of the Lord begins to unfold on the earth.

Where will it occur?

The Church will "**meet the Lord in the air and so shall we ever be with the Lord.**"[60]

Why does it occur?

The purpose of his coming for the Church is to save and deliver it from death and from the wrath of God that will come on the world. It is when the Church receives the object of its calling in Christ – "**the obtaining of the glory of our Lord Jesus Christ.**"[61] It is when the Church will "**appear with Him in glory**."[62] This is the concluding event in the Administration of the Grace of God.

---

[53] II Thessalonians 2:1.

[54] I Thessalonians 4:17.

[55] II Thessalonians 2:3.

[56] Ephesians 4:30.

[57] I Thessalonians 5:9.
[58] I Timothy 3:16.

[59] I Corinthians 15:23.

[60] I Thessalonians 4:17.

[61] II Thessalonians 2:14.

[62] Colossians 3:4.

Glorious New Bodies

The power of Christ's resurrected and glorified body is unlimited in the scope of its activity. It is not bound by natural laws; it operates according to higher spiritual laws. In his new body, Christ could exist on the earth or in the heavenly realm equally as well, and . . . we will be like him!

Philippians 3:20 and 21 AV
For our conversation [citizenship] is in heaven; from whence also we look for the Saviour, the Lord Jesus Christ:

Who shall change our vile body, that it may be fashioned like unto his glorious body, according to the working whereby he is able even to subdue all things unto himself.

Does God's Word teach us that we are to look for death as our entrance into glory or are we to look for the Savior, the Lord Jesus Christ? We are to look for our Savior. At his coming, the Lord Jesus Christ will change our body of humiliation so that it will be fashioned like his glorious body.

Where is our citizenship? We are the citizens of the heavenly realm. While we are here on earth, we are ambassadors and represent our true home in the heavenlies. When our Lord returns for us, he will take us to our true home in the heavenlies.

II Thessalonians 2:14 AV
Whereunto he called you by our gospel, to the obtaining of the glory of our Lord Jesus Christ.

What was God's purpose in calling us? He called us to the obtaining, to the acquisition of the glory of our Lord Jesus Christ! This is our Father's desire. All of His plans for the Church are to this end.

Romans 8:29 Weymouth New Testament
For those whom He has known beforehand He has also pre-destined to bear the likeness of His Son, that He might be the Eldest in a vast family of brothers;

Who decided that we will be conformed to the image of God's Son, that we will bear his likeness? God, our Father determined it. If no one believes it, it is still the truth of God's Word. God's grace and love for His children is beyond anything we could ask or think.

In the U.S. Supreme Court, justices are appointed to rule on constitutional issues. Their decisions are made in light of a longer view of time – centuries. Our Heavenly Father took eternity into account when He made this ruling about His children; not mere centuries. He ruled that we will bear the likeness of His Son.

Ephesians 1:13 and 14 AV
In Whom [Christ] **ye also trusted, after that ye heard the word of truth, the gospel of your salvation: in Whom also after that ye believed, ye were sealed with that holy Spirit of promise,**

which is the earnest of our inheritance until the redemption of the purchased possession, unto the praise of His glory.

Until we receive our inheritance in Christ, we are sealed with holy spirit. The gift of holy spirit is God's down payment to us of the full inheritance that is ours in Christ. Our inheritance encompasses everything that is ours in Christ. It includes the redemption of our bodies at his coming, our glorification with Christ and much more.

It will take our Father the ages to come to demonstrate the riches of His grace to us, which He has purposed in Christ.

Our inheritance embraces "every spiritual blessing in the heavenlies in Christ."

Ephesians 4:30 AV
And grieve not the Spirit of God, whereby ye are sealed unto the day of redemption.

Ephesians twice reveals that we are "sealed." We are sealed with the gift of holy spirit, the spirit of God. It is the down payment against our inheritance. We are sealed for the day of redemption, the day that we will receive our inheritance. That is the day that our Lord will return and gather us together into the heavenlies.

The day is approaching that Christ will return, and we will not only be *with him*, but we will be *like him*! Would you not agree that this is utterly extraordinary? Yet, this is the marvelous "hope of glory" that is ours in Christ.

Ephesians 4:13 AV

Till we all come in the unity of the faith, and of the knowledge of the Son of God, unto a perfect man, unto the measure of the stature of the fulness of Christ:

This will not occur until Christ returns for the Church. Note the measure that we will receive, ". . . **unto a perfect man, unto the measure of the stature of the fullness of Christ.**" When Christ returns for us, we will acquire the salvation for which we have long hoped.

The apostle Paul prayed:

Ephesians 1:17-20 AV

That the God of our Lord Jesus Christ, the father of glory, may give unto you the spirit of wisdom and revelation in the knowledge of Him:

The eyes of your understanding being enlightened, that ye may know what is the hope of His calling, and what the riches of the glory of His inheritance in the saints,

And what *is* the exceeding greatness of His power to us-ward who believe, according to the working of His mighty power,

Which He wrought in Christ, when He raised Him from the dead, and set *Him* at His own right hand in the heavenly places, . . .

When we realize that all of this was our Father's desire for us, and that He planned for its accomplishment by the work of Christ, it is overwhelming. This is the good pleasure of His will for us beloved!

Our Father wants us to understand the hope of His calling and the riches of the glory of His inheritance in the saints and the exceeding greatness of His power to us – the same power that He demonstrated when He raised Christ from the dead and set him at His right hand in the heavenlies.

He did not do it because we deserved it but because of His great love for us. Almighty God, our Heavenly Father, desired to do this for us. With all our shortcomings and sins, we fall so short of deserving such riches of glory, and yet, because of His great love and kindness, it is ours in Christ by His exceeding great grace.

The only way that we could obtain such glory is by the grace and love of God that we see demonstrated in Christ Jesus our Lord.

Philippians 3:20 and 21 Weymouth New Testament

We, however, are free citizens of Heaven, and we are waiting with longing expectation for the coming from Heaven of a Saviour, the Lord Jesus Christ,

who, in the exercise of the power which He has even to subject all things to Himself, will transform this body of our humiliation until it resembles His own glorious body.

There is no hope of eternal life apart from the coming of the Lord Jesus Christ for the Church.

In Christ, we are the free citizens of heaven. From God's perspective, we are no longer of this world. Our citizenship is in the heavenlies. We are no longer of the brotherhood of man but of the household of God.

The day that Christ returns to gather us together and take us to our true home in the heavenlies is quickly approaching. Nothing can keep our Heavenly Father from performing His Will. When it arrives, the Lord will transform our bodies to be like his glorious body. God, His Father, gave him the power to accomplish this glorious reality.

I John 3:2 AV

Beloved, now are we the sons of God, and it doth not yet appear what we shall be: but we know that, when he shall appear, we shall be like him; for we shall see him as he is.

Today, this very moment, we are the sons of God! When Christ appears, **"we shall be like him; for we shall see him as he is."** We may not know all there is to know about eternity, but we do know that we will be like Christ.

I Corinthians 13:12 NAGENT

For now we see in a mirror dimly, but then face to face. Now I know in part; then I shall understand fully, even as I have been fully understood.

Our face to face with Christ Jesus our Lord could occur any moment. Does anyone know the exact day when this will take place?

Matthew 24:36 ASV

But of that day and hour knoweth no one, not even the angels of heaven, neither the Son, but the Father only.

Jesus Christ said that no one knows the time of his coming; the Father did not even reveal it to him. The second someone says that he knows when he is coming, you know that he is contradicting God's Word, and he does not know what he is talking about.

Who would take any man's word over God's Word? God gave us His Word so that we could know His Will. We can check what anyone may say against what the Word of God says. God's Word enables us to separate the truth from error.

Colossians 3:4 AV
When Christ, who is our life, shall appear, then shall ye also appear with him in glory.

We may be vexed with the evil of this world today, but our hope is in Christ's return to deliver, to save, and to redeem us from this present evil world or from the grave itself, if it has overtaken us.

I Corinthians 15:35 AV
But some man will say, How are the dead raised up? and with what body do they come?

Who does "**they**" refer to in verse 35? It is speaking of "**the dead**" mentioned in the first part of the verse. These words were purposely left out of the verse to draw our attention to the remaining words. This is the use of the figure of speech, *ellipsis*. The words "**the dead**" from the context of the first question were omitted to emphasize the remaining words, which deal with the body; ". . . **and with what body do they come** [from the dead]**?**"

The dead are not alive today in heaven, nor do they come back from heaven to get their body from the grave at a later time. If we read what is written, this verse is plainly speaking of the dead.

I Corinthians 15:36-49 AV
Thou fool, that which thou sowest is not quickened, except it die: And that which thou sowest, thou sowest not that body that shall be, but bare grain, it may chance of wheat, or of some other grain: But God giveth it a body as it hath pleased him, and to every seed his own body.

All flesh is not the same flesh: but there is one kind of flesh of men, another flesh of beasts, another of fishes, and another of birds.

There are also celestial bodies, and bodies terrestrial: but the glory of the celestial is one, and the glory of the terrestrial is another. There is one glory of the sun, and another glory of the moon, and another glory of the stars: for one star differeth from another star in glory.

So also is the resurrection of the dead. It is sown in corruption; it is raised in incorruption: It is sown in dishonour; it is raised in glory: it is sown in weakness; it is raised in power: It is sown a natural body; it is raised a spiritual body. There is a natural body, and there is a spiritual body.

And so it is written, The first man Adam was made a living soul; the last Adam [Jesus Christ] was made a quickening [life-giving] spirit. Howbeit that was not first which is spiritual, but that which is natural; and afterward that which is spiritual.

The first man is of the earth, earthy: the second man is the Lord from heaven. As is the earthy, such are they also that are earthy: and as is the heavenly, such are they also that are heavenly. And as we have borne the image of the earthy, we shall also bear the image of the heavenly.

There are terrestrial, or earthly bodies, and there are celestial, or heavenly bodies. "**As we have borne the image of the earthy, we shall also bear the image of the heavenly.**" When the dead in Christ are raised, what will their resurrected body be like?

- It will be incorruptible. It will no longer be subject to death, humiliation, and corruption. It will be imperishable.

- It will be raised in glory. We will obtain the glory of our Lord Jesus Christ.

- It will be raised in power. Christ will exert the vast power that God gave him over the gates of death. He will raise us in power.

- It will be raised a spiritual body. We will be transformed to have glorious bodies like our Lord's. We will bear the image of the heavenly.

When will this occur? Verses 22 and 23 reveal the answer.

For as in Adam all die, even so in Christ shall all be made alive. But every man in his own order: Christ the firstfruits; afterward they that are Christ's at His coming.

"At His coming," we will be with him and we will be like him.

I Corinthians 15:46-49 AV
Howbeit that was not first which is spiritual, but that which is natural; and afterward that which is spiritual.

The first man is of the earth, earthy: the second man is the Lord from heaven. As is the earthy, such are they also that are earthy: and as is the heavenly, such are they also that are heavenly.

And as we have borne the image of the earthy, we shall also bear the image of the heavenly.

Absent from the Body and Present with the Lord

Tradition and the Word of God do not usually agree. The truth of God's Word always makes sense, while tradition usually prevents us from understanding the Word of God.

If we are to rightly-divide the Word of God, every verse concerning the identical subject must agree. If there seems to be a problem in understanding a particular verse or passage, we must understand the difficult passage in light of the many passages that are clear. The Word of God will interpret itself; it will unfold the meaning to us if we will consider its testimony.

We cannot pull a statement or verse out of its context, and use it in a way that contradicts the many scriptures that are clear and understandable.

We are now going to consider a frequently misquoted and misunderstood scripture and apply the principles of biblical study to discover what the Word of God says.

We are going to deal with a section of scripture in II Corinthians 5. Some teach that this section says, that if we are absent from the body we are then present with the Lord, meaning that when you die you go to heaven. Is this the correct teaching concerning this section of Scripture?

The first thing we must realize is that this is not what the Scripture says. It is misquoted and lifted from the context in which the complete statement is made.

Let us pick up the context in II Corinthians 4:14, and allow the Word of God to unfold its own interpretation to us. The subject that the apostle is dealing with is affliction and why he did not "faint."

II Corinthians 4:14 WT

Knowing that he which raised the Lord Jesus shall raise up us also by Jesus, and shall present *us* with you.

God raised Jesus Christ from the dead by His glorious power, and He will raise Paul (the writer to the Corinthians), and Timothy (see 1:1), and bring us, referring to Paul (himself) and Timothy, with you (the believers in Christ) into God's presence by the same mighty power.

There is no release from death and the grave except by resurrection when the Lord raises them to life again at his coming.

II Corinthians 4:16-18 AV

For which cause we faint not; but though our outward *man* perish, yet the inward man is renewed day by day.

For our light affliction, which is but for a moment, worketh for us a far more exceeding *and* eternal weight of glory;

While we look not at the things which are seen, but at the things which are not seen: for the things which are seen *are* temporal; but the things which are not seen *are* eternal.

What are we to look for that makes our present affliction seem light? It is the return of Christ and "**the far more exceeding and eternal weight of glory**" we will then receive. He will raise the dead in Christ to life and change those who are still alive to be immortal.

This present affliction is truly light when compared to the reality of eternity and the far more exceeding and eternal heavy weight of glory we will receive.

We will be renewed day by day if we choose to think about God's Word concerning our hope in Christ. If we choose to keep our eyes on our hope of Christ's return instead of on the world around us, it will keep us radiant.

II Corinthians 5:1 AV

For we know that if our earthly house of *this* tabernacle were dissolved, we have a building of God, an house not made with hands, eternal in the heavens.

The first word in the verse is the corresponding conjunction "for." This word ties the verse together with the verse preceding it in the previous chapter. There should not be a chapter division here because this is a continuation of the subject from chapter 4.

Chapter divisions are made-made additions to the text. They were not a part of the God-breathed original text. Stephen Langton, the Archbishop of Canterbury is believed to apply a systematic chapter division while he worked in the Vulgate (the Latin Bible) around A.D. 1227. Wycliffe published a protestant Bible with chapter divisions in 1382.[63] These divisions are helpful when you are trying to find a reference, but they do not carry any God-given authority when it comes to interpretation.

This chapter begins an *allegory*[64], which is a figure of speech based on comparison.

The word "tabernacle" in verse 1 is *skenos*, a "tent." The tabernacle represents our earthly body, which is a temporary dwelling. The word "dissolved" means "taken down, as a tent is taken down." If our earthly tent [our mortal body] was taken down [meaning we died], we have a building of God that is eternal in the heavens.

The records in I Thessalonians 4 and I Corinthians 15 clearly tell us that we will inherit this spiritual body at the coming of our Lord. Our bodies will be conformed to be like our Lord's glorious body at his appearing.

II Corinthians 5:2 AV
For in this [tent, our earthly body] **we groan, earnestly desiring to be clothed upon with our house which is from heaven:**

"Groan" means "to sigh, as of persons in distress."[65]   It is to ache for something that you currently do not have.

Our earnest desire is not to be unclothed, (which is to die), but **"to be clothed upon with our house from heaven,"** (which is to have a new body like Christ's glorious body that we will receive at his return).

"Our house which is from heaven" will be a permanent spiritual body like Christ's resurrected and glorified body.

When will we be **"clothed upon"** with this body? Death is not the entrance into glory, it is the end of life, and the body corrupts in the grave.

---

[63] Daniell, D. (2003). *The Bible in English: History and Influence.*

[64] "There are three figures involving comparison: *Simile* is comparison by resemblance; *metaphor* is comparison by representation; *hypocatastasis* is comparison by implication. In the first the comparison is stated; in the second it is substituted; in the third it is implied. Thus *allegory* is a continuation of the latter two, *metaphor* or *hypocatastasis*; while the *parable* is a continuation of the *simile*. Bullinger. (1975 ed.). p.748.

[65] Bullinger (1999 ed.). *A Critical Lexicon and Concordance to the English and Greek New Testament.* p. 346.

We are not "**clothed upon**" at death. This will not occur until Christ returns for the Church. Our earnest desire is that Christ will return, and we will be clothed upon with new spiritual bodies like his glorious body.

II Corinthians 5:3 and 4 AV
If so be that being clothed we shall not be found naked. For we that are in *this* tabernacle do groan, being burdened: not for that we would be unclothed, but clothed upon, that mortality might be swallowed up of life.

"**Not be found naked**" is referring to death, when the body corrupts and perishes. In this earthly tent, our mortal body, we groan, we are burdened or weighed down with the affliction spoken of in chapter four.

Our heart's desire is not to be "**unclothed**," which is to die, but to be "**clothed upon**," which is to put on a glorious body at the return of Christ. Then "**mortality**" will "**be swallowed up of life**." When Christ returns for us we will be "**clothed upon**" with new bodies like his.

Notice that it says, "**that mortality might be swallowed up of life**" and not "that corruption might be swallowed up of life." Mortal means though we are alive, we are subject to death, while corruption is what takes place at death. This again points to Paul's desire for the return of Christ, not for death.

II Corinthians 5:5-8 AV
Now he that hath wrought us for the selfsame thing *is* God, who also hath given unto us the earnest of the Spirit.

Therefore *we are* always confident, knowing that, whilst we are at home in the body, we are absent from the Lord:

(For we walk by faith, not by sight:)

We are confident, *I say*, and willing rather to be absent from the body, and to be present with the Lord.

God has prepared that when Christ returns we will have new bodies like his. He is the One that promises us new bodies like Christ's glorious resurrected body. The Nestle-Aland Greek text reads, "**He who has prepared us for this very thing is God, who has given us the spirit as a guarantee.**"

Until then, God gave us the "**earnest of the spirit**," the down payment, which is the pledge that He will perform what He has promised.

Verse six says, "**whilst we are at home in the body, we are absent from the Lord.**" In verse eight, it reads "**willing rather to be absent from the body, and to be present with the Lord.**"

In these verses, we have the words: "**at home,**" "**absent,**" "**absent,**" and "**present**" (which is the same word as "**home**" in the Greek). The two verses use the words in the reverse order.

This is the figure of speech *antimetabole*. "This figure repeats the word or words in a reverse order, for the purpose of opposing one thing to another, or of contrasting two or more things."[66]

The two things that Paul is contrasting are the temporary mortal body we have today and the permanent spiritual body we will have at the return of our Lord.

Today, while we are at home in this earthly tent, in this temporary mortal body we are absent from the presence of the Lord, when we will be clothed upon with a new spiritual body. There is a day coming that we will both be present with the Lord and clothed with a body like his glorious body.

We earnestly desire, we ache for this day's arrival. Until then, we are full of hope and confidence that God will bring it about. He is faithful who promised, and He will perform it. We walk by believing God's promise, not by sight.

We are confident and much more willing to be absent from this mortal body and be present with our Lord at his return and clothed with new glorious bodies that are permanent.

The only way for those in Christ to be with the Lord is for him to return for his Church to clothe us with spiritual bodies like his glorious body

This section of scripture contrasts the temporary body we have today with the permanent body we will have at Christ's return for us. While we are at home in this temporary tent, we cannot have that permanent house.

The context teaches us that we know both that we will be present (verses 1 and 6) with the Lord, and we earnestly desire (verse 2) to be present with the Lord.

This section does not teach that when we die we are present with the Lord. The teaching of the Word of God is that we know, and we earnestly desire to be clothed upon with our heavenly bodies. While we are at home

---

[66] Bullinger (1975 ed.). *Figures of Speech Used in the Bible: Explained and Illustrated.* p. 301.

in this mortal body, we are absent from the Lord – from his return and the glorious spiritual body, like his body, that we will receive at his coming.

We earnestly desire, our hearts ache for Christ to return and gather us together into the heavenlies. When he comes for us, we will not have any more afflictions, sorrow or death – only glory, and that forever.

I Corinthians 5:9 NAGENT
So whether we are at home or away, we make it our aim to please him.

This record in I Corinthians is certainly not speaking of death. Death does not please God; He calls it an enemy. Until Christ returns, we ought to live to please Him.

The Judgment Seat of Christ

The only judgment remaining for the saints in the Administration of the Grace of God will be that of rewards at the *Bema* of Christ. This expression appears in Romans 14:10 and II Corinthians 5:10. Since we are already in II Corinthians 5, let's continue with it.

II Corinthians 5:9 and 10 AV
Wherefore we labour, that, whether present or absent, we may be accepted of him.

For we must all appear before the judgment seat of Christ; that everyone may receive the things *done* in *his* body, according to that he hath done, whether *it be* good or bad.

What is this "judgment seat"? The judgment seat of Christ is called the *Bema*, where the members of the Church will stand before Christ to be rewarded for the things they have done in their mortal bodies. The word literally means "a raised step." It was where rewards were handed out in the Greek games. It is not a judicial bench.

The word "**labour**" is *philotimeomai*, which means that we make it a point of honor to lovingly and diligently work to please Him.

Why do we labor? The word "**accepted**" in verse 9 is *euarestos*,[67] which means well-pleasing. We labor in our walks, in this earthly body to please the Lord by doing his will with diligence and love, and we do it as a point of honor.

The word for "**done**" is *prasso*, which emphasizes the manner in which the works are done, that is, the heart and love with which they are done. It is not only what we do, but also how we do it that will be considered for the reward of service.

If the things done are "good," they will receive a reward. If the things done are "bad" [*phaulos*: unproductive evil], meaning worthless, they will not be worthy of any reward.

II Corinthians 5:11 AV
Knowing therefore the terror of the Lord, we persuade men; but we are made manifest unto God; and I trust also are made manifest in your consciences.

"**Terror**" is the word *phobos* which means "reverence." We know the reverence of the Lord, and therefore, we persuade men to reverence him also.

The judgment seat of Christ will occur sometime after Christ's return for the Church, not at death.

This is not a judgment seat set up for a sentencing of judicial condemnation (*katakrino*) to determine whether one will be saved or not. That matter has already been settled in Christ, and there is no more condemnation coming to believers in Christ Jesus [Romans 8:1, 30-38].

Once we are saved, we will be rewarded for our labor "in Christ."

Let's consider another passage that discusses rewards given for service. Verses in I Corinthians 3 use two allegories: one about planting and watering (verses 6-9a) and the other about builders and the building (verses 9b-17) to teach us about this subject.

I Corinthians 3:6 and 7 AV
I have planted, Apollos watered; but God gave the increase. So then neither is he that planteth any thing, neither he that watereth; but God that giveth the increase.

---

[67] The word also appears in Romans 12:1 and 14:18; Ephesians 5:10; Philippians 4:18; Colossians 3:20; and Hebrews 13:21, revealing much about how we are to be well-pleasing of the Lord.

God is the One who appointed both of them to serve in the body of Christ, the Church, and He is the One that gives the increase, the growth in the body.

We plant and water as God's laborers, but we do not give the growth, no more so than a farmer gives the growth in his field. The ability for the plant's growth is in its seed. The farmer just provides the most suitable conditions for the plant so that it can grow.

For example, we may serve by speaking the Word about salvation, but God is the One that provides the new birth and gives the eternal life in Christ.

Verse 8:

Now he that planteth and he that watereth are one: and every man shall receive his own reward according to his own labour.

Whether we plant or water, we serve the same God; we have the same purpose.

The judgment seat of Christ will consider each saint's labor or work, not his salvation or standing in Christ. This judging will be for rewards. Christians will receive rewards according to their own labor.

I Corinthians 3:9 AV

For we are labourers together with God: *ye are* **God's husbandry,** *ye are* **God's building.**

"For we are labourers together with God:" We plant or water, but God gives the increase. **"Ye are God's Husbandry."** God is the one Who gives the growth in this garden. The garden in this allegory is the body of Christ. The allegory changes in the last half of verse 9, from watering and planting in God's tilled field, to building a building, His temple.

I Corinthians 3:10 AV

According to the grace of God which is given unto me, as a wise masterbuilder, I have laid the foundation, and another buildeth thereon. But let every man take heed how he buildeth thereupon.

Each one who builds must consider how he builds on the foundation. The foundation is Christ and his completed work of redemption. The apostle Paul was the wise master builder. He laid a foundation concerning Christ and his accomplishments in the Epistles of Romans through II Thessalonians. These Epistles teach us what Christ has accomplished for us, who we are in him, and how we are to walk and serve in the body of Christ.

I Corinthians 3:11 AV

For other foundation can no man lay than that is laid, which is Jesus Christ.

There is no other foundation that we can build on other than Jesus Christ. He accomplished the work that provided salvation and all that comes with it. His work made the spirit available once again; he enabled us. His work is not an adornment to Christianity – he is Christianity!

I Corinthians 3:12- 15 AV

Now if any man build upon this foundation gold, silver, precious stones, wood, hay, stubble; [These are all satisfactory building materials that the builders use in this allegory.]

Every man's work shall be made manifest: for the day shall declare it, because it shall be revealed by fire; and the fire shall try every man's work of what sort it is.

If any man's work abide which he hath built thereupon, he shall receive a reward,

If any man's work shall be burned, he shall suffer loss: but he himself shall be saved; yet so as by fire.

These verses speak of a man's "**work**" and his "**reward**" that will be given for his work after he is saved, not his works to obtain salvation. It is speaking of how we build on the foundation that is laid, which is Jesus Christ. The whole context is speaking of our works; how we build on the foundation once we are saved.

If the Church were to be brought into judgment again concerning salvation, the death of Christ would have been deficient. We would still be dead in sin, ungodly, and enemies of God. Who would dare claim that the death of Christ failed to accomplish its purpose? Salvation is by the grace of God and by the work of the Lord Jesus Christ. Rewards will be given for our labor once we are saved.

"**If any man's work shall be burned, he shall suffer loss: but he himself shall be saved; yet so as by fire.**" It is the man's work that is tried by fire, that is, how he built on the foundation. If the man's work is burned, he will lose the reward. The man will still be saved.

Verse 14 says if the work passes the test by fire, he will receive a reward.

Verses 13 and 15 speak of fire and work being burned. How can you literally burn work? This is part of the allegory. The man's work will be proved like metal is assayed by fire; it assesses the purity of the metal. What the man built on Christ will pass the test, and he will receive a reward.

I Corinthians 3:16 and 17 Murdock

Know ye not, that ye are the temple of God? and that the Spirit of God dwelleth in you? Whoever shall mar the temple of God, God will mar him [his work]: for the temple of God is holy, which temple ye are.

If a man mars[68] God's Temple, which is the body of Christ, the Church, God will mar "him." This refers to the man's work, as we learned in the previous verse. This verse has to agree with the context of verse 15, which says that his work will be burned, and he shall suffer loss of reward, but he himself shall be saved.

We should go back to the earlier part of the chapter, and consider what the Corinthians were doing that prompted this teaching.

I Corinthians 3:2-5 AV

I have fed you with milk, and not with meat: for hitherto ye were not able *to bear it*, neither yet now are ye able.

For ye are yet carnal: for whereas *there is* among you envying, and strife, and divisions, are ye not carnal, and walk as men? For while one saith, I am of Paul; and another, I *am* of Apollos; are ye not carnal?

Who then is Paul, and who *is* Apollos, but ministers by whom ye believed, even as the Lord gave to every man?

They were carnally minded, and there was envy, strife, and divisions among them. These works mar or spoil believers who make up God's temple. This is not how God would have us build on the foundation of Christ.

The context, dealing with rewards for service as God's ministers of Christ and stewards of the mysteries of God, continues in chapter 4.

I Corinthians 4:5 AV

Therefore judge nothing before the time, until the Lord come, Who both will bring to light the hidden things of darkness, and will make

---

[68] "The Greek is *ptheiro*, to spoil, corrupt, to bring into a worse state, deprave, mar." Bullinger (1999 ed.) p. 220.

manifest the counsels of the hearts: and then shall every man have praise of God.

When the Lord returns, each steward will receive praise from God for his work and faithfulness.

I Corinthians 4:6 AV
And these things, brethren, I have in a figure transferred to myself and *to* Apollos for your sakes; that ye might learn in us not to think *of men* above that which is written, that no one of you be puffed up for one against another.

The teaching is plain, is it not? We must not confuse our standing in Christ concerning our salvation, with our walk and works of service after we are saved. Our standing in Christ is permanent, but our walk may fluctuate. They are two separate issues. The book of Corinthians continues to deal with the error in their walks.

God's perspective, concerning those whose standing is now in Christ, is that we died with Christ, and we are therefore dead to sin and its condemnation. In our association with Christ as members of his body, we are alive unto God, raised with Christ, seated in the heavenlies in him, and we will be manifested with him in glory as joint-heirs at his coming. We are judged in Christ as the righteousness of God [II Corinthians 5:21].

The members of the body of Christ, the Church, will appear at the *Bema* in their glorified bodies resembling Christ's own glorified body.

We are **"as he is," "complete"** in Christ, and we will be **"perfect** [or full grown] **men, unto the measure of the stature of the fullness of Christ."**

"And then shall every man have praise of God" for what we have done in the body of Christ, whether it is well-pleasing and worthy of praise or whether it is not worthy of a reward [I Corinthians 4:5; I Corinthians 3:9-17].

The Scriptures teach us that **"the Day of Christ"** is going to be a day of rest [II Thessalonians 1:7], comfort [Romans 15:4], joy [I Thessalonians 2:19], and glory [Colossians 3:4].

All that we anticipate concerning this day is ours due to the kindness of our Father and His great love for us, and it is available to us because of the accomplished work of His Son, our Lord Christ Jesus. It is Christ in you, the hope of glory!

It was God's idea to justify us from sin in Christ, making us the righteousness of God in Christ, and giving us the gift of eternal life. Christ is the one who dealt with our sin by giving his life for ours, and today, he intercedes for us at the right hand of God.

The Father tells us that as members of the body of Christ, we are complete in Christ, and that it is Christ in us the hope of glory. Oh, such grace and glory that is ours in Christ!

That which occurs at the *Bema* judgment of the Church cannot contradict what God has revealed to us in the many clear Scriptures of the Church Epistles. We must never confuse our standing in Christ with our walks. They are two different things.

Philippians 1:6 AV
Being confident of this very thing, that He which hath begun a good work in you will perform it until the day of Christ Jesus.

We can be absolutely confident of this truth. We have been called unto **"the obtaining of the glory of the Lord Jesus Christ."**

Nothing will ever **"be able to separate us from the love of God which is in Christ Jesus our Lord."**

Our Father sees us as **"in Christ,"** united with him in his accomplishments, incorporated into his body as members in particular. Our standing before God will always be in Christ.

All that we are and all that we hope for is ours in Christ. It is **"Christ in you, the hope of glory."** We are forever united with Christ in his accomplishments as members of his body . . . nothing can separate us.

We *definitely know* these things to be true because God revealed them to us by His Word. Anyone can understand His will for the Church if they will go to the Scriptures, and read what they have to say.

There is much we do not know about the future, but what is written is well-defined and certain, and what remains to be seen and understood will not – it cannot – contradict that which God has revealed to us in His written Word.

Nothing should trouble us concerning Christ's coming for the Church. We should live each day with the joyful anticipation of Christ's coming to gather us together, and take us to our true home in the heavenlies, to be glorified with him, as joint-heirs. God gave us our hope in Christ for our comfort.

I Corinthians 15:58 AV
Therefore, my beloved brethren, be ye stedfast, unmoveable, always abounding in the work of the Lord, forasmuch as ye know that your labour is not in vain in the Lord.

We can stand today, and serve God as a point of honor, love and diligence. Christ will return for us, and our work will not be for naught. God will recompense us at the *Bema*.

This Same Jesus

There is an expression in the Word of God that provides us with tremendous insight concerning Jesus's resurrection. As you read the following verses, take note of the words, **"this same Jesus."**

Acts 1:11 AV
Which also said, Ye men of Galilee, why stand ye gazing up into heaven? this same Jesus, which is taken up from you into heaven, shall so come in like manner as ye have seen him go into heaven.

When the Lord Jesus returns, he will be the same Jesus that ascended.

Acts 2:36 AV
Therefore let all the house of Israel know assuredly, that God hath made that same Jesus, whom ye have crucified, both Lord and Christ.

God made that same Jesus that they crucified, both Lord and Christ.

Ephesians 4:9 and 10 AV
(Now that he ascended, what is it but that he also descended first into the lower parts of the earth?

He that descended is the same also that ascended up far above all heavens, that he might fill all things.)

The same Jesus that descended into the grave is the same one that ascended far above all heavens. When he ascended up on high, he fulfilled God's Will and led captivity captive!

Hebrews 13:8 AV
Jesus Christ the same yesterday, and today, and for ever.

The same Jesus that was born, lived, died, and was raised from the dead, who ascended far above all heavens, will be the same forever.

God made the same Jesus that they crucified, both Lord and Christ.

Jesus Christ is the same "yesterday" when he lived on the earth, as he is today living at the right hand of God in the heavenlies, and he will be the same forever.

God's only begotten Son, Jesus Christ, is the same, and he is entirely preserved forever.

Colossians 1:18 AV
And he is the head of the body, the church: who is the beginning, the firstborn from the dead; that in all things he might have the preeminence.

Jesus Christ was the firstborn from the dead. God gave him preeminence in all things. The same man who died is the same man that God raised to eternal life, and he is head of the body, the church.

Romans 8:29 AV
For whom he did foreknow, he also did predestinate to be conformed to the image of his Son, that he might be the firstborn among many brethren.

The Lord Jesus was the firstborn among many brethren that will have eternal life. When Christ returns for us, each of us will be the same person that we are today, and we will be conformed to the image of God's Son.

I Thessalonians 5:23 AV
And the very God of peace sanctify you wholly; and *I pray God* your whole spirit and soul and body be preserved blameless unto the coming of our Lord Jesus Christ.

Those who confess Jesus as Lord and believe that God raised him from the dead will be entirely preserved at Christ's coming.

When Christ returns to save and redeem the Church, he will come to save and redeem you, the same individual, the same person that you are today.

Philippians 3:20 and 21 AV

For our conversation [citizenship] is in heaven; from whence also we look for the Saviour, the Lord Jesus Christ: Who shall change our vile body, that it may be fashioned like unto his glorious body, according to the working whereby he is able even to subdue all things unto himself.

Our new spiritual bodies will be like our Lord's. They will be unlimited in the scope of their activity.

We will no longer be mortal. We will no longer be subject to death or disease. Our new bodies will be fashioned like unto Christ's glorious body.

Our minds will no longer be as frail as they are today. We will no longer be burdened with fear, worry, doubt, sorrow, condemnation or any such thing.

Job 19:26 and 27 AV

And though after my skin *worms* destroy this *body*, yet in my flesh shall I see God:

Whom I shall see for myself, and mine eyes shall behold, and not another; *though* my reins be consumed within me.

Job said that *he* would see God *for himself.* He knew that God would resurrect *him*, the same person that was then living.

The same Jesus who lived and died is the same one that arose from dead, ascended, and sat down at the right hand of God in the heavenlies. It is he himself.

The same is true of us; we will be the same ones when he returns for us, and either raises us to life or changes us if we are yet alive. It will be *you yourself*, only glorified.

The Riches in the Ages to Come

Ephesians 2:7 AV
That in the ages to come he might shew the exceeding riches of his grace[69] in *his* kindness toward us through Christ Jesus.

It will take our Father **"the ages to come"** – eternity – to completely demonstrate the exceeding riches of His grace in kindness to us through Christ Jesus.

There are simply no human words capable of completely describing the vastness of the riches of His grace. Today these riches are beyond the boundaries of our limited understanding. What do we know of the riches of His grace?

Ephesians 1:7 AV
In whom we have redemption through his blood, the forgiveness of sins, according to the riches of his grace;

The book of Ephesians mentions grace twelve times. Grace is God's undeserved, divine favor towards man. God's grace towards us is free. Our sins do not hinder God's offer of it, nor is it contingent upon our works. It is ours solely because God desired to make it available to us by the work of Jesus Christ. Our redemption and forgiveness of sins is ours exclusively by **"the riches of his grace."** God freely gave it to us in Christ.

Ephesians 2:5 AV
Even when we were dead in sins, hath quickened us together with Christ, (by grace ye are saved;)

Ephesians 2:7 and 8 AV
That in the ages to come he might shew the exceeding riches of his grace in *his* kindness toward us through Christ Jesus.

---

[69] In the expression "The exceeding riches of His grace," "exceeding" is a figure of speech using *huperballo*. It means "to throw or cast over or beyond, (i.e., beyond a certain limit), also, to throw beyond or farther than another, to surpass in throwing, hence generally, to surpass, excel, exceed." Bullinger (1975 ed.).

For by grace are ye saved through faith; and that not of yourselves: *it is* the gift of God: Not of works, lest any man should boast.

How could God communicate it more plainly? How did God forgive our sins? How did God redeem us? When we were dead in sins, how did He make us alive? How did He save us? The answer to these questions is "in Christ," and what he achieved is ours solely by the grace of God. Salvation is the gift of God so that we cannot boast that it came through our own work.

Ephesians 3:2 AV
If ye have heard of the dispensation of the grace of God which is given me to you–ward:

It should be patently obvious as to why God calls this period "**the dispensation** [or administration] **of the grace of God.**" What do we have from God that we did not receive by His grace? The answer is a resounding, "Nothing!"

Colossians 1:26 and 27 AV
Even the mystery which hath been hid from ages and from generations, but now is made manifest to his saints:

To whom God would make known what *is* the riches of the glory of this mystery among the Gentiles; which is Christ in you, the hope of glory:

"**The exceeding riches of His grace**" connected with the mystery of Christ will end in "**the riches of the glory of this mystery among the Gentiles; which is Christ in you, the hope of glory.**" These riches are exceeding abundantly above all that we could ever ask or think. We will not be disappointed in our expectation of hope in Christ.

The realities that God is revealing to us in His Word are a foregone conclusion. We should be confident that God will perform His Word concerning our hope, the same as He did when He brought Christ the first time. The certainty of Christ's return for the Church is as certain as the fact that you are now reading these words. He is coming!

Ephesians 2:7 AV
That in the ages to come He might shew the exceeding riches of his grace in *his* kindness toward us through Christ Jesus.

I have no idea just how magnificent eternity will be, but I do know that our Father reveals that it will take Him all the ages to come to demonstrate all of His kindness to us in Christ.

It is not only the extraordinary amount of blessing, or the extent of time that it will take Him to demonstrate every spiritual blessing to us that is conspicuous here, but the Father's disposition toward us is also conspicuous. These exceeding riches of grace will come from a loving Father with an intense desire to demonstrate His loving kindnesses and tender mercies to His beloved children.

All we know about eternity is the opening event and yet how incredible it is! It is breathtaking. Such joy unspeakable is ours by the grace of our Heavenly Father.

What more can we say other than, "**Thanks be to God who gives us the victory through our Lord Jesus Christ**"! Beloved, we will obtain the glory of God, the acquisition of the glory of our Lord Jesus Christ! This is why He called us.

I Corinthians 13:12 AV
For now we see through a glass [mirror]**, darkly; but then face to face: now I know in part; but then** [at the return of Christ for the Church] **shall I know even as also I am known.**

The word for "**glass**" is *esoptron*, which is a looking glass or mirror. In the lands and times of the Bible, it was usually made of polished metal such as brass. When one looked into the mirror of polished metal, one did not see the exact reality, but a blurry reflection.

The word "**darkly**" means, "to hint obscurely." Today, we only see a glimpse of what we hope for, but when Christ returns we will see and know the reality of our hope, firsthand.

We will have come unto the measure of the stature of the fullness of Christ. We will know even as we are known.

I Corinthians 2:9 AV
But as it is written, Eye hath not seen, nor ear heard, neither have entered into the heart of man, the things which God hath prepared for them that love him.

God has revealed to us what was once a mystery, but much of the hope following our gathering together unto Him into the glory of the heavenlies is an enigma still to be revealed.

Our Heavenly Father has only drawn back the curtain of eternity and given us a peek into the future glorious realities that await us in Christ.

Colossians 2:2 and 3 WT
So that their hearts may be encouraged, united in love, even unto all riches of the complete certainty of understanding, unto the knowledge [acknowledgement] **of the mystery of God concerning Christ, in which all the treasures of wisdom and knowledge are hidden.**

When you consider all that our Father previously kept secret concerning the Mystery of Christ, and, if it is going to take Him the ages to come to show us all of His kindness in Christ Jesus, just think of the treasures He must still have hidden away from our view concerning our glorious hope!

All the treasures of wisdom and knowledge are hidden within the mystery concerning Christ!

Colossians 1:25-27 AV
Whereof I am made a minister, according to the dispensation of God which is given to me for you, to fulfil the word of God;

***Even* the mystery which hath been hid from ages and from generations, but now is made manifest to his saints:**

To whom God would make known what is the riches of the glory of this mystery among the Gentiles; which is Christ in you, the hope of glory:

God assures the Church that it will partake of a glorious hope. "**The riches of the glory of this mystery**" pertain to the mystery concerning Christ that God revealed to His apostle, Paul.

From the opening event to the closing event, this entire period was a mystery. It was not hidden in prophecy – it was hidden in God. The prophets diligently searched for it, but it remained a mystery to them. No man knew it until God revealed it to the apostle Paul.

As with every spiritual blessing, the glorious riches concerning our hope are solely dependent on the Father's desire to make them available to us by the work of our Lord, Jesus Christ. They are ours by God's grace and by His grace alone.

God has revealed "**the riches of the glory of this mystery . . ..**" Had God not revealed them to us, they would remain His secret - forever hidden, and we would remain ignorant of them.

However, God *did* choose to reveal these riches to us. All that we hope for is ours "in Christ," and Christ is in us by the spirit of sonship. It is "**Christ in you, the hope of glory!**"

Philippians 1:6 AV
Being confident of this very thing, that He Which hath begun a good work in you will perform it until the day of Jesus Christ.

We have a hope today, but the day is swiftly approaching when our hope will become a reality! We can be confident that our Father will bring the good work of salvation that He began in us to its completion, to its full end. He will fulfill the good pleasure of His will concerning us in Christ.

Christ is coming for his church on the day of redemption and we will obtain the glory of the Lord Jesus Christ! He called us to obtain it beloved!

The Second Stage: The Day of the Lord

Revelation 1:10
I was in the Spirit on the Lord's day, and heard behind me a great voice, as of a trumpet . . ..

Overview

The second stage of Christ's coming to the earth is in "the Day of the Lord." The Word of God does not tell us how long this period will last. It could last as long as his first coming or even longer. Only seven years are specifically mentioned.

The only way we can understand this period is to go to the Word of God, and allow the scriptures to reveal it to us. The Old Testament prophets foretold of this day. The Lord Jesus Christ described the different stages of it in the four gospel records. The book of Revelation describes it in detail.

The record in I Thessalonians distinguishes between the two stages of Christ's coming, also. First, we read about his coming concerning the Church in the Administration of the Grace of God.

I Thessalonians 4:13-18 AV
But I would not have you to be ignorant, brethren, concerning them which are asleep, that ye sorrow not, even as others which have no hope.

For if we believe that Jesus died and rose again, even so them also which sleep in Jesus will God bring with him.

For this we say unto you by the word of the Lord, that we which are alive *and* remain unto the coming of the Lord shall not prevent [precede] them which are asleep.

For the Lord himself shall descend from heaven with a shout, with the voice of the archangel, and with the trump of God: and the dead in Christ shall rise first:

Then we which are alive *and* remain shall be caught up together with them in the clouds, to meet the Lord in the air: and so shall we ever be with the Lord.

Wherefore comfort one another with these words.

Immediately following the comfort of the revelation concerning the Lord's coming for the Church, we read:

I Thessalonians 5:1-11 AV

But of the times and the seasons, brethren, ye have no need that I write unto you. For yourselves know perfectly [*akribos*: accurately] that the day of the Lord so cometh as a thief in the night.

For when they shall say, Peace and safety; then sudden destruction cometh upon them, as travail upon a woman with child; and they shall not escape.

But ye, brethren, are not in darkness, that that day should overtake you as a thief. Ye are all the children of light, and the children of the day: we are not of the night, nor of darkness. Therefore let us not sleep, as *do* others; but let us watch and be sober.

For they that sleep sleep in the night; and they that be drunken are drunken in the night.

But let us, who are of the day, be sober, putting on the breastplate of faith and love; and for an helmet, the hope of salvation.

For God hath not appointed us to wrath, but to obtain salvation by our Lord Jesus Christ, Who died for us, that, whether we wake or sleep, we should live together with him.

Wherefore comfort yourselves together, and edify one another, even as also ye do.

Verse one begins with the contrasting conjunction "**but**." This signals that we are no longer dealing with the gathering together of the Church; we are now dealing with a different subject. The two parts of Christ's coming are set in contrast to each other in these chapters.

Christ first comes for his Church to gather them into the heavenlies, and then later he comes to the earth in the Day of the Lord. The first part of his coming will be for salvation and deliverance, while the second part will involve wrath and judgment for those left on the earth.

Next, we have the mention of "**times and seasons**." Christ's coming for the Church in the Administration of the Grace of God or the Mystery, has no prophetic teaching concerning times or seasons.

The apostles believed that the return of Christ for the Church was imminent. They did not instruct the saints to look for signs and seasons, but for the return of the Lord from heaven.

Christ could return for the Church at any time since the Day of Pentecost following his ascension into the heavenlies. Not a single scripture in the

Church Epistles indicates particular signs or seasons, which must be fulfilled as a prerequisite to Christ's coming for the Church in the Administration of the Grace of God.

When we read verse 3, "**For when they shall say, Peace and safety; then sudden destruction cometh upon them, as travail upon a woman with child; and they shall not escape**," it is like reading Isaiah 13:6-9 or Jeremiah 30:6. This describes something totally different than the coming of Christ for the Church in the previous chapter. If you know a woman who has delivered a baby, she can explain the comparison to you better than I could.

In verse one, what does the phrase "**the times and seasons**" concern? The next verse explains it for us.

I Thessalonians 5:2 AV
For yourselves know perfectly that the day of the Lord so cometh as a thief in the night.

We know perfectly (*akribos*, the Greek word means "accurately"), or accurately, that the Day of the Lord comes as a thief.

II Peter 3:10, Revelation 3:3 and 16:15 also speak of his coming as a "**thief.**" A thief does not announce that he is coming. These verses all describe his coming in the Day of the Lord. The Lord himself spoke of this.

Matthew 24:42-44 AV
Watch therefore: for ye know not what hour your Lord doth come.

But know this, that if the goodman of the house had known in what watch the thief would come, he would have watched, and would not have suffered his house to be broken up.

Therefore be ye also ready: for in such an hour as ye think not the Son of man cometh.

The Lord was speaking to his disciples who were Judeans. He told them that ". . . **the Son of man cometh**." This expression is used in connection with the earth. The Son of man will regain the dominion on the earth that Adam lost.

What the Lord said here does not concern the Church in the Administration of the Grace of God. The Church in the Administration of the Grace of God and the Mystery was still a secret known only to God at this particular time.

What is "the Day of the Lord"?

If we will go to the first time it is used and follow its subsequent uses in the Word of God we will have the biblical definition of the term. The first use is in the book of Isaiah.

Isaiah 2:12 AV
For the day of the LORD of hosts *shall be* **upon every** *one that is* **proud and lofty, and upon every** *one that is* **lifted up; and he shall be brought low:**

The Day of the Lord is the time when everyone that is proud and lofty and everyone that is lifted up . . . shall be brought low.

The expression, the Day of the Lord, appears in:

- Isaiah 2:12; 13:6,9
- Ezekiel 13:5; 30:3
- Joel 1:15; 2:1, 11, 31; 3:14
- Amos 5:18, 20
- Obadiah 1:15
- Zephaniah 1:7, 14
- Zechariah 14:1
- Malachi 4:5
- Acts 2:20
- I Thessalonians 5:2
- II Thessalonians 2:2
- II Peter 3:10
- Revelation 1:10

The expression, the Day of the Lord, is also translated as the Lord's Day in the New Testament.

The Day of the Lord is the only way to express it in the Hebrew because the Hebrew does not contain the possessive adjective "Lord's."

The Greek can express it two ways. It can use two nouns, "the Day of the Lord," the same as the Hebrew or it can use the adjective Lord's as in "the Lord's Day."

They both describe the same day. The difference is in which word receives the emphasis. "The Day of the Lord" places the emphasis on the word "Lord." "The Lord's Day," by using an adjective to qualify the noun, places the emphasis on the noun "day."

The phrase, in combination with other words such as anger, wrath, vengeance, sacrifice, etc., occurs a number of times. "That day" or "the great day" or "the day" when used to refer to the Day of the Lord occurs more than 75 times in the Old Testament. Numerous other scriptures also speak of the events that will occur in that day.

Let's read the context surrounding the first occurrence of the day of the Lord in Isaiah.

Isaiah 2:11-22 AV
The lofty looks of man shall be humbled, and the haughtiness of men shall be bowed down, and the LORD alone shall be exalted in that day.

For the day of the LORD of hosts *shall be* upon every *one that is* proud and lofty, and upon every *one that is* lifted up; and he shall be brought low:

And upon all the cedars of Lebanon, *that are* high and lifted up, and upon all the oaks of Bashan, And upon all the high mountains, and upon all the hills *that are* lifted up, And upon every high tower, and upon every fenced wall, And upon all the ships of Tarshish, and upon all pleasant pictures.

And the loftiness of man shall be bowed down, and the haughtiness of men shall be made low: and the LORD alone shall be exalted in that day.

And the idols he shall utterly abolish.

And they shall go into the holes of the rocks, and into the caves of the earth, for fear of the LORD, and for the glory of his majesty, when he ariseth to shake terribly the earth.

In that day a man shall cast his idols of silver, and his idols of gold, which they made *each one* for himself to worship, to the moles and to the bats; To go into the clefts of the rocks, and into the tops of the

ragged rocks, for fear of the LORD, and for the glory of his majesty, when he ariseth to shake terribly the earth.

Cease ye from man, whose breath is in his nostrils: for wherein is he to be accounted of?

This does not sound like "**the riches of the glory**" concerning the Church's hope in Christ, does it? No, it does not. Is this the comfort, rest, joy, and glory that we are to hold in mind concerning Christ's coming for the Church? No, it is not. Does this sound like a time that we will obtain salvation or does it sound like a time of judgment?

The Day of the Lord is the time of God's judgment, when the Lord will do the judging – not man.

I Corinthians 4:3 Interlinear Greek- English New Testament
But to me the smallest matter it is that by you I be examined, or by man's day. But neither myself do I examine.

Today is "**man's day**" because man is the one who does the judging. God is silent today as far as judgment is concerned. This is not the case during the time of the Lord's Day. He will be the judge of all the earth when this period unfolds.

If we are to understand the revelation in Isaiah, we must first determine to whom it is addressed and of whom it speaks.

Isaiah 1:1 AV
The vision of Isaiah the son of Amoz, which he saw concerning Judah and Jerusalem in the days of Uzziah, Jotham, Ahaz, and Hezekiah, kings of Judah.

The book of Isaiah concerns Judah and Jerusalem, not the Church in the Administration of the Grace of God.

Remember, the Church of the Grace of God was a mystery until God revealed it to the apostle Paul. The Church is the Church, not Judah. Judah is not the Church, it is Judah and Jerusalem is Jerusalem; the city where the King of Judah will reign.

We cannot read Judah and Jerusalem and interpret them as the Church if we are to rightly divide the Word of God. God's Word says exactly what it means and it means precisely what it says. All Scripture is addressed to either the Judeans[70], the Gentiles, or to the Church of God.

The Church in the Administration of the Grace of God and the Mystery is not under consideration in the book of Isaiah.

Likewise, if we read "Israel" but think that Israel is "the Church" or if we read what belongs to the "Administration of the Law" and think that it is the same as "the Administration of the Grace of God," we will not have the truth. We will have error and be left with confusion if we conclude that the Gospels and Church Epistles are both speaking about the same time and about the same people.

The scenes about which we are reading in Isaiah take place on the earth, and they are not scenes of salvation and glory, but of *grave judgment*.

Christ's coming in the Lord's Day occurs on the earth, and it involves judgment for the Judeans and the Gentile, not the Church in the Administration of the Grace of God. The Church was judged in Christ as righteous, and its hope is to be received up into glory and into the heavenlies when Christ comes for them.

The next record concerning the Day of the Lord is Isaiah 13.

Isaiah 13:6-9 AV

Howl ye; for the day of the LORD *is* at hand; it shall come as a destruction from the Almighty.

Therefore shall all hands be faint, and every man's heart shall melt: And they shall be afraid: pangs and sorrows shall take hold of them; they shall be in pain as a woman that travaileth: they shall be amazed one at another; their faces *shall be* as flames.

Behold, the day of the LORD cometh, cruel both with wrath and fierce anger, to lay the land desolate: and he shall destroy the sinners thereof out of it.

---

[70] "Originally, Judah was a son of Jacob. Judah fathered only one of the tribes of Israel. Many centuries after the founding of the twelve tribes in the Old Testament, the tribes split into two kingdoms. The northern kingdom kept the name of 'Israel' because ten of the twelve tribes were located there. The southern kingdom was called 'Judah' or 'Judea' because, though other tribes were represented (including all of Benjamin), the tribe of Judah was dominant. Over and over again God's Word differentiates between the House of Israel and the House of Judah. Judeans by descent were only those of the House or Kingdom of Judah." After the splitting of the twelve tribes, the terms 'Judah' and 'Judea' referred to the southern kingdom and to its geographical location. V.P. Weirwille, *Jesus Christ Our Passover*, pp. 437-438.

The Day of the Lord will be a time of "**destruction from the Almighty**." It will be a time characterized by pangs and sorrows, pain as a woman has in the labor of childbirth. It will be a time of wrath and fierce anger. This is what we read in II Thessalonians 5. The land, referring to Israel, will be made desolate. The Lord Jesus Christ will destroy the sinners in that land. The next use of the Day of the Lord is in Ezekiel.

Ezekiel 13:5 AV
Ye have not gone up into the gaps, neither made up the hedge for the house of Israel to stand in the battle in the day of the Lord.

The Day of the Lord will be a time of battle for Israel.

Ezekiel 30:3 AV
For the day is near, even the day of the lord is near, a cloudy day; it shall be the time of the heathen.

It will be the time of the heathen or Gentile nations. The context goes on to tell us that they shall be judged and broken. The prophecy begins "**Howl ye, Woe be to the day!**"

Joel 1:15 AV
Alas for the day! For the day of the Lord is at hand, and as a destruction from the Almighty shall it come.

Again we read that is a time of "**destruction from the Almighty**."

Joel 2:1 AV
Blow ye the trumpet in Zion, and sound an alarm in My holy mountain: let all the inhabitants of the land tremble: for the day of the Lord cometh, for it is nigh at hand.

The Day of the Lord will be a time of alarm and great fear for those in the land of Judah.

Joel 2:11 AV
And the LORD shall utter his voice before his army: for his camp is very great: for he is strong that executeth his word: for the day of the LORD is great and very terrible; and who can abide it?

The Lord will lead His army in battle in the Day of the Lord.

Joel 2:31 AV

The sun shall be turned into darkness, and the moon into blood, before the great and terrible day of the LORD come.

If the sun is turned into darkness it will cause cataclysmic events on the earth. Acts 2:20 also refers to this.

Joel 3:14 AV

Multitudes, multitudes in the valley of decision: for the day of the LORD is near in the valley of decision.

"The valley of decision" is the valley of Jehoshaphat where God will assemble the nations to judge them. The entire chapter of Joel 3 deals with this.

Amos 5:18-20 AV

Woe unto you that desire the day of the Lord! to what end is it for you? the day of the Lord is darkness, and not light.

As if a man did flee from a lion, and a bear met him; or went into the house, and leaned his hand on the wall, and a serpent bit him.

Shall not the day of the Lord be darkness, and not light? even very dark, and no brightness in it?

This is not very comforting is it? This describes one calamity after another.

Obadiah 1:15 AV

For the day of the Lord is near upon all the heathen: as thou hast done, it shall be done unto thee: thy reward shall return upon thine own head.

The Day of the Lord will not be a good day for those who have rejected God.

Zephaniah 1:7-13 AV

Hold thy peace at the presence of the Lord GOD: for the day of the LORD is at hand: for the LORD hath prepared a sacrifice, he hath bid his guests.

And it shall come to pass in the day of the LORD'S sacrifice, that I will punish the princes, and the king's children, and all such as are clothed with strange apparel.

In the same day also will I punish all those that leap on the threshold, which fill their masters' houses with violence and deceit.

And it shall come to pass in that day, saith the LORD, that there shall be the noise of a cry from the fish gate, and an howling from the second, and a great crashing from the hills.

Howl, ye inhabitants of Maktesh, for all the merchant people are cut down; all they that bear silver are cut off.

And it shall come to pass at that time, that I will search Jerusalem with candles, and punish the men that are settled on their lees: that say in their heart, The LORD will not do good, neither will he do evil.

Therefore their goods shall become a booty, and their houses a desolation: they shall also build houses, but not inhabit them; and they shall plant vineyards, but not drink the wine thereof.

The Lord will search Jerusalem to find the guilty. It will not be a good day for the royal house. They will be punished for sending their servants into people's homes to steal from them. This will be a day of judgment. The Day of the Lord will be a time of loss for the guilty.

Zephaniah 1:14-2:3 AV
The great day of the LORD is near, it is near, and hasteth greatly, even the voice of the day of the LORD: the mighty man shall cry there bitterly.

That day is a day of wrath, a day of trouble and distress, a day of wasteness and desolation, a day of darkness and gloominess, a day of clouds and thick darkness,

A day of the trumpet and alarm against the fenced cities, and against the high towers.

And I will bring distress upon men, that they shall walk like blind men, because they have sinned against the LORD: and their blood shall be poured out as dust, and their flesh as the dung.

Neither their silver nor their gold shall be able to deliver them in the day of the LORD'S wrath; but the whole land shall be devoured by the fire of his jealousy: for he shall make even a speedy riddance of all them that dwell in the land.

Gather yourselves together, yea, gather together, O nation not desired;

Before the decree bring forth, before the day pass as the chaff, before the fierce anger of the LORD come upon you, before the day of the LORD'S anger come upon you.

Seek ye the LORD, all ye meek of the earth, which have wrought his judgment; seek righteousness, seek meekness: it may be ye shall be hid in the day of the LORD'S anger.

The Day of the Lord will be a day of wrath, trouble, distress, "wasteness," desolation, darkness, and gloominess. It will be the time when the Lord's wrath will be unleashed against his enemies. Their blood will be poured out as dust and their flesh thrown out as the dung. There will be a speedy riddance of the sinners in the Land – Judah. Neither their strength, nor their wealth, nor their intelligence will be able to deliver them from the wrath of God.

Zechariah 14:1-3 AV
Behold, the day of the Lord cometh, and thy spoil shall be divided in the midst of thee.

For I will gather all nations against Jerusalem to battle; and the city shall be taken, and the houses rifled, and the women ravished; and half of the city shall go forth into captivity, and the residue of the People shall not be cut off from the city.

Then shall the Lord go forth, and fight against those nations, as when He fought in the day of battle.

The entire fourteenth chapter in Zechariah deals with events that pertain to the Day of the Lord. The Lord will go forth and fight against the nations. He will come to the earth and stand on the Mount of Olives, which is before Jerusalem, and it will be split in the midst. The Lord will come and all his saints with him. Verse seven says that it will be one day, which shall be known to God. When it occurs, Jesus Christ will be the King over all the earth. Under his reign, Jerusalem will be inhabited and God's people will dwell safely.

Malachi 4:5 AV
Behold, I will send you Elijah the prophet before the coming of the great and dreadful day of the LORD:

You may recognize some of the expressions in these records from the four gospel accounts. Remember, these records teach that the Day of the Lord will be a day of wrath, trouble, alarm, distress, wasteness, and destruction, a day of darkness, gloominess, etc. It will be a period of judgment on the earth when the ungodly, and sinners will be judged.

The Lord Jesus described this time in the book of Matthew. After the Lord told his disciples that the Temple in Jerusalem would be destroyed, they asked him a question about it.

Matthew 24:3 AV
And as He sat upon the mount of Olives, the disciples came unto Him privately, saying, Tell us, when shall these things be and what shall be the sign of Thy coming, and of the end of the world?

His answers to their questions span the next two chapters. The word for "coming" is *parousia*, which concerns his coming and presence. The word for "end" is *sunteleia*. The times of the *sunteleia* are the times, which lead up to the consummation of the age. It is not the end of the world, but the time of one age leading into another.

Matthew 24:4-8 AV
And Jesus answered and said unto them, "Take heed that no man deceive you,

For many shall come in My name, saying, 'I am Christ;' and shall deceive many.

And ye shall hear of wars and rumours of wars: see that ye be not troubled: for all these things must come to pass, but the end is not yet.

For nation shall rise against nation, and kingdom against kingdom: and there shall be famines, and pestilences, and earthquakes, in divers places.

All these are the beginning of sorrows.

The Lord describes the *sunteleia,* or the end times, leading to his coming to the earth. He tells his disciples there will be false Christs, wars, famines, and earthquakes. He says, "**All these things are the beginning of sorrows.**"

The revelation concerning the six seals in the book of Revelation, chapter 6, gives the same order of these events as the record here in the book of Matthew. Both books are referring to the time of the Lord's Day.

In Matthew 24, the Lord tells them about persecution and martyrdom and that those who endure unto the end (*telos*) shall be saved. After the gospel of the kingdom is preached throughout the inhabited earth for a witness unto the nations, then the end (*telos*) will come.

The abomination of desolation spoken of in Daniel will be set up, followed by the great tribulation such as there never was before or ever will be again. False prophets will try to deceive them with great signs and wonders.

Then he reveals what his coming will be like.

Matthew 24:27 and 28 AV

For as the lightening cometh out of the east, and shineth even unto the west; so shall also the coming [*Parousia*] of the Son of man be.

For wheresoever the carcase is, there will the eagles [vultures] **be gathered together.**

Revelation 19:17 and 18 refer to this event as "**the supper of the great God**." The carcasses are from those who fight against the Lord and his army. The vultures will feed on their dead bodies.

Matthew 24:29 AV

Immediately after the tribulation of those days shall the sun be darkened, and the moon shall not give her light, and the stars shall fall from heaven, and the powers of the heavens shall be shaken;

Joel 2:31 also refers to this. Both Joel and Matthew are speaking of the same time – the Day of the Lord.

Matthew 24:30 AV

And then shall appear the sign of the Son of man in heaven: and then shall all the tribes of the earth mourn, and they shall see the Son of man coming in the clouds of heaven with power and great glory.

When the Son of man comes, in the Lord's Day, the people on the earth will mourn, not rejoice.

Unparalleled celestial events will announce Christ's coming to the earth. The sun will be darkened (Isaiah 13:10 and 34:1-5). The moon will not give off its light. The stars (not just a star or two) will fall from heaven. It will be as if "the light switch" in the heavens was turned off.

In the midst of this darkness, the sign of the Son of man will appear in heaven. He will come "**as the lightning cometh out of the east, and shineth**

even unto the west." The Lord will come in incomparable, magnificent glory as the King of kings and the Lord of lords.

Do you see why it will be unmistakable? Darkness will engulf the earth, and then, the glorious, brilliant light of the Lord's coming will break forth as lightning flashes out of the east unto the west. The only light in the heavens above or in the earth beneath will be the glory of the Lord. It will be unmistakable!

When he comes to the earth every eye will see him, and all the tribes of the earth will mourn, because he is coming to take dominion over the earth, to judge the ungodly and sinners.

Matthew 24:31 AV
And He shall send His angels with a great sound of a trumpet, and they shall gather together His elect from the four winds, from one end of heaven to the other.

This is not the gathering of the Church into the heavenlies; this is the gathering of the living saints of Israel who were carried away into captivity by other nations. After he comes to the earth, the Lord will send his angels to gather the 144,000 of Israel who were sealed before the great tribulation and who are still alive. They will bring them back to their King in Jerusalem.

Revelation chapter one also describes this coming.

Revelation 1:7 AV
Behold, He cometh with clouds; and every eye shall see Him [the Lord Jesus Christ]**, and they also which pierced Him: and all kindreds of the earth shall wail because of Him.**

This record agrees with the record in Matthew 24:29. Those who killed him are dead now, but they will see him again in the resurrection of the unjust. All the "**kindreds of the earth**" will wail at his coming because he comes to judge and make war, to reap the earth.

What does the book of Revelation call this coming?

Revelation 1:10 AV
I was in the Spirit on the Lord's day, and heard behind me a great voice, as of a trumpet,

The book of Revelation is about "**the Lord's Day.**" This is when the Lord will carry out judgment.

John 5:22 AV

For the Father judgeth no man, but hath committed all judgment unto the Son:

John 5:27 AV

And hath given him authority to execute judgment also, because he is the Son of man.

In John 5:22 and 27, we are told that the Father has "**committed all judgment unto the Son**" and that he has been given the authority to execute it "**because he is the Son of man.**" The book of Revelation speaks of "**the Son of man**" and the time that he will execute this judgment.

Revelation 1:13 – 18 AV

And in the midst of the seven candlesticks *one* like unto the Son of man, clothed with a garment down to the foot, and girt about the paps with a golden girdle.

His head and *his* hairs *were* white like wool, as white as snow; and his eyes *were* as a flame of fire;

And his feet like unto fine brass, as if they burned in a furnace; and his voice as the sound of many waters.

And he had in his right hand seven stars: and out of his mouth went a sharp two-edged sword: and his countenance *was* as the sun shineth in his strength.

And when I saw him, I fell at his feet as dead. And he laid his right hand upon me, saying unto me, Fear not; I am the first and the last:

I *am* he that liveth, and was dead; and, behold, I am alive for evermore, Amen; and have the keys of hell and of death.

The Day of the Lord is the time that the Son of man, the Lord Jesus Christ, will execute judgment. They killed him the first time he was on earth. God raised him from the dead, and today he lives at the right hand of God in the heavenlies. He possesses the keys that will unlock the graves and bring his people release from death.

The title "Son of man" is always used in connection with the earth. It is used the second time in chapter 14.

Revelation 14:14-20 AV

And I looked, and behold a white cloud, and upon the cloud *one* sat like unto the Son of man, having on his head a golden crown, and in his hand a sharp sickle.

And another angel came out of the temple, crying with a loud voice to him that sat on the cloud, Thrust in thy sickle, and reap; for the time is come for thee to reap; for the harvest of the earth is ripe.

And he that sat on the cloud thrust in his sickle on the earth; and the earth was reaped.

And another angel came out of the temple which is in heaven, he also having a sharp sickle.

And another angel came out from the altar, which had power over fire; and cried with a loud cry to him that had the sharp sickle, saying, Thrust in thy sickle, and gather the clusters of the vine of the earth; for her grapes are fully ripe.

And the angel thrust in his sickle into the earth, and gathered the vine of the earth, and cast it into the great winepress of the wrath of God.

And the winepress was trodden without the city, and blood came out of the winepress, even unto the horse bridles, by the space of a thousand *and* six hundred furlongs.

The Son of man will carry out the judgment of the wrath of God. He comes to the earth as the King of kings and Lord of lord's to reap the harvest of the world.

The first time he was on earth he came as the Savior, but they rejected him and the Word of God that he spoke. In the end, they placed a crown of thorns on his head and crucified him.

When he returns to the earth, he will be wearing a golden crown that God has placed on his head. This crown of gold symbolizes the dominion he is about to claim as King of kings and Lord of lords.

In the four Gospels, the Son of man comes as the sower that went forth to sow. In the book of Revelation, he comes as the reaper that harvests the earth.

Revelation 1:10 AV

I was in the Spirit on the Lord's day, and heard behind me a great voice, as of a trumpet,

The apostle John was given the revelation concerning the events that will take place during the Lord's day," and he was told to write them down.

Revelation 1:19 Rotherham
Write therefore – what things thou hast seen and what they are; and what things are about to come to pass, after these things:

He was told to write what he saw by revelation and what "**they are**," meaning, what "they signify." Throughout the book, we are shown the sequence of events that "**are about to come to pass**" during the Lord's Day.

The Lord's Day is not a day of the week such as Saturday or Sunday.

The Hebrews numbered their days: the first day of the week, the second day, etc., as did the early Church. The Sabbath was the seventh day of the week.

The names that we call our days all come from secular origins, for example: Saturn's Day, Sun's Day, Moon-day, etc. The names of our days come from planets and/or the gods these planets represented to ancient pagans.

The Greco-Roman tradition credits Vettius Valens, an astrologer who wrote in 170 A.D, with the names of the seven days. He named them after the Sun, Moon, and the gods Ares, Hermes, Zeus, Aphrodite, and Cronos.

When we read "the Lord's Day" or "the Day of the Lord" in the Word of God, it is referring to the period when the Lord will judge the earth as we have read in passage after passage.

The whole, extended period recorded in the book of Revelation concerns the Lord's Day. It consists of the times that follow the gathering together of the Church [I Thessalonians 4: 14-17; II Thessalonians 2:1-3] until the end of the second heaven and earth [II Peter 3:10-13].

The times of the Lord's Day are quite different from what we read in the Church Epistles concerning the first part of Christ's coming or *Parousia* for the Church in the Administration of the Grace of God and the Mystery.

After the Church is received up into glory, when the Lord gathers them together, the Lord's Day, and the time of His judgment begins to unfold on the earth. We will consider this in even more detail in the chapter that we compare the Lord's two comings in the books of I and II Thessalonians.

There are no scriptures that reveal the length of this period. It could cover a period as long as Christ's first coming or longer. Only the last seven years are specifically mentioned.

The Lord Jesus Christ foretold the events that will lead up to the end of the age or the *sunteleia*. He spoke of "**the beginning of sorrows**," wars, famines, pestilences, and earthquakes in many places. He spoke of "**great tribulation**," and the time when they would be hated of all nations for His name's sake. They will be afflicted and killed.

He told them that all the tribes of the earth will mourn when he comes "**in the clouds of heaven with power and great glory**." You can read about it in Matthew 24.

The Seven Seals

The book of Revelation covers this same period. It covers the *sunteleia* or the times leading up to the very end – the *telos*.

Revelation 5:1 AV
And I saw in the right hand of Him That sat on the throne a book written within and on the backside, sealed with seven seals.

The book of Revelation deals with the times that lead up to the coming of the Lord in chapter 19.

Revelation 5:2 AV
And I saw a strong angel proclaiming with a loud voice, "Who is worthy to open the book, and to loose the seals thereof?"

The rest of the chapter answers the question by describing him.

- He is "**the Lion of the tribe of Juda, the Root of David, hath prevailed to open the book and to loose the seven seals thereof.**"
- "**Thou art worthy to take the book, and to open the seals thereof; for Thou wast slain, and hast redeemed them to God by Thy blood out of every kindred, and tongue, and people, and nation;**"
- "**Worthy is the Lamb That was slain to receive power, and riches, and wisdom, and strength, and honour, and glory, and blessing.**"

The Lord Jesus Christ is the one worthy to open the book and loose the seals. When he was on earth the first time, they killed him, but God raised him from the dead. He is the Redeemer. He prevailed over the grave. God made him both Lord and Christ, and He gave him the authority over death. He is worthy to loose the seven seals of the book.

The seven seals outline the period that ends with Christ's coming to the earth as King of kings and Lord of lords.

Revelation 6:1 and 2 AV
And I saw when the Lamb opened one of the seals, and I heard, as it were the noise of thunder, one of the four beasts saying, "Come and see." And I saw, and behold, a white horse: and he that sat on him had a bow: and a crown was given unto him: and he went forth conquering, and to conquer.

This is the first of the seven seals that the Lamb opens. The rider on the white horse is not Christ.

Who is he?

- Isaiah
  14:4 "the king of Babylon"
  14:25 "the Assyrian"

- Daniel
  7:7 and 8 "little horn" (see also verse 8:9)
  8:23 "a king of fierce countenance"
  9:26 "the prince that shall come"
  11:21-30 "vile person"
  11:36 "the willful king"

- II Thessalonians
  2:3 "the man of sin" and "the son of perdition"
  2:8 "the wicked one"

- Revelation
  13:2-7 "the beast"
  13:1-18 "a beast...having seven heads and ten horns"

He rises to power in turbulent times as the arbiter of peace, safety, and prosperity. After three and a half years, he makes war against the saints. Revelation 13:7a says, **"And it was given unto him to make war with the saints and to overcome them."**

Revelation 6:3 and 4 AV

And when He had opened the second seal, I heard the second beast say, "Come and see."

And there went out another horse that was red: and power was given to him that sat thereon to take peace from the earth, and that they should kill one another; and there was given unto him a great sword.

Verses about the second seal pertain to wars and their casualties.

Revelation 6:5 and 6 AV

And when He had opened the third seal, I heard the third beast say, "Come and see." And I beheld, and lo, a black horse; and he that sat on him had a pair of balances in his hand.

And I heard a voice in the midst of the four beasts say, "A measure of wheat for a penny, and three measures of barley for a penny; and see thou hurt not the oil and the wine.

Verses about the third seal speak of famines; when bread is spoken of by weight, it denotes scarceness.

Revelation 6:7 and 8 AV

And when He had opened the fourth seal, I heard the voice of the fourth beast say, "Come and see."

And I looked, and behold, a pale horse: and his name that sat on him was Death, and Hell followed with him. And power was given unto them over the fourth part of the earth, to kill with sword, and with hunger, and with death, and with the beasts of the earth.

The fourth seal record describes the extent of the judgment during this time; a fourth part of the earth will die. Death is followed by the Grave. The two are personified here and said to have the power to kill a fourth part of the earth.

Revelation 6:9-11 AV

And when He had opened the fifth seal, I saw under the altar the souls of them that were slain for the word of God, and for the testimony which they held;

And they cried with a loud voice, saying, "How long, O Lord, holy and true, dost Thou not judge and avenge our blood on them that dwell on the earth:

And white robes were given unto every one of them; and it was said unto them, that they should rest yet for a little season, until their fellowservants also and their brethren, that should be killed as they were, should be fulfilled.

The record in verses 9 through 11 reveals what happens to martyred saints. They are dead, not living ones. In the revelation that John saw, they are personified and said to speak.

In verse 9, the word "souls" is put for "persons" by the figure of speech, *synecdoche*, which puts a part of man for the whole man. This usage of "soul" is quite frequent in the Word of God.

For example, Genesis 46:18 says ". . . **she bare unto Jacob, even sixteen souls.**" She had sixteen children. The record in Romans 13:1 says **"Let every soul be subject unto the higher powers."** Every believer in Christ is to be subject to the higher powers, those in the Church with gift ministries of apostles, prophets, evangelists, pastors, and teachers. Acts 7:14 says ". . . **and all his kindred, threescore and fifteen souls.**" His kindred were 75 people. "Soul" is put for "people" in these verses, the same as it is in Revelation 6:9.

In Genesis 4:10 we read, ". . . **the voice of thy brother's blood crieth unto Me from the ground.**" Abel's blood was said to cry from the ground. Abel was no more alive than the slain saints who were under the altar. In both instances, we have the use of the figure of speech, *prosopopceia* or personification, where the dead are spoken of as alive, and they speak. The revelation that John saw in this vision was for his instruction.

These saints will not live again until the first resurrection, which will not take place until the Lord raises them in Revelation 20:4. When they are resurrected, they will be clothed with white robes as foretold in Revelation 3:4 and 5.

Until that time, they must **"rest yet for a little season."** They will have to wait until the time of their resurrection from the dead.

These verses teach us that saints will be martyred during this time, the same as the ones speaking were martyred. Martyrdom marks this period.

Revelation 6:12-17 AV

And I beheld when He had opened the sixth seal, and, lo, there was a great earthquake; and the sun became black as sackcloth of hair, and the moon became as blood;

And the stars of heaven fell unto the earth, even as a fig tree casteth her untimely figs, when she is shaken of a mighty wind.

And the heaven departed as a scroll when it is rolled together; and every mountain and island were moved out of their places.

And the kings of the earth, and the great men, and the rich men, and the chief captains, and the mighty men, and every bondman, and every free man, hid themselves in the dens and in the rocks of the mountains;

And said to the mountains and rocks, "Fall on us, and hide us from the face of Him That sitteth on the throne, and from the wrath of the Lamb;

For the great day of His wrath is come; and who shall be able to stand?"

The signs in the sixth seal signal the coming of the wrath of the Lord. The events that occur in the sixth seal lead up to the Lord's coming in chapter 19.

Revelation 8:1 AV

And when He had opened the seventh seal there was silence in heaven about the space of half an hour.

This silence separates the first six seals from the seventh. The seventh seal contains a new series of judgments set forth by the seven trumpets (of which the last three are spoken of as "woe trumpets") and the seven vials.

The records in Revelation 8:7-11:14 describe the judgments pertaining to the seven trumpets.

The Seven Trumpets:

1. The earth: hail and fire mingled with blood cast upon the earth – a third of the trees and grass burnt up.

2. The sea: smitten as it were with a great burning mountain cast into it, and a third of the sea became blood – a third of the living creatures in the sea die, and a third of the ships in the sea are destroyed.

3. The waters: a great star (wormwood) fell upon the third part of the rivers and fountains of waters, and they become bitter – many men die of the waters.

4. The third part of the sun, of the moon, and of the stars darkened: third part of the day and night darkened.

5. (First woe) The pit is opened. Locusts. Men without the seal of God in their foreheads tormented for five months but cannot die.

6. (Second woe) Four angels in Euphrates loosed: Horsemen. Three plagues of fire, smoke, and brimstone kill the third part of men.

7. (Third woe) The seventh trumpet sounds – the seven vials.

Revelation 16:1 through 18:24 describes the judgments pertaining to the seven vials. The Lord's coming immediately follows these judgments.

The Seven Vials of the Wrath of God poured out upon the earth:

1. Noisome and grievous sores on those with the mark of the beast.

2. Sea becomes as the blood of a dead man: every living soul in the sea dies.

3. Rivers and fountains of waters become blood.

4. Vial is poured upon the sun: men scorched with fire, great heat.

5. Vial is poured on the seat of the beast: his kingdom is full of darkness; they gnaw their tongues out of pain.

6. The Euphrates River is dried up to prepare the way for the kings from the east. The beast and false prophet operate devil spirits that work miracles to bring the armies to the battle of Armageddon; that great day of God Almighty.

7. The vial is poured into the air: the great earthquake, greater than any since there were men on the earth (it divides the city of Babylon into three parts); the cities of the nations fall; every island flees away; the mountains were not found; a great plague of hail falls upon men, each stone about the weight of a talent (114 pounds troy weight).

These judgments are continuous once they begin. Once they are finished, the Lord comes from heaven with power and great glory to take possession of the earth.

Revelation 19:11-16 AV

And I saw heaven opened, and behold, a white horse; and He that sat upon him *was* called Faithful and True, and in righteousness He doth judge and make war. His eyes *were* as a flame of fire, and on His head *were* many crowns; and He had a name written, that no man knew, but He Himself. And He was clothed with a vesture dipped in blood; and His name is called the Word of God. And the armies *which were* in heaven followed Him upon white horses, clothed in fine linen, white and clean. And out of His mouth goeth a sharp sword, that with it He should smite the nations: and he shall rule them with a rod of iron; and he treadeth the winepress of the fierceness and wrath of Almighty God. And He hath on *His* vesture and on His thigh a name written, KING OF KINGS AND LORD OF LORDS.

Since the Lord's Day is a time of judgment, the Church, which is of the Administration of the Grace of God, cannot be present on the earth, because God tells us that it was judged "in Christ" as righteous and will never again come into condemnation. The Word of God says that there is no more condemnation coming to it, only glory and praise from God our Father. The only judgment left for the Church of the Grace of God is for rewards.

Comparing Christ's Two Comings

II Thessalonians 1:5-10 WT

It is evidence of the just judgment of God for you to be considered worthy of the kingdom of God, for which you also suffer,

since *it is* just with God to repay affliction to those who afflict you

and to you who are afflicted along with us *to repay* rest at the revelation of the Lord Jesus from heaven with his messengers of power.

With flaming fire, he will give vengeance against those who do not know God and who do not obey the gospel regarding our Lord Jesus {OR/Lord Jesus Christ}.

They will be sentenced to eternal destruction from the face of the lord and from the glory of his prevailing ability

after he comes to be glorified in his holy [*sanctified*] ***ones*** and to be admired in that day by all those who have believed (for our witness to you was believed).

The Epistles of I and II Thessalonians

Now we are going to the Church Epistles of I and II Thessalonians to read what they reveal to us about the two stages of Christ's second coming.

After the Church is gathered unto the Lord into the heavenlies, the events concerning the second part of his coming, the Lord's Day, begin to unfold on the earth. II Thessalonians distinguishes between Christ's coming for the Church and the Lord's Day that will occur on the earth.

II Thessalonians 2:1-3 AV
Now we beseech you, brethren, by the coming of our Lord Jesus Christ, and *by* our gathering together unto Him,

That ye be not soon shaken in mind or be troubled, neither by spirit, nor by word, nor by letter, as from us, as that the day of Christ is at hand.

Let no man deceive you by any means: for *that day shall not come*, except there come a falling away first, and that man of sin be revealed, the son of perdition,

There is nothing disturbing or troubling about the coming of our Lord Jesus Christ for the Church; it is our glorious hope. His coming is the joy and rejoicing of our hearts. The Lord gave us the revelation regarding it for our comfort, but this is not the case with the Day of the Lord.

The coming of our Lord Jesus Christ for the Church (in verse 1) is set in contrast to his coming in the Day of the Lord (in verse 3). The apostle Paul exhorted the saints not to be disturbed by those who said that they were then in the Day of the Lord; it didn't matter if they received the information from a spirit, by some teaching, or an alleged letter supposedly written by Paul.

The Greek textual critics, Griesbach, Lachmann, Tischendorf, Tregelles, Alford, Westcott, and Hort, as well as Nestle-Aland, and the translators of the Revised Version, all translate verse 2 as "the Day of the Lord," not "the day of Christ" as the King James or Authorized Version does.

Notice how the same record reads in the following translations:

II Thessalonians 2:1 and 2 NAGENT
Now concerning the coming of our Lord Jesus Christ and our assembling to meet him, we beg you, brethren, not to be quickly shaken in mind or excited, either by spirit, or by word, or by letter purporting to be from us, to the effect that the day of the Lord has come.

II Thessalonians 2:1 and 2 WT
[1] **Now with regard to the coming of our Lord Jesus Christ and our gathering together up to him, brothers, we ask you**

[2] **that you not be hastily shaken in mind or disturbed, neither by spirit, nor by word, nor by an epistle as if it were from us, as saying that the Day of the Lord is present.**

How does the Aramaic translate it?

II Thessalonians 2:1 and 2 Aramaic-English Interlinear New Testament, Volume II
But we entreat you, my brothers, concerning the coming of our lord Jesus the Messiah and concerning our gathering together to him,

that you neither quickly be shaken in your minds, nor be troubled, not by word, nor by spirit, nor by a letter, as though from us, [saying] **namely, Behold, the day of our lord has arrived.**

Both the Greek and Aramaic read "**the day of the Lord**," not "**the day of Christ**." After considering every use of "the day of the Lord" in the Word of God, the importance of this verse of scripture should become clear. In the Word of God, God says what He means and His words mean what He intends to say.

"**The Day of the Lord**" is an altogether different period than "**our gathering together unto him**" mentioned in verse one. From the revelation of the Word of God, we are told that the Church will not go through this period, so the believers were not be disturbed by those who were saying "**Behold, the day of our lord has arrived.**"

The Day of the Lord was foretold throughout the Old Testament. It will involve Israel and the Gentiles, not the Church (The Church is the body of Christ, and it belongs to the Administration of the Grace of God, the Mystery). The Day of the Lord will be a period of judgment.

II Thessalonians 2:3 AV

Let no man deceive you by any means: *for that day shall not come,* **except there come a falling away first, and that man of sin be revealed, the son of perdition;**

The Day of the Lord will not occur before ". . . **the falling away come first, and the man of sin be revealed . . .**" What is "the falling away"?

Apostasia

The words "**falling away**" are the Greek noun *apostasia*, from "*apo*", and "*stasia*." "*Apo*" means "away from", and "*stasia*" means "to stand." The word occurs in II Thessalonians 2:3 and Acts 21:21.

Apostasia is translated as "a falling away" here. To determine what this is, the Word of God will have to supply us with the answer. First, we will consider the verse where the words are used. Within the verse, we will study the biblical usage of the word *apostasia*. Next, we will consider the use of the Greek article, *he*, and its bearing on the subject.

After that, we will consider the verse in light of its context, both immediate and in a remote context. The verse has to agree with the context without any contradiction, if we are to rightly divide the Word of God.

Lastly, we will compare our findings in the verse and context with other scriptures that speak about the identical subject. Every scripture regarding the identical subject has to agree if we are to have the word of truth.

The biblical definition of a word is determined by how it is used in the Scriptures, not by its secular usage. The word *apostasia* only appears twice in the New Testament, in II Thessalonians 2:3, and here in Acts 21:21.

Acts 21:21 AV

And they are informed of thee, that thou teachest all the Jews[71] which are among the Gentiles to forsake Moses, saying that they ought not to circumcise *their* **children, neither to walk after the customs.**

Apostasia is translated "forsake" here in the Authorized Version. James, and the elders in Jerusalem accused the apostle Paul of teaching the Judeans

---

[71] *Ibid.*

to "forsake" Moses' teachings, such as circumcision and other customs that they held. This was a departure from their teachings.

So we see that in II Thessalonians 2:3, *apostasia* is translated "falling away," and in Acts 21:21, it is translated "forsake." If we consider the uses of the verb we will gain a better understanding of the meaning of *apostasia*, since the noun form is derived from the verb.

The noun, *apostasia*, comes from the verb, *aphisteemi*. *Aphisteemi* comes from *apo* "away from" and *histemi* "to stand." It appears 15 times in the New Testament. Although *apostasia* and *aphisteemi* do not look alike, they come from the same root. They are merely different forms of the same root.

Listed below are the fifteen times that *aphisteemi* appears in the New Testament. Again, I highlighted the English word translated from *aphisteemi*.

Luke 2:37 AV
And she was a widow of about fourscore and four years, which **departed** not from the temple, but served God with fastings and prayers night and day.

Luke 4:13 AV
And when the devil had ended all the temptation, he **departed** from him for a season.

Luke 8:13 AV
They on the rock are they, which, when they hear, receive the word with joy; and these have no root, which for a while believe, and in time of temptation **fall away**.

Luke 13:27 AV
But he shall say, I tell you, I know you not whence ye are; **depart** from me, all ye workers of iniquity.

Acts 5:37 AV
After this man rose up Judas of Galilee in the days of the taxing, and **drew away** much people after him: he also perished; and all, even as many as obeyed him, were dispersed.

Acts 5:38 AV
And now I say unto you, **Refrain** from these men, and let them alone: for if this counsel or this work be of men, it will come to nought:

Acts 12:10 AV

When they were past the first and the second ward, they came unto the iron gate that leadeth unto the city; which opened to them of his own accord: and they went out, and passed on through one street; and forthwith the angel **departed** from him.

Acts 15:38 AV

But Paul thought not good to take him with them, who **departed** from them from Pamphylia, and went not with them to the work.

Acts 19:9 AV

But when divers were hardened, and believed not, but spake evil of that way before the multitude, he **departed** from them, and separated the disciples, disputing daily in the school of one Tyrannus.

Acts 22:29 AV

Then straightway they **departed** from him which should have examined him: and the chief captain also was afraid, after he knew that he was a Roman, and because he had bound him.

II Corinthians 12:8 AV

For this thing I besought the Lord thrice, that it might **depart** from me.

I Timothy 4:1 AV

Now the Spirit speaketh expressly, that in the latter times some shall **depart** from the faith, giving heed to seducing spirits, and doctrines of devils;

I Timothy 6:5 AV

Perverse disputings of men of corrupt minds, and destitute of the truth, supposing that gain is godliness: from such **withdraw** thyself.

II Timothy 2:19 AV

Nevertheless the foundation of God standeth sure, having this seal, The Lord knoweth them that are his. And, Let every one that nameth the name of Christ **depart** from iniquity.

Hebrews 3:12 AV

Take heed, brethren, lest there be in any of you an evil heart of unbelief, in **departing** from the living God.

Aphisteemi is translated "depart," "departing" or "departed" eleven of the fifteen times it is used. Once it is translated "withdraw," once "refrain," once "fall away," and once "drew away."

In these verses, the clear sense of the word is that of "departing" whether it is physically departing or spiritually departing. The departing may be either positive or negative. We must determine the nature of the particular departure from the information given in the verse and its context.

Apostasia and *aphisteemi* both convey the sense of departing. It is a standing away from, a drawing out from among or a separation away from. It is a departure.

The English versions prior to the Authorized or King James Version translated *apostasia* in II Thessalonians 2:3 as "**a departing**."

The King James or Authorized Version was the first to translate *apostasia* as "falling away." Jerome's Latin translation of the Vulgate around 400 A.D, translated the Greek *apostasia* as the Latin *discessio* meaning "departure." The Tyndale Bible of 1534, the Geneva Bible, and the Cranmer Bible, first published in 1537, translated *apostasia* as "a departing." These versions precede the King James Bible printed in 1611.

Kenneth Wuest, author of *The New Testament: An Expanded Translation of the Greek New Testament*, comments in his preface to II Thessalonians:

> If *apostasia* and *aphisteemi* meant what our word 'apostasy' and 'apostatize' mean, why did Paul when using *aphisteemi* in I Timothy 4:1 feel the need of adding the qualifying phrase, 'from the faith' to complete the meaning of *aphisteemi* in that instance of its use? The word *apostasia*, therefore, in its original, and pure meaning, unadulterated by the addition of other ideas imposed upon it by the contexts in which it has been used, means a 'departure.'

Rev. Walter Cummins, in *A Journey Through Acts and Epistles* on page 487, makes the following comments:

> **2:3 falling away**: Greek: *apostasia* = departure. The cognate neuter noun *apostasion* occurs three times (Matthew 5:31; 19:7; Mark 10:4) of "divorce," the departure of a husband and wife from each other. The word used here is a feminine noun with only one other occurrence in the New Testament, namely, in Acts 21:21 regarding a "departure" from Moses, that is, a

departure from the Mosaic law. The departure referred to here is explained in verses 6-8 as the removal of a restraint. Verse 1 began this discussion with regard to the coming of the Lord Jesus Christ and our gathering up together to him. This passage in chapter 2 taken together with the previous verses in the first chapter suggests that the "departure" refers to the gathering together of the holy ones, which precedes both the appearance of the lawless one and the Day of the Lord.

Therefore, we can conclude that the biblical definition of the word, *apostasia*, is "departure."

The Usage of the Greek Article

II Thessalonians 2:3 AV
Let no man deceive you by any means: for *that day shall not come*, except there come a falling away first, and that man of sin be revealed, the son of perdition,

The King James or Authorized Version reads, "a falling away." The Greek texts read *he apostasia*. *He* is the article "the" so the expression should be translated as "the departure."

The Greek does not need the article to make the noun definite as we use it in English. In the Greek a substantive is definite without the article.

The article originally came from the demonstrative pronoun (such as "this" or "that"), which calls attention with special emphasis to a designated object. Its function is to point out an object or to draw attention to it. "Its use with a word makes the word stand out distinctly. Whenever the Greek uses the article, it points out individual identity . . . it marks a specific object of thought."[72]

The Greek uses the article with infinitives, adjectives, adverbs, prepositional phrases, and clauses or even with whole sentences. We do not have a corresponding English usage even remotely similar.

---

[72] Dana & Mantey. (1957). *A Manual Grammar of the Greek New Testament.* p.136: reference 146 (3).

When the article, *he*, appears in the Greek, it always signals some special significance.

We need to look at the matter from the Greek point of view, not the English, if we are to discover the reason that the article is used.

The usage of the article draws our attention to the identity and special significance of this particular departure.

According to Dana and Mantey in, *A Manual Grammar of the Greek New Testament*, page 141, reference 147 (2), "The article may be used to point out an object, the identity of which is defined by some previous reference made to it in the context."

Wuest acknowledges this particular usage in his expanded translation. In his preface to II Thessalonians, he says,

> The word 'previous' is all-important here. The translators of the A. V. looked for the definition of the word in the *subsequent* context, whereas the Greek article points here to a *previous* context, namely, to the coming of the Lord Jesus into the air and the gathering together of the saints to Him and their consequent ascent to heaven.

> Thus, instead of speaking of a departure of men from the true Faith, Paul is referring to the departure of the saints to heaven. The departure of the Church must occur before the day of the Lord sets in and the identity of the man of lawlessness is revealed.

His translation of the Greek reads:

II Thessalonians 2:3 Wuest's Expanded Translation of the Greek New Testament
Do not begin to allow anyone to lead you astray in any way, because that day shall not come except the aforementioned departure [of the Church to heaven] **comes first and the man of lawlessness is disclosed** [in his true identity], **the son of perdition.**

Wuest comments:

> The fatal mistake the translators made was in failing to take into consideration the definite article before the word *apostasia* which appears in the Greek text of Eberhard Nestle, in that of his son, Erwin Nestle, and in that of Westcott and Hort.

A. T. Robertson in his monumental work, *A Grammar of the Greek New Testament in the Light of Historical Research*, asserts that the translators of the A. V., under the influence of the Vulgate, dealt with the Greek article in a loose and inaccurate way (p. 756). It is vital to look at the matter in hand from the Greek angle and find a reason for the use of the article in any given instance.
(Kenneth S. Wuest, The New Testament: An Expanded Translation.)

Let's read the previous context.

II Thessalonians 2:1-4 Wuest
Now, I am requesting you, brethren, with regard to the coming and personal presence of our Lord Jesus Christ, even our being assembled together to Him,

not soon to become unsettled, the source of this unsettled state being your minds, neither be thrown into confusion, either by a spirit, or through a word as from us or through a letter falsely alleged to be written by us, to the effect that the day of the Lord has come and is now present.

Do not begin to allow anyone to lead you astray in any way, because that day shall not come except the aforementioned departure comes first and the man of the lawlessness is disclosed, the son of perdition,

he who sets himself in opposition to and exalts himself above everyone and everything that is called a god or that is an object of worship, so that he seats himself in the inner sanctuary of God, proclaiming himself to be deity.

"**The departure**" previously mentioned in the context is "**the coming and personal presence of our Lord Jesus Christ, even our being assembled together to Him**." In light of this, Paul instructed the saints not to be disturbed by those who were saying that the Day of the Lord had set in, because it cannot occur until after the Church departs with their Lord into the heavenlies.

The Aramaic translation agrees with the Greek.

Do not let anyone deceive you in any way, because [it will not come] **except an escape should come first and the man of sin be revealed, the son of destruction,**

The context of II Thessalonians 2:1-3 assures the saints that they will not go through the judgment of the ungodly when it occurs in the Day of the Lord. The apostle Paul instructed the saints not to be disturbed, nor deceived by anyone who said that the Day of the Lord was then present. The saints of the Church, which is the body of Christ, will escape the coming judgment in the Day of the Lord. Their escape or departure will be the closing event to the Administration of the Grace of God.

It is comforting to know that the Lord will return for the Church of the Grace of God, and remove it from the earth before the events concerning the Day of the Lord unfold.

The revelation of the Lord's coming for his Church is revealed in I Thessalonians 4.

I Thessalonians 4:15-17 AV
For this we say unto you by the word of the Lord, that we which are alive and remain unto the coming of the Lord shall not prevent[73] **[precede] them which are asleep.**

For the Lord himself shall descend from heaven with a shout, with the voice of the archangel, and with the trump of God: and the dead in Christ shall rise first:

Then we which are alive and remain shall be caught up together with them in the clouds, to meet the Lord in the air: and so shall we ever be with the Lord.

The Lord will descend from the heavenlies, and gather the members of his body together (both the living and those who have died) to meet him in the air, and then depart with him into the heavenlies. That is, both the dead in Christ, and the living of the Church will be caught up in the clouds to meet the Lord in the air, and they will depart with him into the heavenlies.

This is the **"word of the Lord,"** and he gave this revelation for our comfort.

---

[73] An archaic English word: "prevent" means precede.

The Church will escape the judgment of the Lord's Day, which will begin to unfold on the earth after their departure.

I Thessalonians 5:1 and following describes the Day of the Lord. It distinguishes between the ungodly and the saints.

I Thessalonians 5:1-11 AV

But of the times and the seasons, brethren, ye have no need that I write unto you.

For yourselves know perfectly that the day of the Lord so cometh as a thief in the night.

For when they shall say, Peace and safety; then sudden destruction cometh upon them, as travail upon a woman with child; and they shall not escape.

But ye, brethren, are not in darkness, that that day should overtake you as a thief.

Ye are all the children of light, and the children of the day: we are not of the night, nor of darkness.

Therefore let us not sleep, as *do* others; but let us watch and be sober.

For they that sleep sleep in the night; and they that be drunken are drunken in the night.

But let us, who are of the day, be sober, putting on the breastplate of faith and love; and for an helmet, the hope of salvation.

For God hath not appointed us to wrath, but to obtain salvation by our Lord Jesus Christ,

Who died for us, that, whether we wake or sleep, we should live together with him. Wherefore comfort yourselves together, and edify one another, even as also ye do.

The revelation begins with the contrasting conjunction **"but"** which distinguishes the previous event when the Church is caught up to meet the Lord in the air with the events that pertain to the Day of the Lord, which will follow on the earth.

The **"brethren"** that the apostle Paul is addressing are the members of the Church, which is the body of Christ. They have no need to know of signs and seasons because they do not involve the Church. The Church will not be on earth when the signs and seasons concerning the Day of the Lord begin to unfold.

Notice the pronouns used in this section of scripture: "**they**" and "**them**," "**we**," and "**ye**." "**We**" are "**the brethren**," God's children, "**the children of light and the children of the day**," spoken of in the previous chapter and here in the context, which will meet the Lord in the air and be snatched out of harm's way before the terrible Day of the Lord breaks forth on the earth.

"**They**" and "**them**" refer to the ungodly, "**those of the night**," who have rejected Christ and the salvation that only he can bring from this day of God's judgment and wrath.

The verses in I Thessalonians 5: 1-11 contrast two groups of people: "**the children of light and the children of the day**" with "**those who are of the night . . . of darkness**." This distinguishes between two different categories of people.

"**The children of light**" are those of the Church, which is the body of Christ and which belongs to the Administration of the Grace of God. They are "in Christ." Their end was spoken of in the previous chapter, an end of deliverance and comfort at Christ's coming for them in the air.

The latter group, those "**of the night . . . and of darkness**," is headed into the Day of the Lord, which includes the wrath of God.

The contrast in these verses is between light and darkness, between wrath and salvation from that wrath. The "**children of light and the children of the day**" are not in darkness, nor are they appointed to "**the wrath of God**."

They have already been judged as the righteousness of God in Christ [See II Corinthians 5:21], and they have been legally justified from sin by the work of Christ [Romans 5:2, 9 and 6:7]. There is no more condemnation and no more judicial judgment concerning those in Christ Jesus [Romans 8:1, 30-39]. They will never again come into condemnation.

The entire period of the Administration of the Grace of God was a mystery hid in God from its beginning on the Feast of Pentecost, following Jesus Christ's resurrection and ascension into the heavenlies, to its end at the gathering together of the saints to meet the Lord in the air. Therefore, we cannot learn about it in the four gospel records, nor in the Old Testament. The records in the Old Testament and Gospels concern Christ's coming to the earth.

The Church Epistles – the books of Romans to II Thessalonians – reveal the doctrine for the Administration of the Grace of God. It begins with grace, and ends when the Church is received up in glory.

"**The coming of our Lord Jesus Christ and our gathering together unto Him**," in II Thessalonians 2:1 is "**the departure**" spoken of in verse 2:3. This gathering is to be, "**caught up together** [the living and the dead of the Church] **in the clouds to meet the Lord in the air**," as in I Thessalonians 4:17. The record in I Timothy 3:16 says that we will be "**received up into glory**."

After the Church is removed from the earth, an administration of judgment will begin to unfold.

The records of both I and II Thessalonians distinguish between Christ's coming for the Church, which occurs in the air when the Lord gathers them together, and they depart with him into the heavenlies, with the Day of the Lord which will afterwards unfold on the earth.

The ungodly shall not escape the Day of the Lord, but it will not overtake the saints of the Church. The saints are not appointed to wrath, but are to obtain salvation by our Lord Jesus Christ.

Returning to II Thessalonians 1:6-10, this record contrasts the Lord's coming for the Church with his coming to the earth in judgment of the ungodly. This remoter context helps clarify the subject even further.

II Thessalonians 1:4-10 ASV
So that we ourselves glory in you in the churches of God for your patience and faith in all your persecutions and in the afflictions which ye endure;

Which is a manifest token of the righteous judgment of God; to the end that ye may be counted worthy of the kingdom of God, for which ye also suffer;

If so be that it is a righteous thing with God to recompense affliction to them that afflict you,

And to you that are afflicted rest with us, [when?] **at the revelation of the Lord Jesus from heaven with the angels** [messengers] **of his power**

In flaming fire, rendering vengeance to them that know not God, and to them that obey not the gospel of our Lord Jesus:

Who shall suffer punishment, even eternal destruction from the face of the Lord and from the glory of his might,

When [after] he shall [have] come to be glorified in his saints, and to be marveled at in all them that believed (because our testimony unto you was believed) in that day.

These verses refer to both parts of the Lord's *Parousia*. The Lord Jesus will have already gathered his Church into the heavenlies and brought them rest before his revelation to the world when he appears with his mighty angels to execute judgment against the ungodly.

The word **"vengeance"** in verse eight means "execution of justice." The Lord Jesus' execution of justice will be rendered to the Gentiles who do not know God and to the Judeans who do not obey the gospel . . . *after* the Lord shall have come to be glorified in his saints and admired in all who believe regarding him.

The words, **"when he shall come,"** in verse 10, are *hotan elthe* from the adverb *hotan* and the second aorist subjunctive of the verb, "to come."

Rev. Walter Cummins remarks in *A Journey Through the Acts and Epistles*, on page 486[74]:

> **1:10: When:** Greek: *hotan* = when, whenever. The verb in this temporal clause is aorist subjunctive, indicating that the action of the temporal clause precedes the action of the main clause in verse 9. Hence, *hotan* may be translated "after" in this construction. Thus verse ten indicates that the return of the Lord Jesus Christ for the holy ones, the gathering together of the Church as described in I Thessalonians 4:13-18, will precede his return with his messengers of power and destruction of the ungodly as described here in verses 5-9. That period of vengeance or wrath following the gathering together of the Church is called the Day of the Lord.

The Interlinear Greek-English New Testament translates it, **"when he shall have come."** The Aramaic-English Interlinear New Testament translates it, **"after he comes."** The period of the Lord's execution of justice on earth will not begin until after he has come to be glorified in his saints.

When the Lord comes to the earth in judgment, he shall already have come forth in the air to take the members of his body to their rest in the

---

[74] Cummins, Walter J. (2006). *Volume 2: A Journey through the Acts and Epistles.*

heavenlies. When he comes to judge the ungodly of the earth with everlasting destruction from his presence and glory, he shall already have come to be glorified in his saints.

The Day of the Lord cannot take place before the departure of the Church from the earth. The departure is the final, concluding event in the present Administration of the Grace of God.

Sometime after the coming of our Lord Jesus Christ and our gathering together unto him in the air, the man of sin will be revealed on earth. He will exalt himself above God and take his seat in the Temple setting himself forth as the mighty one.

After the Church departs from the earth, his time will have come – though short-lived it will be.

II Thessalonians was written to reassure the saints of the Lord's coming and their gathering together unto him. The purpose of his coming for the Church is to save it, to redeem his purchased possession and to deliver it from the coming judgment of the ungodly.

The saints of the Church of the Grace of God will not go through the day of the Lord's judgment with the ungodly of the earth. The saints have already been judged in Christ as righteous, and we will never again come into condemnation.

Romans 5:2 AV
By Whom [the Lord Jesus Christ] **also we have access by faith into this grace wherein we stand, and rejoice in hope of the glory of God.**

How is the Church to view the coming of Christ for it? We are to **"rejoice in hope of the glory of God."** What began in grace will end in glory for the saints of the Church.

Colossians 1:27 AV
To whom God would make known what is the riches of the glory of this mystery among the Gentiles; which is Christ in you, the hope of glory:

What are the glorious riches of the Mystery pertaining to the Gentiles? It is **"Christ in you, the hope of glory!"** When our Lord returns for us, we will be glorified together with him. We will obtain the glory of our Lord Jesus Christ.

"I told you these things"

II Thessalonians 2:1-4 ERV
Now we beseech you, brethren, touching the coming of our Lord Jesus Christ, and our gathering together unto him; to the end that ye be not quickly shaken from your mind, nor yet be troubled, either by spirit, or by word, or by epistle as from us, as that the day of the Lord is now present; let no man beguile you in any wise: for it will not be, except the falling away come first, and that man of sin be revealed, the son of perdition, He that opposeth and exalteth himself against all that is called God or that is worshipped; so that he sitteth in the temple of God, setting himself forth as God.

Immediately following these verses, the apostle Paul asked the saints a question that has an important bearing on our understanding of the subject.

II Thessalonians 2: 5 AV
Remember ye not, that, when I was yet with you, I told you these things?

The saints in Thessalonica were well aware of the coming of the Lord Jesus Christ and our gathering together unto him - the departure, when we are caught up in the clouds to meet the Lord in the air and return with him into the heavenlies.

What do we know that the apostle Paul previously told them? What he said is recorded in I Thessalonians 1:9-10; 2:19; 3:13; 4:13-18 and 5:1-11. The scriptures in II Thessalonians 1:7-10, 12; 2:1ff; 2:13-17 and 3:5 cannot contradict those of I Thessalonians. Please take the time to look them up. Both books refer to the Lord's coming for the Church to gather them together to meet him in the air and his coming to the earth in the Day of the Lord.

It is inconceivable to think that when the apostle was with them, he said something different from the Word of the Lord in his letters to them. The very reason he wrote to them in II Thessalonians was to remind them of what he said. The one letter cannot contradict the other. Immediately after he gives them the revelation, the apostle reminds them that he previously told them these things when he was with them. His letter confirmed what he previously said in person.

The revelation of the Lord's coming for the Church is one of great comfort. I Thessalonians 4:18 says, "**Wherefore comfort one another with these words**." "**Wherefore comfort yourselves together . . .**" is God's instruction to the Church in I Thessalonians 5:11.

"Salvation," "redemption," "glory," "rest," "joy" and "comfort" are the words used in the New Testament to describe Christ Jesus' coming for the Church.

II Thessalonians 2:14 reveals that the Church was called "**to the obtaining of the glory of the Lord Jesus Christ**," not to undergo judgment with the ungodly of the world.

I Thessalonians 5:9 and 10 reveals to us that "**God hath not appointed us to wrath, but to obtain salvation by our Lord Jesus Christ, who died for us, that, whether we wake or sleep, we should live together with Him**." Today, we have God's promise of salvation; when he comes for his body, the Church, we will obtain the reality itself.

In I Thessalonians 4:15, Christ's coming for the Church of the Grace of God is called "**the coming of the Lord**," and in 4:17, it refers to it as "**caught up together with them in the clouds to meet the Lord in the air**."

II Thessalonians 2:1 refers to it as "**. . . the coming of our Lord Jesus Christ, and by our gathering together unto Him**." This is "**the departure**" mentioned in 2:3.

The revelation of the coming of the Lord Jesus Christ for the Church is given as expressively as possible with words that make it unmistakably clear. God does not want us ignorant of our hope.

The Day of the Lord is not his coming for the members of his body, the Church. The Day of the Lord is a time of judgment on the earth. It will begin to unfold after God sends His Son on the Day of Redemption to redeem the members of the Church from the grave and from this evil world.

The Word of God instructs us that the Church has been delivered from the wrath to come. It will not undergo the judgment of the ungodly, which takes place during the Lord's Day.

- **God hath not appointed us to wrath but to obtain salvation by our Lord Jesus Christ, who died for us, that, whether we wake or sleep, we should live together with Him** (I Thessalonians 5:1-11);

- **Much more then, being now justified by his blood, we shall be saved from wrath through him.** (Romans 5:9 AV);

- **And to wait for his Son from heaven, whom he raised from the dead, even Jesus, which delivered us from the wrath to come.** (I Thessalonians 1:10 AV).

The record in II Thessalonians 1:10 assures the saints that the judgment of the world spoken of in verses seven and eight, previously, will not come until **"after he shall have come to be glorified in His saints."**

The very purpose of the Lord Jesus Christ's coming to gather the Church of the Grace of God together (both the living and the dead) into the heavenlies is to save it, to redeem it, to remove it from the earth before the coming period of judgment breaks forth on the earth in the Day of the Lord. He comes to be glorified in the Church, and to glorify it with him in the heavenlies.

What comfort is there for the Church if it were to go through the Day of the Lord, which includes the time of Jacob's trouble, the wrath of God, and the judgment of the ungodly? How can the Church be saved from these events and still go through them, as some say? That makes no sense whatsoever.

There is nothing mentioned about looking for a "falling away," which was more recently termed "an apostasy" in some versions or as some contemporary versions say, "a rebellion" of the Church. This is not the biblical definition of the word. Nothing in the Church Epistles suggests an apostasy or rebellion of the saints as a sign of the coming of the Lord for his Church.

There has always been apostasy or unbelief. Where do you want to begin, with Adam in the garden, in the times of Noah, Nimrod, and the Babylonians, Moses' day in the wilderness of Sin, during the times of Israel's judges, or later, with their kings, during Jesus Christ's earthly ministry (they killed him)? In the first century, we read that all Asia turned away from the apostle Paul and the Word of God that he taught them.

If there was such a great apostasy in the Church, who would be left to recognize it as a sign?

This verse is also not speaking of apostasy caused by the man of sin. It says ". . . **except there come a falling away first, and that man of sin be revealed, the son of perdition.**" The falling away – the departure – comes first, and then the man of sin will be revealed. It does not say he is the source of this falling away or departure.

What does God's Word instruct the Church to look for in the Administration of the Grace of God, which was a mystery until God revealed it to the Apostle Paul?

Philippians 3:20 AV
For our conversation [citizenship] **is in heaven; from whence also we look for the Saviour, the Lord Jesus Christ:**

The Word of God instructs the saints to look for the Lord Jesus Christ – not for apostasy. We are to look for the object of our hope – the coming of the Lord Jesus from heaven. God's Word does not instruct us to look for signs or seasons that will announce Christ's coming for the Church of the Grace of God – there are none given in the Church Epistles, the books of Romans through the books of II Thessalonians.

We are to live in anticipation of the coming of our Lord Jesus Christ and our gathering together unto him. When he returns for us, we will receive the glorious fulfillment of our salvation. He could come for us at any time; it could even be today.

The Church in the Administration of the Grace of God is not associated with the Day of the Lord.

The Day of the Lord is the object of Old Testament prophecy, and it concerns Judeans and Gentiles, not the Church of the Grace of God. The Old Testament, including the four Gospels, declares the Day of the Lord and the signs and seasons that will precede it. "The Lord's Day" is the subject of the book of Revelation.

The Church Epistles mention the "Day of the Lord" twice, once in I Thessalonians 2:2 and once in II Thessalonians 5:2. The context in both instances assures us that the Church will not be a part of it. God appointed the Church to obtain salvation, and we are not to be deceived by anyone who tells us that we will go through the Day of the Lord.

"And now ye know. . ."

II Thessalonians 2:3-8 AV
Let no man deceive you by any means: for that day shall not come, except there come a falling away [*he apostasia*: the departure] **first, and that man of sin be revealed, the son of perdition; Who opposeth and exalteth himself above all that is called God, or that is**

worshipped; so that he as God sitteth in the temple of God, shewing himself that he is God.

Remember ye not, that, when I was yet with you, I told you these things?

And now ye know what withholdeth that he might be revealed in his time.

For the mystery of iniquity doth already work: only he who now letteth *will let*, until he be taken out of the way.

And then shall that Wicked be revealed, whom the Lord shall consume with the spirit of his mouth, and shall destroy with the brightness of his coming:

Verse 6 says "**And now ye know what withholdeth that he might be revealed in his time.**" What did Paul tell them in verse 3, that was withholding the man of sin? He said ". . . **except there come** *he apostasia* **first . . .**" (v.3). The man of sin cannot be revealed until the departure first occurs. After the departure of the Church occurs, "**his time**" (v.6) will have come.

We cannot mix events in the Administration of the Grace of God with the events that will occur in the Administration of the Lord's Day if we are to understand the *sunteleia* – the times of the end. The Lord's Day cannot begin until the Administration of the Grace of God concludes with our gathering together unto the Lord in the air.

In verse 6, what is "**what withholdeth**" and in verse 7, who is "**he who now letteth**"? "**What withholdeth**" and "**he who now letteth**" are translations of the same Greek word, *katecho*. The word means "to hold fast or restrain." They are both present participles, the first is neuter and the second is masculine.

Verses 6 and 7 read, "**And now ye know what withholdeth** [that which restrains; the departure] **that he might be revealed in his time. For the mystery of iniquity doth already work: only he who now letteth** [restrains], **until he be taken out of the way.**"

"**Until he be taken out of the way**" in verse 7 corresponds with "**a falling away**" in verse 3 and "**the coming of our Lord Jesus Christ, and by our gathering together unto Him**" in verse one.

Once the saints, who have the spirit of sonship, the seed of holy spirit, are "**taken out of the way**" by their Lord, nothing will be left to restrain the revealing of the man of sin and the working of the mystery of iniquity. God will have removed His restraining power.

"**And then shall that Wicked be revealed . . .**" His time will have come, but it will not last; ". . . **whom the Lord shall consume with the spirit of his mouth, and shall destroy with the brightness of his coming.**"

II Thessalonians 2:8-12 AV

And then shall that Wicked be revealed, whom the Lord shall consume with the spirit of his mouth, and shall destroy with the brightness of his coming:

***Even him,* whose coming is after the working of Satan with all power and signs and lying wonders,**

And with all deceivableness of unrighteousness in them that perish; because they received not the love of the truth, that they might be saved.

And for this cause God shall send them strong delusion, that they should believe a lie:

That they all might be damned who believed not the truth, but had pleasure in unrighteousness.

The Lord's coming spoken of here is the one in which he consumes the wicked one. This coming is in the Lord's Day spoken of in the book of Revelation 19:11-21. The Lord will come in that day in righteousness to judge and make war with him and his followers. He will come as King of kings and Lord of lords! He will fulfill the words in his prayer; ". . . **Thy kingdom come, Thy will be done on earth as it is in heaven.**"

The entire period of the Administration of the Grace of God was a mystery hid in God from its beginning on the Feast of Pentecost following Jesus Christ's resurrection and ascension into the heavenlies, to its end at the gathering together of the saints to meet the Lord in the air. Therefore, we cannot learn about it in the four Gospel records, nor in the Old Testament. Those records concern the Day of the Lord and his coming to the earth.

"**The coming of our Lord Jesus Christ and our gathering together unto Him**" is "**the departure,**" "**caught up together** [both the living and the dead of the Church] **in the clouds to meet the Lord in the air.**" I Timothy 3:16 says that we will be "**received up into glory.**"

The Church Epistles – the books of Romans to II Thessalonians – reveal the doctrine for the Administration of the Grace of God. It begins in grace and ends when the Church is received up in glory.

After the Church is removed from the earth, an administration of judgment will begin to unfold. Both records in I and II Thessalonians distinguish between Christ's coming for the Church (which occurs in the air, and we depart with him into the heavenlies) from the Day of the Lord.

The purpose of the revelation in II Thessalonians 2:1-3 is to reassure the saints that they were not in the Lord's Day as certain ones were teaching.

The Word of God assures the saints that the Day of the Lord could not take place until *after* "the departure" – the gathering together of the saints unto their Lord in the air. The man of lawlessness cannot be revealed on earth before then.

Confusion occurs concerning these events when we do not determine *to whom* the Scripture is addressed and *of whom* it is speaking.

The Scripture concerns three distinct groups of people: The Judeans, the Gentiles, and the Church of God. We need to determine the people involved, the different administrations of time about which the scripture is speaking and the subject under consideration if we are to have a correct understanding of what God is revealing to us.

We must not categorize the different times and events concerning Christ's *Parousia* as all being identical. We must allow the Scripture to reveal its interpretation to us in the verse and the context where it is given, as well as how the event is spoken of elsewhere in the scriptures.

When we read the Old Testament, the four Gospels, or the General Epistles, such as I and II Peter or the book of Revelation, as though they are addressed to the Church of the Grace of God, which was before a mystery hid in God, we may walk away with confusion and think that there are apparent contradictions. These records are not addressed to the Church. We must distinguish to whom these records are addressed and who is involved in each record.

Instead of the comfort that God intended us to have with the knowledge of Christ's coming for his Church, we may be distressed or even terrified if we think that we are going to go through the Lord's Day. The events spoken of in the records outside the Church Epistles are as much the Word of God as that which we read in the Church Epistles, but they do not concern the Church during the Administration of the Grace of God.

All is true of whom it speaks, and to whom it is addressed, in the administration that it concerns.

Chart Comparing the Two Stages of Christ's *Parousia*

The comparison chart below contrasts some of the differences between the two stages of Christ's *Parousia*: his coming for the Church in the air and his coming to the earth. This is not a complete listing of differences, but enough to demonstrate that they are not the same event.

Christ's Coming for the Church	*Christ's Coming in the Lord's Day*
The Great Tribulation occurs on earth **after** the Church is gathered in the air. **I Thessalonians 4:16-5:11** **II Thessalonians 1:7-10; 2:1 & 2;** **2:6 & 7**	The Great Tribulation occurs **before** Christ comes to earth in the Lord's Day. **Matthew 24:29- 31;** **Isaiah 26:19-21**
The gathering together and departure of the Church in the air comes **before** the wrath of God is poured out on earth. **I Thessalonians 4 and 5;** **II Thessalonians 1 and 2**	The resurrection of the just comes **after** the wrath of God is poured out. **Job 14:13;** **Isaiah 26;** **Revelation 19 and 20**
There is no more condemnation to those in Christ Jesus. The Church is judged in Christ, and it stands before God clothed in his righteousness, spared from the wrath to come. **Romans 8; I John 1:10**	The Lord's Day is a period of judgment and wrath on the unrighteous and ungodly. **Romans 1:18-32; 2:1-29;** **Isaiah 2:11-22**
When Christ comes for the Church it is to remove it from the earth. The dead in Christ will be raised to life, and the living will be changed to be like him. **I Thessalonians 4:13-18**	When Christ comes to the earth it is to judge and make war, to establish an earthly kingdom, and reign as King of kings and Lord of lords. He will gather living Israel to Jerusalem and raise the dead saints in the Resurrection of the Just **Revelation 19:10-20:6**
After Christ comes for the Church, evil increases. **II Thessalonians 2:3-4; 8-12**	When Christ comes to the earth in the Lord's Day, all that is evil will be judged: Israel, the nations, Satan, devil spirits, the dead. **Revelation 20**

Christ's Coming for the Church	Christ's Coming in the Lord's Day
Before Christ comes for the Church, there is a restrainer holding back the mystery of iniquity. **II Thessalonians 2:6-7**	After Christ gathers the Church into the heavenlies, nothing restrains the man of sin. **II Thessalonians 2:8-9**
When Christ comes for his Church, they will see him face to face. **I Corinthians 13:12; I John 3:3**	Every eye on the earth will behold Christ's coming to the earth in the Lord's Day; there will be weeping and gnashing of teeth. **Revelation 1:7**
When Christ comes for the Church, those who pierced him are still dead.	When Christ comes to the earth, those who pierced him shall see him in the resurrection of the unjust. **Revelation 1:7**
The hope of Christ's coming for the Church is a message of comfort. **I Thessalonians 4:18**	The coming of Christ to the earth on the Lord's Day is a message of judgment. **Revelation 1:10; Isaiah 21:10-23**
Christ will give the Church rest when he comes **II Thessalonians 1:7-10**	When Christ comes to the earth, he will come to make war and to judge. **Revelation 19:11ff**
Satan is not bound when Christ comes for his Church.	Satan is bound for 1000 years when Christ comes to the earth in the Lord's Day. **Revelation 20:1-3**
Death is not destroyed but the Church is delivered from it. **I Corinthians 15:22-23; 15:51-55**	Death is destroyed at the end of Christ's 1000-year rule on earth. **I Corinthians 15:26; Revelation 20:14**
The creation will get worse after Christ comes for the Church. See the events that occur during the opening of the seven seals in the book of Revelation. **Revelation 6 ff**	When Christ comes to the earth creation will undergo wonderful changes **Isaiah 29:17; 35:1-7 and v. 15; 51:3; 55:13; 62:8-9; Jeremiah 31:27-28, Ezekiel 34:27; 36:29-35; Romans 8**

Christ's Coming for the Church	*Christ's Coming in the Lord's Day*
When Christ comes for the Church, Gentile dominion is not yet fulfilled.	The times of the Gentiles will end when Christ comes to the earth in the Lord's Day as King of kings and Lord of lords
The Church has its seat of government in the heavenlies. **Philippians 1:20; Romans 5:2**	During the times of the Lord's Day, Israel will have their government in Jerusalem.
Today is "man's day"; man does the judging. **I Corinthians 4:13**	In the Lord's Day, the Lord will do the judging. All judgment is committed unto him. **Isaiah 2:11 and v17; John 5:22**
The Church will be gathered into the heavenlies with Christ. **I Thessalonians 4:16-17; II Thessalonians 2:1**	Israel is finally gathered to their promised land on earth. **Isaiah 11:11,12; Hosea 1:10-2:1; Micah 2:12; Ezekiel 39:27-29; Matthew 24:31; Mark 13:27**
The Church will be judged at the Bema in the heavenlies, receiving praise and rewards from God for deeds done. **I Corinthians 4:5**	Judeans and Gentiles are judged on earth for works done, receiving condemnation, sentences, and rewards. **Revelation 20**
After the Church is gathered together, the mystery of iniquity breaks forth in full. **II Thessalonians 2:7-8**	When Christ comes to the earth, the mystery of iniquity ends. **Revelation 19**
After Christ gathers his Church, the man of sin will be revealed and rises to power. **II Thessalonians 2:3-4**	When Christ comes to the earth, the man of sin is judged and destroyed. **Revelation 19**
Christ comes in the air for the Church to glorify it. **II Thessalonians 2:14**	When Christ comes to the earth it will be to judge and rule with a rod of iron. **Psalm 2:8-9**

Christ's Coming for the Church	Christ's Coming in the Lord's Day
When Christ gathers the Church into the heavenlies it will be like him and it will obtain his glory. **Philippians 3:21;** **II Thessalonians 2:14**	When Christ gathers Israel to Jerusalem, they will rule with him for 1000 years on earth. **Revelation 20:4**
The Church's expectation is to be received up into the heavenlies. **I Timothy 3:16;** **I Thessalonians 4:16-17**	Israel's expectation is: *Thy Kingdom come, Thy will be done on earth.* **Matthew 6**

Come Quickly Lord Jesus!

Conclusion

Ephesians 2:7AV
That in the ages to come he might shew the exceeding riches of his grace in his kindness toward us through Christ Jesus.

Our Hope in Christ

We were called to obtain the glory of our Lord Jesus Christ. It is a hope of comfort, joy, and glory. It is the day of our salvation and redemption. It is joy unspeakable!

The new birth is indeed glorious, but compared to our hope of obtaining the glory of our Lord Jesus Christ it pales by comparison. The birth is only the beginning.

The gathering together of the saints in the air by our Lord is the first event, the beginning of an eternity of our Father's tender mercies and loving kindnesses for us in Christ. We will participate in the exceeding riches of our Father's great grace to us in Christ and behold glory that surpasses our every expectation.

The records in I Corinthians 15 give us a brief outline of the events concerning Christ's coming.

I Corinthians 15:19 AV
If in this life only we have hope in Christ, we are of all men most miserable.

Today, the spirit that is born within us as children of God seals us for eternal life. The down payment we have is not the reality that we hope for in Christ.

Our hope is of eternal life, to receive the full reality of the promise of life in Christ Jesus, to have glorious new bodies fashioned to be like Christ's glorious body, and to be joint-heirs with him, to be glorified together with him.

If what we have today in Christ, as wonderful as it is, is all there is we should be pitied more than all men for wasting our lives hoping in Christ for something that does not exist, but this is not the case.

I Corinthians 15:20-23 AV

But now is Christ risen from the dead, and become the firstfruits of them that slept.

For since by man came death, by man came also the resurrection of the dead.

For as in Adam all die, even so in Christ shall all be made alive.

But every man in his own order: Christ the firstfruits; afterward they that are Christ's at his coming.

Christ was the first to rise from the dead, ascend into the heavenlies, and actually experience eternal life. He is called the author and finisher of our faith because he is the only man that began the course of believing God and has actually received the promise of eternal life. God raised him from the dead, he ascended into heaven, and he lives forevermore, seated at the right hand of God in the heavenly realm.

After God raised him from the dead, Christ presented himself to the Father in the Temple as the first fruit offering of the harvest. Leviticus 23:9-14 describes this offering.

When will the rest of the crop be harvested? I Corinthians 15:23 indicates there is an order involved in this process. Christ was the first fruit offering. The next time the dead will be raised is "**at his coming.**"

God gave Christ the authority to exercise this power, and he will exercise it at his coming and not before.

The Church of the Grace of God will be raised if dead, or changed if living when Christ gathers us together and we are caught up into the clouds to meet him in the air.

There are two other times that Christ will raise the dead, and they occur during the Lord's Day. They are the resurrection of the just and the resurrection of the unjust.

The resurrection of the just is also called the first resurrection, the better resurrection, and the resurrection unto life. Those who participate in it are called, "Children of God, being children of the resurrection."

The resurrection of the unjust is also called the resurrection of damnation, the one to shame, and everlasting contempt.

It is the resurrection of dead people, when the rest who have no hope in Christ are raised. If their name is not written in the book of life they will die the second death when they are cast in the lake of fire, the *gehenna*, and they will be destroyed.

The teaching that when we die we go to heaven or hell came from Greek philosophers, it is not found in the Word of God. The only time the dead will be resurrected is at the coming of Christ and by the authority of his command.

The resurrection of the just takes place toward the beginning of his earthly reign of 1000 years, and the resurrection of the unjust occurs at the end of it according to Revelation 20.

I Corinthians 15:24-26 AV
Then cometh the end, when he shall have delivered up the kingdom to God, even the Father; when he shall have put down all rule and all authority and power. For he must reign, till he hath put all enemies under his feet. The last enemy that shall be destroyed is death.

Verses 24 through verse 28 digress from the discussion of resurrection, to discuss the end, after Christ puts down all rule, and all authority, and power, until all enemies are subdued. The last enemy that shall be destroyed is death. Verse 29 then continues with the discussion of resurrection. This digression forms a parenthesis.

I Corinthians 15:27 and 28 AV
For he [God] hath put all things under his [Christ's] feet. But when he [God] saith all things are put under him [Christ], it is manifest that he [God] is excepted, which did put all things under him [Christ].

And when all things shall be subdued unto him [Christ], then shall the Son [Christ] also himself be subject unto him [God] that put all things under him, that God may be all in all.

The book of Revelation, chapters 19-22 cover this period. After the Son has accomplished all that His Father has entrusted to him, Christ will himself be subject to God. The book of II Peter sheds light on this as well.

II Peter 3:1-4 AV
This second epistle, beloved, I now write unto you; in both which I stir up your pure minds by way of remembrance: That ye may be mindful of the words which were spoken before by the holy prophets, and of the commandment of us the apostles of the Lord

and Saviour: Knowing this first, that there shall come in the last days scoffers, walking after their own lusts, And saying, Where is the promise of his coming? for since the fathers fell asleep, all things continue as they were from the beginning of the creation.

The First Century saints needed to be reminded and have their minds stirred up by the Word of God concerning Christ's coming.

II Peter 3:5-7 ASV
For this they willfully forget, that there were heavens from of old, and an earth compacted out of water and amidst water, by the word of God;

by which means the world that then was, being overflowed with water, perished:

but the heavens that now are, and the earth, by the same word have been stored up for fire, being reserved against the day of judgment and destruction of ungodly men.

Perhaps the ungodly have underestimated God's Word, and they should reconsider their position of unbelief. As the Lord Jesus Christ demonstrated by his resurrection from the dead, the Word of God cannot be broken. The reason that the Word of God cannot be broken is that God's power and authority backs it up. He is the All Powerful God, and nothing will keep Him from His purposes.

The current heaven and earth will have a different end than that of the first heaven and earth.

The previous world was deluged with water. It perished. The word is *apollumi*, which means, "to destroy, cause to perish, to be utterly and finally ruined and destroyed, brought to nothing." It expresses final and irretrievable destruction.

The first heaven and earth of Genesis 1:1 and 2a, "**became without form and void**." It became waste, without form and empty. Nothing survived this cataclysmic event: it was utterly destroyed.

The ungodly and scoffers have willfully failed to consider this judgment, and likewise they arrogantly ignore the judgment that will overtake them concerning the second heaven and earth.

II Peter 3:8 and 9 AV

But, beloved, be not ignorant of this one thing, that one day is with the Lord as a thousand years, and a thousand years as one day.

The Lord is not slack concerning his promise, as some men count slackness; but is longsuffering to us-ward, not willing that any should perish, but that all should come to repentance.

God does not want any person to perish; He would have all men come to the knowledge of the truth and be saved. He is not slack concerning His promise, but He is longsuffering. He made His offer of salvation available for any person. If they will confess Jesus as Lord and believe that He raised him from the dead, they will be saved. Such grace!

II Peter 3:10-12 AV

But the day of the Lord will come as a thief in the night; in the which the heavens shall pass away with a great noise, and the elements shall melt with fervent heat, the earth also and the works that are therein shall be burned up [discovered or exposed].

Seeing then that all these things shall be dissolved [destroyed], **what manner of persons ought ye to be in all holy conversation and godliness. Looking for and hasting unto the coming of the day of God, wherein the heavens being on fire shall be dissolved, and the elements shall melt with fervent heat?**

Even though God is longsuffering, and His Will is only good towards people, if they choose to reject His offer they are on their own, and they will perish. They reject their only hope of surviving the judgment of the Day of the Lord.

The verse speaks of the end of the Day of the Lord and the beginning of the Day of God, when this heaven and earth pass away.

The Word of God instructs us that after the end of this current, second heaven and earth there will be a third heaven and earth.

II Peter 3:13 AV

Nevertheless we, according to his promise, look for new heavens and a new earth, wherein dwelleth righteousness.

This speaks of "**new heavens and a new earth**" which are yet future. These will be the third heaven and earth. The apostle Paul mentions these also.

II Corinthians 12:1-4 AV

It is not expedient for me doubtless to glory. I will come to visions and revelations of the Lord.

I knew a man in Christ above fourteen years ago, (whether in the body, I cannot tell; or whether out of the body, I cannot tell: God knoweth;) such an one caught up [*harpazo*: to catch away, not up] **to the third heaven.**

And I knew such a man, (whether in the body, or out of the body, I cannot tell: God knoweth;)

How that he was caught up [*harpazo*: to carry away] **into paradise, and heard unspeakable words, which it is not lawful for a man to utter.**

God gave Paul such vivid revelation that he could not tell whether he was actually there or if he had had a vision of this future reality. He could not tell if he was "**in the body**", meaning that he was actually there or if he was "**out of the body**", meaning that he received revelation. It was that vivid.

The revelation concerned the third heaven and paradise, which will exist on the third earth. God showed him the future concerning the third heaven and paradise but He did not permit him to communicate the revelation.

God gave the revelation of these things to come, including the new heaven and earth to His apostle John, and He instructed him to record it.

Revelation 21:1-5 AV

And I saw a new heaven and a new earth: for the first [protos] **heaven and the first earth were passed away; and there was no more sea.**

And I John saw the holy city, new Jerusalem, coming down from God out of heaven, prepared as a bride adorned for her husband.

And I heard a great voice out of heaven saying, Behold, the tabernacle of God is with men, and he will dwell with them, and they shall be his people, and God himself shall be with them, and be their God.

And God shall wipe away all tears from their eyes; and there shall be no more death, neither sorrow, nor crying, neither shall there be any more pain: for the former [*protos*] **things are passed away.**

And he that sat upon the throne said, Behold, I make all things new. And he said unto me, Write: for these words are true and faithful.

In verse one, the word "**first**" is *protos*, the same word that is translated "**former**" in verse four. *Protos* may mean either "first" or "former." The word "former" gives us the correct sense here and fits with all the other scriptures concerning the identical subject.

The "**former heaven and earth**" is the second heaven and earth that exists today.

The word "**new**" concerns the new quality of life on the new heaven and earth. "**There will be no more death, neither sorrow, nor crying, neither shall there be any more pain: for the former things are passed away.**"

This is not the quality of life we currently enjoy, is it? In the third heaven and earth, God will make all things new again, and the former things shall pass away.

The Three Final Administrations		
The Administration of the Mystery and the Grace of God	**The Lord's Day**	**The Day of God and the Third Heaven and Earth**
Begins at the Feast of Pentecost with the pouring out of the spirit, after God raised Jesus from the dead, he ascended into heaven, and he sat down at the right hand of God.	Begins after the Church is gathered together unto Christ in the air.	Begins with the heavens being on fire and they are destroyed. The elements will melt with fervent heat. God will make all things new again in the Third Heavens and Earth.
Ends with the gathering together of the Church (both those who are living and those who died) to meet the Lord in the air **I Thessalonians 4:13-18**	Ends at the destruction of the Second Heavens and Earth. **I Thessalonians 5:2; II Thessalonians 2:2 and 3; Revelation 1:10** All judgment is committed unto the Son. **John 5:27** Ends when All enemies are subdued, and the Lord Jesus delivers the Kingdom over to God. **I Corinthians 5:24-28**	He makes all things new again **II Peter 3:12 and 13 Revelation 21:5** This administration has no end. It is a period of unending glory. **Revelation 21:1-22**

And he that sat upon the throne said, Behold, I make all things new. And he said unto me, Write: for these words are true and faithful.

And he said unto me, It is done. I am Alpha and Omega, the beginning and the end. I will give unto him that is athirst of the fountain of the water of life freely.

He that overcometh shall inherit all things; and I will be his God, and he shall be my son.

But the fearful, and unbelieving, and the abominable, and murderers, and whoremongers, and sorcerers, and idolaters, and all liars, shall have their part in the lake which burneth with fire and brimstone: which is the second death.

And there came unto me one of the seven angels which had the seven vials full of the seven last plagues, and talked with me, saying, Come hither, I will shew thee the bride, the Lamb's wife.

And he carried me away in the spirit to a great and high mountain, and shewed me that great city, the holy Jerusalem, descending out of heaven from God,

Having the glory of God: and her light was like unto a stone most precious, even like a jasper stone, clear as crystal;

And had a wall great and high, and had twelve gates, and at the gates twelve angels, and names written thereon, which are the names of the twelve tribes of the children of Israel:

On the east three gates; on the north three gates; on the south three gates; and on the west three gates.

And the wall of the city had twelve foundations, and in them the names of the twelve apostles of the Lamb.

And he that talked with me had a golden reed to measure the city, and the gates thereof, and the wall thereof.

And the city lieth foursquare, and the length is as large as the breadth: and he measured the city with the reed, twelve thousand furlongs. The length and the breadth and the height of it are equal [This makes a cube 1377 miles long x 1377 miles wide x 1377 miles high].

And he measured the wall thereof, an hundred and forty and four cubits, according to the measure of a man, that is, of the angel.

And the building of the wall of it was of jasper: and the city was pure gold, like unto clear glass.

And the foundations of the wall of the city were garnished with all manner of precious stones. The first foundation was jasper; the second, sapphire; the third, a chalcedony; the fourth, an emerald;

The fifth, sardonyx; the sixth, sardius; the seventh, chrysolite; the eighth, beryl; the ninth, a topaz; the tenth, a chrysoprasus; the eleventh, a jacinth; the twelfth, an amethyst.

And the twelve gates were twelve pearls; every several gate was of one pearl: and the street of the city was pure gold, as it were transparent glass.

And I saw no temple therein: for the Lord God Almighty and the Lamb are the temple of it.

And the city had no need of the sun, neither of the moon, to shine in it: for the glory of God did lighten it, and the Lamb is the light thereof.

And the nations of them which are saved shall walk in the light of it: and the kings of the earth do bring their glory and honour into it.

And the gates of it shall not be shut at all by day: for there shall be no night there.

And they shall bring the glory and honour of the nations into it.

And there shall in no wise enter into it any thing that defileth, neither whatsoever worketh abomination, or maketh a lie: but they which are written in the Lamb's book of life.

And he shewed me a pure river of water of life, clear as crystal, proceeding out of the throne of God and of the Lamb.

In the midst of the street of it, and on either side of the river, was there the tree of life, which bare twelve manner of fruits, and yielded her fruit every month: and the leaves of the tree were for the healing of the nations.

And there shall be no more curse: but the throne of God and of the Lamb shall be in it; and his servants shall serve him:

And they shall see his face; and his name shall be in their foreheads.

And there shall be no night there; and they need no candle, neither light of the sun; for the Lord God giveth them light: and they shall reign for ever and ever.

And he said unto me, These sayings are faithful and true: and the Lord God of the holy prophets sent his angel to shew unto his servants the things which must shortly be done.

Behold, I come quickly: blessed is he that keepeth the sayings of the prophecy of this book.

The purpose of the ages, which God accomplished in Christ Jesus our Lord, will all be fulfilled. The first time Jesus came, he suffered as the Lamb of God. The next time he comes it will not be to bear sin, but to bring salvation to those who are waiting for him.[75]

Acts 3:18-21 AV
But those things, which God before had shewed by the mouth of all his prophets, that Christ should suffer, he hath so fulfilled.

Repent ye [have a change of heart] **therefore, and be converted, that your sins may be blotted out, when the times of refreshing shall come from the presence of the Lord;**

And he shall send Jesus Christ, which before was preached unto you:

Whom the heaven must receive until the times of restitution [the times of restoration] **of all things, which God hath spoken by the mouth of all his holy prophets since the world began.**

All of this makes up our hope in Christ. It begins with our gathering together unto him in the air, and then stretches throughout eternity, glory after glory after glory.

Isaiah 46:9 and 10 AV
Remember the former things of old: for I am God, and there is none else; I am God, and there is none like me, Declaring the end from the beginning, and from ancient times the things that are not

yet done, saying, My counsel shall stand, and I will do all my pleasure:

---

[75] Hebrews 9:28.

God has revealed the end from the beginning, beloved. Rejoice!

I Corinthians 15:58 AV

Therefore, my beloved brethren, be ye stedfast, unmoveable, always abounding in the work of the Lord, forasmuch as ye know that your labour is not in vain in the Lord.

Verses from Paul's Epistles to Consider in Light of the Hope

In the Church Epistles:

Romans
Chapter 1:16-3:20;
Chapter 4:13-17;
Chapter 5:1, 2, 5, 9, 10, 21;
Chapter 8:11, 17-25, 28-39
Chapter 11:25-27
Chapter 12:12
Chapter 13:11
Chapter 14:10-12
Chapter 15:4-13
Chapter 16:20
I Corinthians
Chapter 1:7-9
Chapter 2:7-9
Chapter 3:8-17
Chapter 4:1-5
Chapter 6:2, 3, 9, 10, 11, 14
Chapter 7:29-31
Chapter 9:24-27
Chapter 13:8-13
Chapter 15:1-58
Chapter 16:22
II Corinthians
Chapter 1:14
Chapter 2:14-17
Chapter 3:7-12, 18
Chapter 4:10-14-17, 18
Chapter 5:1-10
Chapter 12:1-5
Galatians
Chapter 5:5
Chapter 6:8, 9
Ephesians
Chapter 1:8-10, 11-14, 18-23
Chapter 2:7, 11-12, 19-22
Chapter 3:6
Chapter 4:4, 13
Chapter 6:6-8, now & at the Return
Chapter 6:13, 17

Philippians
Chapter 1:6, 10, 20-23
Chapter 2:16
Chapter 3:11-14, 20, 21
Chapter 4:1
Colossians
Chapter 1:5, 12-14,
Chapter 1:18-20,
Chapter 1:22, 23, 26, 27
Chapter 2:16, 19
Chapter 3:13
Chapter 4:13-18
Chapter 5:1-10, 23
I Thessalonians
Chapter 1:3, 10
Chapter 2:16, 19
Chapter 3:13
Chapter 4:13-18
Chapter 5:1-10, 23
II Thessalonians
Chapter 1:5-12
Chapter 2:1-17
Chapter 3:5

In the Pastoral Epistles:

I Timothy
Chapter 1:16
Chapter 2:4, 5, 6
Chapter 4:8-10
Chapter 6:12-16, 19
II Timothy
Chapter 1:1, 9, 10, 12, 18
Chapter 2:10-12
Chapter 3:15
Chapter 4:8, 18
Titus
Chapter 1:2
Chapter 3:13-14
Chapter 3:7
Philemon - None

Are You Looking for Christ?

Philippians 3:20-21 WT

On the other hand, our citizenship is in heaven, from where we also patiently wait for the Savior, the Lord Jesus Christ,

Who will transform our humiliated body *that it may have* the same form as his glorious body according to the energizing by which he is able to subordinate all *things* to himself.

Are You Looking for Him?

II Corinthians 4:16-18 AV
For which cause we faint not; but though our outward man perish, yet the inward *man* is renewed day by day.

For our light affliction, which is but for a moment, worketh for us a far more exceeding *and* eternal weight of glory;

While we look not at the things which are seen, but at the things which are not seen: for the things which are seen *are* temporal; but the things which are not seen *are* eternal.

Oh, that it was today! There are times that the pressures of life overwhelm us. From a five senses perspective there are times that may seem insurmountable and we are tempted to faint in our minds. In times like these, we need to keep our eyes fixed on our hope in Christ and the riches of glory that our Father guarantees that we will inherit.

The understanding of our hope will renew us day by day. It gives us the stamina we need to endure the trials of life and stand as sons of God in this present evil world. The hope of Christ's return is the anchor of our soul.

The Day of Salvation is coming and the light affliction we endure today is not worth comparing to the **"far more exceeding *and* eternal weight of glory"** that we will share together with Christ as joint-heirs.

Today, we are sealed with the gift of holy spirit which is the down payment of our inheritance until the Day of Redemption; the day that our Lord will redeem those whom he purchased with his life.

God had the prophet Joel write to Israel and say, **"I will restore to you the years that the locust hath eaten . . .."**

The adversary wants to devour what God has blessed us with in our lives, as a swarm of locusts devours what is in its path. Day by day we must remember that we are more than conquerors through Him that loved us; both now and throughout eternity. When our Lord returns, he will restore all that the adversary has stolen from us.

Our Father puts the enduring of **"our light affliction"** for the moment in the proper perspective, does He not? This, **"far. . . more . . . exceeding. . . and eternal . . . weight . . . of glory;"** will be ours when Christ comes for the Church, which is his body.

Keep your eyes fixed on Christ. He is the head of the body, the Church. All that we now are, all that we now have and all that we will be is permanently fixed in Christ and in what he achieved.

God sees us in Christ and nothing will ever separate us from this glorious reality. We have every spiritual blessing in the heavenlies, sonship rights, abilities and privileges associated with this esteemed position. We are citizens of heaven, seated together with Christ. We are God's habitation by the spirit and members of His household.

When we decide to look at things from God's point of view, we have a much better perspective than the limited earthly viewpoint that the senses register.

If we will allow the light of God's Word to enlighten our understanding and we believe it, we will not faint in our minds. The light affliction we endure today is nothing compared to the glory we will share with Christ.

What we believe concerning our hope in Christ will have a dynamic bearing on how we live day by day.

The First Century saints believed in Christ's imminent return. Read the book of Acts to see how they lived and walked with God. They stood on God's Word and held it forth with boldness. They walked by the spirit of God and manifested it to move God's Word and minister deliverance to others. If we truly believed that Christ's return for us could be today, how would we live?

We should keep our eyes fixed on Christ and ardently expect his return. As we look at him it will keep us joyful as we live in this crooked and perverse world of darkness.

The adversary wants us to look within ourselves or to measure our lives by others. If we look within and dwell on our past sins, failings or entertain doubts concerning our standing in Christ, we will be miserable.

If we decide to look at the world and measure ourselves by others it will distract us from the glorious realities that are ours in Christ.

If we look at ourselves in the mirror of Christ's accomplishments, as our Heavenly Father looks on us, we will have the peace of God, fullness of joy, the comfort of our hope and we will be radiant. It is Christ in you, the hope of glory!

II Thessalonians 2:1 AV
Now we beseech you, brethren, by the coming of our Lord Jesus Christ, and *by* our gathering together unto him,

This is the sure hope of the Church. When our Lord Jesus Christ comes he will take us into the glory of the heavenlies. We will be gathered together unto him; we will see him face to face, we will be like him, having bodies conformed unto his glorious body, we will be as he is and we will return with him into the heavenlies as joint-heirs. The Church was called, ". . . **to the obtaining of the glory of our Lord Jesus Christ**"!

The revelation concerning our being "in Christ" is the apex, the zenith, the climax of all revelation. It embraces the realities that are ours both now and throughout eternity. We can live day by day in the comfort and absolute certainty of God's Word. It's ". . . **Christ in you, the hope of glory**"!

The end of this Age of Grace and the Mystery will occur when Christ comes to gather us together into the heavenlies and we ascend with him into the Father's presence to enjoy exceeding rich glory together with Christ.

When Christ returns for the Church, there will be no more sorrow, sickness, pain or death for the members of his body. We will no longer be vexed with evil day after day. There will be no more struggling against sin. The Lord will deliver us from this present evil world and heal all of our wounds. There will only be glory and that beyond anything that we can possibly imagine.

Thanks be to God Who gives us the victory over the grave and this evil world through our Lord Jesus Christ! He has revealed the absolute certainty of His Will to us in the Scriptures of truth and every jot and tittle of it shall come to pass as He has said. Nothing can hinder our Heavenly Father from performing all that He has purposed in Christ Jesus our Lord.

Remember the words of our Lord Jesus Christ, ". . . **the Word of God cannot be broken**." He staked his life on God's Word and so can we because, "**It stands written!**" Comfort yourself with this wonderful truth.

Ephesians 1:9 and10 Nestle-Aland Greek-English New Testament
For he has made known to us in all wisdom and insight the mystery of his will, according to his purpose which he set forth in Christ as

a plan for the fullness of time, to unite all things in him, things in heaven and things on earth.

The coming of Christ for the Church is the conclusion of this present Administration of the Mystery, the Administration of the Grace of God.

In the next administration, Christ will subdue all of God's enemies. His Father will make them his footstool. He will head up everything in the heavens and on the entire earth.

Once Christ has accomplished all of God's will, God will make all new again in the third heaven and earth. God will successfully carry out His purpose, the purpose of the ages, by Christ Jesus our Lord.

Ephesians 3:9-11 Darby
And to enlighten all *with the knowledge of* what is the administration of the mystery hidden throughout the ages in God, who has created all things, in order that now to the principalities and authorities in the heavenlies might be made known through the assembly [the church] the all-various wisdom of God, according to *the* purpose of the ages, which he purposed in Christ Jesus our Lord,

God is demonstrating His infinitely diversified wisdom through the church to the heavenly principalities and powers concerning the purpose of the ages which He purposed in Christ Jesus our Lord.

The book of Ephesians gives us God's point of view concerning the work of Christ and what he accomplished by it.

By the same exceeding great power that God exerted to raise Christ from the dead, He made us alive with Christ, raised us up with him and made us sit together with him in the heavenlies. He blessed us with every spiritual blessing in the heavenlies in Christ.

God considers the Church to be "in Christ." He expresses the revelation in language like "the body of Christ" and "members of his body" and "one flesh." God considers the Church to be united with Christ in his accomplishments.

How could God communicate the revelation concerning our association with Christ any plainer? Our hope lies in the reality of who we are in Christ. There is no hope apart from him. Our standing in Christ is framed with the exceeding riches of God's grace and glory. We are joint heirs with him and we will be glorified together with him.

Ephesians 2:7 AV

That in the ages to come he might shew the exceeding riches of his grace in *his* kindness toward us through Christ Jesus.

It will take the unveiling of eternity for our Father to demonstrate all the treasures that He purposed for us in Christ Jesus. Our Father's exceeding rich grace concerning His purposes in Christ will be demonstrated in His kindness towards us. We are truly the objects of His affection.

I Corinthians 2:9 and 10 AV

But as it is written, Eye hath not seen, nor ear heard, neither have entered into the heart of man, the things which God hath prepared for them that love him. But God hath revealed *them* unto us by his Spirit: for the Spirit searcheth all things, yea, the deep things of God.

At one time this revelation was a mystery, a secret hidden in God, but now He has revealed a glimpse of the riches of the glory of this mystery to us by the revelation knowledge of the Church Epistles.

It is Christ in you, the hope of glory! Our hope in Christ makes the sufferings of this present time insignificant compared to the glory that shall be revealed in us.

The coming of Christ for the Church is the conclusion to the Administration of the Mystery, the Administration of the Grace of God.

When Christ comes the next time, it will not be to bear our sin, but to bring the reality of salvation to those who are waiting for him.

Philippians 1:6 NIV

Being confident of this, that he who began a good work in you will carry it on to completion until the day of Christ Jesus.

What a tremendous comfort this is. Our hope is of salvation, redemption, eternal life and of obtaining the glory of Christ Jesus our Lord.

Our Father loves us and His only begotten Son gave His life for us. We can be certain that He who began a good work in us will carry it on to its completion, until the coming of Christ Jesus our Lord. When he returns for us we will receive everything that He promised us in Christ.

These are the last days before our Lord returns to gather us into the glory that our loving Father has reserved for us in the heavenlies.

Philippians 3:20 and 21 ERV

For our citizenship is in heaven; from whence also we wait for a Saviour, the Lord Jesus Christ: who shall fashion anew the body of our humiliation, *that it may be* **conformed to the body of his glory, according to the working whereby he is able even to subject all things unto himself.**

We can rejoice daily in our hope of seeing Christ Jesus our Lord face to face and being transformed to be like him.

Just think . . . when we see him, as glorious as it will be, it will only be the inaugural event of the rest of eternity for us.

Our hope in Christ Jesus our Lord is exceeding, abundantly, above all that we could ever ask or think.

Titus 2:13 AV

Looking for that blessed hope, and the glorious appearing of the great God and our Saviour Jesus Christ;

It should read, **"Looking for that blessed hope and appearing of the glory of the great God even our Savior Jesus Christ."** Jesus Christ's coming is our blessed hope. His appearing will be the realization of our hope of obtaining the glory of the Lord Jesus Christ. When he comes it will be to save us.

We should expect the return of our Lord with great anticipation. If we keep our eyes on the hope of his return, the cares of this world will not be as burdensome. They are only temporary compared to the far more exceeding and eternal weight of glory which God reserved for us. The hope of our Lord's return to save and redeem us should ever be before our eyes.

The Word of God instructs us to look for, to patiently wait for Christ, to ardently expect him.

Philippians 3:20 RV

For our conversation [citizenship] **is in heaven; from whence also we look[76] for the Saviour, the Lord Jesus Christ:**

---

[76]The Greek word is *apekdechomai.* Twice it is translated "look for" and five times as "wait for" in the Authorized Version. It means "to wait out, wait long for, await ardently." Bullinger, (1999).

Hebrews 9:28 NIV
. . . and he [Christ] **will appear a second time, not to bear sin, but to bring salvation to those who are waiting** [AV: looking] **for him.**

I Corinthians 1:7 AV
. . . waiting for the coming of our Lord Jesus Christ:

Galatians 5:5 AV
For we through the spirit [by the complete new birth reality] **wait for the hope of righteousness by faith.**

I Thessalonians 1:10 RV
And to wait[77] **for his Son from heaven, whom he raised from the dead,** *even* **Jesus, which delivereth**[78] **us from the wrath to come.**

The one object of hope for the church is the return of Christ. The apostles believed that it was imminent. They did not instruct the saints to look for signs and seasons, but for the return of the Lord from heaven.

Colossians 3:1 and 2 AV
If ye then be risen with Christ, seek those things which are above, where Christ sitteth on the right hand of God. Set your affection on things above, not on things on the earth.

Since we are risen with Christ, we should occupy ourselves with the realities that it involves. We should live as dead men who were raised to life! We should serve in the newness of the spirit. Our thoughts and affections should be centered in the spiritual realm and in what God made us in Christ because Christ is our life. All that remains is his return for us, and then:

Colossians 3:4.
When Christ, *Who* **is our life, shall appear, then shall** *ye* **also appear with Him in glory.**

What works could we possibly do to deserve this glory? It is so priceless, so costly that God had to make it available to us by His grace.

---

[77] "Wait" is *anameno,* to wait with patience and confident expectancy. (Vine 1981) "To wait for as the coming of the morning sun, etc." *See* above reference.

[78] Delivereth is, *rhuomai,* to draw or snatch to one's self; hence, *gen.* to draw or snatch from danger, to rescue, to deliver. (Bullinger 1999). The word means to rescue as you would snatch a child out of the danger of an oncoming car.

Romans 5:2 Amplified

Through Him [Jesus our Lord] **also we have "our" access** (entrance, introduction) **by faith into this grace** (state of God's favor) **in which we "firmly and safely" stand. And let us rejoice** *and* **exult in our hope of experiencing** *and* **enjoying the glory of God.**

The Lord Jesus gave us the introduction and entrance into the state of God's Divine favor. We now firmly and safely stand in His grace towards us. We do not have to earn this access; it is now ours through the work of our Lord Jesus Christ. We now stand in God's grace, not in our works. We rest in God's grace; that is why we can exult; we can rejoice in the hope of enjoying the glory of God!

We have gone from dead in sin to alive before God; from condemned to redeemed; from headed into the wrath of God to saved from wrath; from enemies of God to beloved sons of God. Our hearts and minds should overflow with thankfulness for the undeserved, Divine favor shown us in Christ.

Romans 15:13 AV

Now the God of hope fill you with all joy and peace in believing, that ye may abound in hope, through the power of the Holy Ghost.

Our God is the God of "the hope" – so all the texts read. He provided our hope in Christ. The hope of Christ's return for the church is the grand finale of revelation in the book of Romans.

We should *abound* in hope. It should govern our stand, our thinking and our resolve. If you took a set of scales and put the hope of Christ's return on one side of the scales and the daily stuff, junk and things of life we endure on the other, it should be obvious that the hope of glory far outweighs the things we endure today. Understanding the hope will give you the stamina required to stand as a son of God day by day.

II Corinthians 3:18 AV

But we all, with open face beholding as in a glass [a mirror] **the glory of the Lord, are changed into the same image from glory to glory,** *even* **as by the Spirit of the Lord.**

When we confessed Jesus as our Lord and believed that God raised him from the dead we received the spirit of God. The spirit of the Lord, the sonship spirit, removed the veil from our eyes. Now we can see spiritually.

When we behold the glory of the Lord, it is like seeing a reflection in a mirror. We are beholding what He created us to be in Christ Jesus. The spirit of the Lord changed us from being natural men, to men who are filled with the spirit of the Lord. We were **"transformed into the same image from glory to glory, *even* as by the spirit of the Lord"**.

We have the glory of the spirit of the Lord today and when our Lord returns, we will have glorious spiritual bodies like his. We will see him face to face and we will be transformed to be like him. It is truly Christ in you, the hope of glory!

What are you looking at? Are you looking at the world or at the glorious hope of Christ's return? You become what you look at. If you look at the world, you will faint from its burdens. If you want to be filled with joy and peace in believing, keep your eyes on the hope of Christ's return.

Abound in hope through the power of the holy spirit in you! Abounding in hope cannot hurt you; it can only strengthen you and keep you joyous and peaceful.

Put on the **"helmet of salvation"** as Ephesians 6:17 instructs, or, as I Thessalonians 5:8 says, **"for a helmet, the hope of salvation."** A helmet protects the head. If we are to stand as God's sons in this crooked and perverse world today, it is essential that we hold the hope foremost in our thinking.

The hope of Christ's return is the anchor of our soul. It is certain and fixed. As Christ Jesus entered the heavenlies, so shall we! The glory of the new birth is only the beginning. The fulfillment of the purpose of the ages awaits us.

I Corinthians 15:58 AV
Therefore, my beloved brethren, be ye stedfast, unmoveable, always abounding in the work of the Lord, forasmuch as ye know that your labour is not in vain in the Lord.

Keep your eyes on the hope of Christ's return and press toward the finish line for the prize of the calling on high. We press on with God's Word, His spirit, our standing in Christ and our sonship rights. We study, renew our minds to who we are in Christ, believe God's Word, and live in the reality of God's love.

We are God's epistle known and read of all men. Until he returns, live in the love of God as you renew your mind and manifest it to others. It's Christ in you, the hope of glory!

Come quickly Lord Jesus!

Appendix A: How The Word of God Interprets Itself

Why do Christians not all agree on the teaching of the Word of God? This question is paramount to our search for the truth. One group believes one thing and another believes something quite contrary. How is this possible if they both claim to believe the truth?

To answer this question, we need some basic knowledge about the Word of God. Next, we need to understand how it interprets itself.

The earliest known manuscripts of the Word of God date from the fourth century A.D. We do not have any originals in existence today.

The oldest manuscripts were written in *uncial* (all capital letters), also known as *majuscule*. An example would read,

FORGODSOLOVEDTHEWORLDTHATHEGAVEHISONLYBE
GOTTENSONTHATWHOSOEVERBELIEVETHINHIMSHOUL
DNOTPERISHBUTHAVEEVERLASTINGLIFE

These manuscripts date from the fourth to ninth century. Early in the ninth century, cursive script began to take its place. Below is an example of cursive script.

Forgodsolovedtheworldthathegavehisonlybegottensonthatwhosove
rbelievethinhimshouldnotperishbuthaveeverlastinglife

There were no punctuation markings, no chapter divisions, or verses in these manuscripts. The editors of the various Bibles added these much later.

The Old Testament texts were originally written in Hebrew, while the New Testament texts were originally written in Estrangelo Aramaic, and Greek. Some texts were later translated into Latin.

An interlinear book of scripture, that places the English words above the Greek, Hebrew or Aramaic words, is helpful in biblical study. You can then check an Analytical Lexicon for the parsing of the words used and their definitions.

A translation is the first copy of a manuscript when converted into another language. The second someone reworks it, in any way, it becomes a version.

No particular translation, much less a version, is the original God-breathed Word of God as it was given to holy men of God by revelation. Since none of these is THE Word of God, how do we get back to what God originally revealed to His holy apostles and prophets?

To get THE Word of God from any version of the Bible, we will have to work it from the information it reveals to us – not from secular or religious sources outside of the Scriptures such as tradition, the early Church Fathers, denominational writings, archeology, history, etc. Man is the origin of all of these references. They may be correct or they may be in error.

To get the Word of God as He originally gave it to holy men of God, it will have to interpret itself in the verse right where it is written, or in the context where the verse appears. If we cannot find the interpretation in the verse or its context, we will have to consider records where the subject is discussed previously.

God gave His Word to reveal His Will to man. He did not reveal it so that men could come up with a meaning independent of the words He used to communicate it. God does not leave it up to us to determine His Will in light of what He did not say. He used words to communicate His Will so that men could understand His intent and meaning. The Scriptures give us a point of reference, a safe check as to what God said.

Within the verse we will have to consider the biblical definition of words, that is, how God uses them in the Scriptures. The usage of words in the Word of God may vary from their secular usage.

We can trace a word from its first use and following uses in the Word of God to find its meaning. A concordance lists every use of the words in the Bible. Young's and Strong's are both good concordances.

A lexicon gives the usages of a word employed in the Bible; it gives their definitions. Bullinger, Vine, Thayer, Liddell, and Scott's[79] are all good examples of lexicons for Greek New Testament words.

---

[79] E. W. Bullinger, *A Critical Lexicon and Concordance to the English and Greek New Testament.* (1999 ed.); W. E. Vine & F. F. Bruce (Ed.), *Vine's Expository Dictionary of Old & New Testament Words.* (1981); J. H. Thayer, *The New Thayer's Greek-English Lexicon of the New Testament Coded with Strong's Concordance Numbers.* (1981); H. G. Liddell and R. Scott, *A Greek-English Lexicon.* (1871). (The latest reprint of Liddell and Scott is 2015.)

We also have to understand the archaic usage of words we find in various versions of the Bible. A word used during one period of history may have a different meaning than the current usage of the word. For example, Noah Webster compiled the *American Dictionary of the English Language* in 1828. It is helpful with versions written around that time.

Within the verse, we must recognize figures of speech and understand their usages. The Holy Spirit places emphasis in His Word by the use of figures of speech. Figures of speech do not lessen the truth stated; they intensify it and draw our attention to what it says in some way that deviates from normal grammatical usage. The figure takes on a different form from its ordinary and natural form.

The most comprehensive work in this field that I am aware of is by Dr. E. W. Bullinger.

We must also understand oriental idioms and customs (Orientalisms) that were common in eastern lands and times in which the Bible was written. These idioms appear throughout the Word of God. Bishop K.C. Pillai[80] did the best work I know of in this field.

If we are to have the Word of God as He originally gave it, it will have to fit together from Genesis 1:1 to Revelation 22:21 without any contradiction.

If there seems to be a discrepancy, it has to be an improper translation of the text or our lack of understanding. Truth is truth.

Using the keys to how the Word of God interprets itself, we will be able to determine the God-breathed original so that it expresses God's Will to us.

The verse must agree with the teaching of the context in which it appears. We cannot lift a verse from its context and use it in a way that contradicts the teaching that surrounds it.

If the verse or the context surrounding it does not give us the interpretation, we will have to search instances where the subject appears previously in the scriptures. If we trace the subject back to where it first appears and then track it through the Word of God, we will find the intended interpretation.

---

[80] Reahard, Bo (1980) Compilation of *Old and New Testament Orientalisms: Teachings of Bishop K. C. Pillai: The Eastern Customs and Manners of the Bible and their Spiritual Application in Understanding the Scriptures.*

Every record regarding the identical subject must agree if we are to rightly-divide God's Word. Once we take into account every scripture dealing with the identical subject we will know all there is to know about it.

We must realize that not everything concerning a given topic may be given in one scripture. As we study the identical subject from other passages, they will complement one another and give us added insight.

One record may give us a part of the truth while other records may supply us with additional details, which when considered together will furnish us with a complete picture of the truth. This is the principle of scripture-buildup.

If we lump scriptures together concerning similar records (even though they may concern different times, people, places or other details), as though they are identical, our handling of the Word of God may be in error. We need to consider the place the record occurs, the time it occurs, the details of what occurs, who is involved, the records that precede it and those that follow it.

We will have to be cognizant of to whom the record is addressed, who it concerns and of whom it is true.

The Scriptures are addressed either to the Jews (Judeans) or to the Gentiles or to the Church of God.[81]

A Gentile is not a Judean and a Judean is not the Church. If we read God's Word as though it all concerns only us, we could walk away with frustration, confusion or fear.

The different times or administrations in which God deals with man must also be taken into account if we are to rightly divide His Word. God dealt with man based on different principles in each of these periods. There are seven administrations of time in the Word of God: Paradise, Patriarchal, Law, Christ, Grace, the Lord's Day, and The Third Heaven and Earth.

Each of these periods of time or administrations began and ended by an act of God.

---

[81] I Corinthians 10:32.

1. Paradise:

God restored the second heaven and earth, and placed Adam and Eve in a garden or paradise. God formed Adam's body, made soul life in him, and created him in His image, which was spirit. He gave Adam a commandment, **"Of every tree of the garden thou mayest freely eat: but of the tree of the knowledge of good and evil, thou shalt not eat of it: for in the day that thou eatest thereof thou shalt surely die."** (*Genesis 2:16b, 17 AV*)

God communicated with Adam - Spirit to spirit - in the Garden. The day he disobeyed, Adam most surely died. He lived for nine hundred and thirty years in a body and soul life existence, so what died that day? He died spiritually. Death is a loss of life. The day Adam disobeyed, he lost the spirit life that God had given him. God could no longer work with him as He did before the condemnation. He lost the spirit of God that had been upon him. The ground was cursed; nature was affected with noxious plants. He could no longer live in the garden; he was driven out of it and had to toil in the field. God set cherubim, powerful spirit-beings, to the east of Eden, to keep the way to the Tree of Life.

2. Patriarchal:

In the Garden or Paradise, Adam was created in the image of God. When Adam had children, Genesis 5:3 says they were born **"in his own likeness, after his image . . ."** not in God's image, which was spirit. So how was God to work with them now? In the generations of Adam, God worked with men who listened to Him and believed what He said. Hebrews 11:1 through verse 29 covers this period of time. During this period, at times God conditionally put his spirit on men to communicate with them. Seth, Enoch, Noah, Abraham, Isaac, and Jacob were men who listened to God and believed what He said. Abraham, Isaac, and Jacob walked with God and believed the promises God made to Abraham.

Jacob had twelve sons, which became the twelve tribes of the nation of Israel. The Patriarchal Administration ended when God gave the law to Moses for Israel.

3. The Law:

This period began when God gave the Law to the prophet Moses for Israel. The Law specified in great detail how Israel was to live and worship. The Law covered every facet of life. It was the standard that God gave to the nation of Israel, who were only body and soul people. It pertained to the flesh and regulated their lives. God covenanted with Israel to be their God and for them to be His people.

4. The Christ Administration:

The Law Administration and the Christ Administration overlap because God sent His Son to Israel to fulfill the Law.

Galatians 3:13 and 14 AV
Christ hath redeemed us from the curse of the law, being made a curse for us: for it is written, 'Cursed is every one that hangeth on a tree: That the blessing of Abraham might come on the Gentiles through Jesus Christ; that we might receive the promise of the spirit through faith.

Chapter three of Galatians explains how Israel was kept under the law until Christ fulfilled it. See also Galatians 3:19-25, and II Corinthians 3:6-18. The Christ Administration ended after Jesus Christ was crucified, died, was buried, and God raised him from the dead. He ministered on earth another 40 days before he ascended into heaven and when God seated him at His right hand.

5. The Administration of the Grace of God, which is also called the Administration of the Mystery:

In this administration, the Judeans and the Gentiles are joint-heirs, and of a joint-body, and joint-partakers of the promise in Christ Jesus. Everything that the saints have in this administration is by the grace of God extended to us because of the accomplishments of Jesus Christ.

This administration began when He poured out the spirit on the Feast of Pentecost that followed Christ's death, resurrection, ascension, and seating at God's Right Hand in the heavenlies.

The proof that the twelve Apostles received the spirit of God was that they spoke in tongues the wonderful works of God. It was the proof that they received the promise of the Father of which Christ told them.

Acts 1:4-5 AV
And being assembled together with them, [Christ] commanded them that they should not depart from Jerusalem, but wait for the promise of the Father, which, saith he, ye have heard of Me. For

John truly baptized with water; but ye shall be baptized with the Holy Ghost not many days hence.

The book of Acts gives us the Divine history of Israel receiving the holy spirit, and later on, the Gentiles receiving it at Cornelius' house, when Peter taught them. The proof they received the same spirit as Israel received, was that they spoke in tongues, the same as the twelve apostles did at the Feast of Pentecost.

The books of Romans through the Epistle of II Thessalonians are addressed to the Church of the Grace of God, which are those in the Administration of the Mystery. See Ephesians 3:2 and 9.

In this current administration, God is dealing with those in the Church based on the accomplishments of the Lord Jesus Christ, and their receiving the spirit of Christ within. In this period, those who believe in the Lord Jesus Christ - Judean or Gentile - are born of the spirit of God. They receive the spirit of sonship.

Romans 10:9 AV
That if thou shalt confess with thy mouth the Lord Jesus, and shalt believe in thine heart that God hath raised him from the dead, thou shalt be saved.

Romans 8:9 AV
But ye are not in the flesh, but in the Spirit, if so be that the Spirit of God dwell in you. Now if any man have not the Spirit of Christ, he is none of his.

Romans 8:14-18 AV
For as many as are led by the Spirit of God, they are the sons of God.

For ye have not received the spirit of bondage again to fear; but ye have received the Spirit of adoption [*huiothesia*: to be placed as a son by adoption or by birth: here it is speaking of the spirit of sonship by birth], **whereby we cry, Abba, Father.**

The Spirit itself beareth witness with our spirit, that we are the ildren of God:

And if children, then heirs; heirs of God, and joint-heirs with Christ; if so be that we suffer with him, that we may be also glorified together.

For I reckon that the sufferings of this present time are not worthy to be compared with the glory which shall be revealed in us.

This administration ends when God sends Christ to remove the Church of the Grace of God from the earth; both the living, and the dead in Christ will be removed at the same time. The living are transformed to have glorious bodies like Christ's, and the dead in Christ are raised with glorious bodies like his, too. See I Thessalonians 4:15-18. II Thessalonians 1 and 2 describes the gathering together of the Church, when we meet him in the air, as the departure.

This must occur before the man of sin is revealed. God restrains him until the Church departs, and Christ gathers them up into the clouds in the air. The Word of God conclusively asserts that the Day of the Lord, and the Lord's revelation to the world will not occur until after the Church is at rest with the Lord.

    6.   The Day of the Lord:

This period is also called The Lord's Day (Revelation 1:10), and it begins after the gathering together of the Church occurs in the air. The Lord's Day concerns Israel and the Gentiles, not the Church of the Grace of God. The book of Revelation describes this period with Christ opening the seven seals of the book given to him from the throne of God.

During this period of time, the man of sin will be revealed, the son of perdition. This is the time of "Jacob's trouble." The wrath of God is poured out on the earth. The battle of Armageddon takes place and Christ returns to the earth to claim his dominion as King of kings and Lord of lords. His return to the earth ends the time of the Gentiles' domination over Israel.

Jesus Christ rules for 1000 years with his saints. The resurrection of the just occurs by the Lord's command. The Lord also gives the angels the command to gather the living saints of Israel from the nations back to their King in Jerusalem.

The judging of Israel, the Gentiles, the beast, the false prophet, and Satan occurs. The resurrection of the unjust, the Great White throne judgment from the books, and the opening of the Book of Life are also events during this administration. The sentence of the second death for those not found in the Book of Life occurs, and they are cast into the lake of fire and destroyed.

7. The New Heaven and the New Earth:

God shall wipe away all tears - no more death, neither sorrow, nor crying, and no more pain. God will make all things new and dwells with His people. New Jerusalem descends out of heaven, having the glory of God (it has its dimensions given as 12,000 furlongs in length, 12,000 furlongs in height, and 12,000 furlongs in width: a cube that is 1377 miles long, high and wide). The bride, the Lamb's wife is described. There is not a temple in the New Jerusalem because the Lord God Almighty and the Lamb are the Temple of it. There is no more sea. The city has no need of the sun, neither moon: the glory of God lightens it, and the Lamb is the light thereof. The nations of them, which are saved, walk in the light of it, and the kings of the earth bring their glory and honor into it. Only those written in the Lamb's Book of Life enter.

It contains the Paradise of God. The river of living waters is in it, and the tree of life yields its fruit every month. There is no more curse. His servants see His face, and they shall reign forever and ever.

The Lord Jesus spoke of it in Luke 23:43. The apostle Paul refers to the third heaven and paradise in II Corinthians 12:2-4. The record in Revelation 2:7 promises it to the over-comers. Revelation 21:1 through Chapter 22:6, describe it. This is an administration of God's unending glory.

In summary, as we study the Word of God as our reference for truth concerning spiritual matters, we must allow it to interpret itself in the verse, in the context, and see how it is used previously.

We must observe the principles of how God's Word interprets itself if we are to study to show ourselves approved unto God. If we rightly divide His Word we will have the Word of Truth that He originally revealed to holy men of God. He wants us to understand His Word and Will.

If it is the Word of God as He originally gave it to holy men of God by revelation, it cannot contradict itself. It will have to fit together from Genesis 1:1 to Revelation 22:21 without contradiction. If we will work the Scriptures in this manner, we will be able to recapture the original "God-breathed Word."

In biblical study, we must be as honest about learning as we would be in any other field. We cannot decide what we believe before we consider the evidence of God's Word. We cannot begin our study of God's Word with predetermined ideas and then look for scriptures that support our point of view.

We must have the same "readiness of mind" as the Bereans we read about in Acts 17:11. If we expect to gain an understanding of spiritual matters, we will have to study the Word of God as our reference for truth, and allow it to reveal the truth to us. It will interpret itself.

We should not make up our minds as to what we believe before we study God's Word and consider the evidence it reveals. If we do, our believing could be in error. Our preconceived ideas or predetermined doctrinal positions could be roadblocks that prevent us from learning.

Someone once said, "It's what you learn after you think you know the answer that is really important."

If we truly want answers, we must allow the Word of God to speak for itself. Sincerity is no guarantee for truth. We cannot afford to be close-minded when it comes to learning what God reveals in His Word.

God does not have to conform to our way of thinking, but we will have to change our minds to conform to His thinking as we learn.

We need to be teachable. This requires humility on our part. We have to put forth the effort to learn and receive God's Word with meekness.

When we come to believe that the Bible is the revealed Word of God, we will have arrived at a position that far too many have overlooked.

When we have the Word of God as God originally gave it to holy men of God, we are standing in the presence of God. We cannot get any closer to God than His Word, no more than you could get closer to me than by my word.

Once we allow the Word of God to interpret itself by studying to show ourselves approved unto God by rightly dividing His Word, we will have the Word of Truth. If we will take God at His Word, we will be in a position that we can learn from the mouth of God Himself.

Appendix B: Works Cited and Suggested Reading

Bruce, F. F. (1982). *I & II Thessalonians: Word Biblical Commentary Series, Vol. 45.* Thomas Nelson.

Bullinger, E. W. (1999 ed.). *A Critical Lexicon and Concordance to the English and Greek New Testament.* Grand Rapids, MI: Kregel Academic & Professional.

Ibid. (1992 ed.). *Figures of Speech Used in the Bible: Explained and Illustrated.* Grand Rapids, MI: Baker Book House.

Ibid. (1960). *Selected Writings.* London Lamp Press. (The Book Contents Includes: The Importance and Accuracy in The Study of Holy Scripture; Rightly Dividing the Word of Truth; The Knowledge of God; God's Purpose in Israel in History; Type and Prophecy; Christ's Prophetic Teaching; The Rich Man and Lazarus; The Spirits in Prison; The Transfiguration; The Resurrection of the Body; The Lord's Day; The Two Prayers in The Epistles to The Ephesians; The Mystery.).

Ibid. (1974, Reprint). *The Companion Bible.* Zondervan Bible Publishers.

Ciardi, John (Translator). (2003). *Dante Alighieri: The Divine Comedy (The Inferno, The Purgatorio, and The Paradiso).* New York: Penguin/New American Library.

Cummins W.J. (2006). *Volume 1 and 2: A Journey Through the Acts and Epistles.* Franklin, Ohio: Scripture Consulting.

Dana, H.E. and Mantey, J.R. (1957). *A Manual Grammar of the Greek New Testament.* Toronto: MacMillan Publishing.

Daniell, David S. (2003). *The Bible in English: History and Influence.* New Haven: Yale University Press.

Daniell, David S. (Ed.). (2000). William Tyndale: The Obedience of a Christian Man (Penguin Classics). Penguin Random House/Penguin Books.

Donaldson, J. and Roberts, A. (Eds.). (1956). *The Ante-Nicene Fathers, Vol. IV: Fathers of the Third Century*. Grand Rapids, MI: Eerdmans.

Edersheim, Alfred. (1993 ed.). *The Life and Times of Jesus the Messiah*. Peabody MA: Hendrickson Publishers.

Elwell, W. A. (Ed.). (1996). *The Evangelical Dictionary of Theology 2nd Ed.* Ada, MI: Baker Publishing Group.

Farrar, F.W. (2003 ed.). *History of Interpretation*. New York; E.P. Dutton and Co.

Garcia, J.E., Reichberg, G.M., and Schumacher, B.N. (Eds.). (2003). *The Classics of Western Philosophy: A Reader's Guide*. Oxford: Blackwell Publishing.

Graham, Billy. (1983). *Peace with God, Revised and Expanded*. Thomas Nelson/Word Books.

Hislop, Alexander. (Pub. Mar 2013). *The Two Babylons*. CreateSpace Independent Publishing Platform.

Jackson, S. Macauley. (2015). *The New Schaff-Herzog Encyclopedia of Religious Knowledge. (Classic Reprint Series)*. London: FB &c Ltd. / Forgotten Books.

Jaeger, Werner. (1959). "*The Greek Ideas of Immortality*," *Harvard Theological Review*, Volume LII: July, Number 3.

Kaufmann, Kohler. *Immortality of the Soul* (late Hebrew, "hasharat ha-nefesh;" hayye 'olam"), at http://www.jewishencyclopedia.com/articles/8092-immortality-of-the-soul.

Liddell, H.G. and Scott, R. A. (1978 ed.). *Greek-English Lexicon (1871): With a Supplement 1968*. Oxford: University Press.

Lightfoot, John. (1989). *A Commentary on the New Testament from the Talmud and Hebraica*. Peabody, MA: Hendrickson Publishers.

Noah Webster's First Edition of An American Dictionary of the English Language (1828), republished in facsimile edition. (1989). San Francisco, CA: Foundation for American Christian Education.

Pentecost, J. Dwight. (1964 ed.). *Things to Come: A Study in Biblical Eschatology*. Grand Rapids, MI: Zondervan/Academie Books.

Ramm, Bernard. (1970*). Protestant Biblical Interpretation: A Textbook of Hermeneutics*. Ada, MI: Baker Publishing Group.

Reahard, Bo. (1980). Compilation of *Old and New Testament Orientalisms: Teachings of Bishop K. C. Pillai: The Eastern Customs and Manners of the Bible and their Spiritual Application in Understanding the Scriptures.* The Way International.

Roller, Duane W. (2014). *The Geography of Strabo: An English Translation, with Introduction and Notes.* Cambridge University Press.

Schaff, Phillip. (2006). *History of the Christrian Church, Vol. II, 3rd Ed.* Peabody, MA: Hendrickson Publishers, Inc.

Tarnas, Richard. (1991). *The Passion of the Western Mind: Understanding the Ideas That Have Shaped Our World View.* New York: Crown Publishing Group/ Harmony Publisher.

Thayer, J.H., Stong, James. (1981). *The New Thayer's Greek-English Lexicon of the New Testament Coded with Strong's Concordance Numbers.* Peabody MA: Hendrickson Publishers, Inc.

The Catholic Encyclopedia. (1990). Broderick, R. C. (Ed.). Thomas Nelson Publishers.

The International Standard Bible Encyclopedia: Vol. 2 (of Vol. 1-5). (1960). Grand Rapids, MI: Wm. B. Eerdmans Publishing Co.

Vine, W.E., Bruce, F.F. (Ed.). (1981). *Vine's Expository Dictionary of Old & New Testament Words.* Tarrytown, NY: Fleming H. Revell Co.

Vos, Howard F. (1960). *Highlights of Church History.* Chicago, IL: Moody Press.

Weimar edition of Luther's Works.

Wierwille, Victor Paul. (1981). *Jesus Christ Our Passover.* New Knoxville, OH: American Christian Press.

Ibid. (1971). *Are the Dead Alive Now.* Old Greenwich, CT: The Devin-Adair Co.

Woodrow, Ralph E. (1981). *Babylon Mystery Religion: Ancient and Modern.* Riverside, CA: Woodrow.

Wuest, Kenneth S. (1984 ed.). *The New Testament: An Expanded Translation of the Greek New Testament.* Grand Rapids, MI: Wm. Eerdmans Publishing Co.

Young, Robert. (1977). *Analytical Concordance to the Holy Bible. (8th Edition).* Guildford and London: Lutterworth Press.

34518339R00152

Made in the USA
Middletown, DE
28 August 2016